THE YEN APPRECIATION AND THE
INTERNATIONAL ECONOMY

THE YEN
APPRECIATION AND
THE INTERNATIONAL
ECONOMY

Dilip K. Das

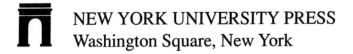

NEW YORK UNIVERSITY PRESS
Washington Square, New York

First published in the U.S.A. in 1993 by
NEW YORK UNIVERSITY PRESS
Washington Square,
New York, N.Y. 10003

Library of Congress Cataloging-in-Publication Data
Das, Dilip K., 1945–
The yen appreciation and the international economy / Dilip K. Das.
p.   cm.
Includes bibliographical references and index.
ISBN 0–8147–1852–3
1. Japan—Economic conditions—1945–   2. Japan—Foreign economic
relations.   3. Economic assistance, Japanese—Developing countries.
4. Monetary policy—Japan.   I. Title.
HC462.95.D37   1993
337.52—dc20   92–25486
                                                                        CIP
Printed in Hong Kong

For
Vasanti, Tanushree and Siddharth

Yang Chu, weeping at the crossroads, said, 'Isn't it here that you take a half-step wrong and wake up a thousand miles astray.' —— **a saying of the Confucian Hsun-tsu**

Contents

List of Tables

List of Figures

Preface

The decision to appreciate the yen was made by the Finance Ministers and central bankers of the Group of Five (G-5) countries during the Plaza accord for the purpose of macroeconomic policy coordination among the large industrial economies. From Japan's perspective, concurring with the decision was of momentous significance because this was the sharpest appreciation among the leading currencies in the recent past. Doubling the value of a currency in such a short time-span, if handled without sagacity and clairvoyance, could lead to stifling of the economy. Little wonder that Yoshio Suzuki called the yen appreciation an 'external shock that was larger than [any of] those experienced before'. Conversely, not consenting to the collective decision to appreciate the yen would have aggravated the international economic imbalances which manifested themselves in the trade and current account imbalances of the major industrialised economies. Allowing the imbalances to persist would have festered the international economy and opened Japan to the charge of being oblivious to its international responsibilities.

The Plaza accord aimed at redressing the international economic imbalances by 'correcting' the currency overvaluations and undervaluations. To this end, the first move that was made was to bring down the high US interest rates which was one of the principal causal factors behind the overvalued dollar. With a decline in the US interest rates, the differential between long-term interest rates in the US on one side and those in Japan and Europe on the other – which had exceeded 5 percentage points before the Plaza accord – shrank to around 2 percentage points. This provided leeway for interest rates to be slashed in Japan and Europe. They slashed interest rates in a concerted manner to stimulate growth in domestic demand, while maintaining approximately a two percentage point interest rate differential. This orchestrated policy move succeeded in depreciating the dollar, appreciating the yen and reducing the external imbalances, albeit after a lag. This macroeconomic co-ordination also succeeded in achieving global economic recovery.

Instead of being smothered by currency appreciation, the Japanese economy after the brief *endaka* recession entered into an upswing of the business cycle. The economic expansion continued and in September 1991 the Japanese economy passed a historic milestone, that is, the uninterrupted economic boom had completed 58 months, making it longer lasting than the *Izanagi* boom, the longest lasting economic boom until thus far in the post-war period. The economy grew at an annual average rate of 5.5 per cent during the current upswing which was lower than 12.1 per cent annual growth rate in the *Izanagi* era but it was still the highest average growth rate for any leading industrialised country over this period.

The post-appreciation economic success seemed to bemuse even the Japanese. Despite the strains of the yen appreciation the economy turned in a stellar performance. No industrialised nation has ever grown so rich so fast. If Japan had not achieved what it did, no one would have believed such a feat was feasible. During the 1986–89 period, it became the largest creditor nation, the largest aid giver, and the largest foreign investing economy. Japan became the banker of the world and its banks and securities firms dominated the international financial markets. Going by the *Fortune* 500 list, of the 500 biggest industrial corporations in the world in 1990, 111 were Japanese. The corresponding numbers for the US, the largest economy, was 164. Britain and France ranked third and fourth, respectively, with 43 and 30 corporations. Many countries felt the full force of the Japanese economy through its exports, imports and investment drives. In an increasingly interdependent world the impact of Japanese economic expansion was felt all the more. Towards the end of the 1980s, Japan's status as a fully-fledged economic superpower was fully established. Its domestic economic policies began to sway the international economic environment.

An amber signal is warranted here. Nowhere in this book do I take the illogical stance of after-it-therefore-due-to-it. That is, nowhere do I argue that Japan became an economic superpower due to the yen appreciation because the economy was riding a long-running wave of economic expansion. Currency appreciation helped it to acquire its new status. A remarkable idiosyncratic ethos prevailed in Japan which shaped Japanese capitalism. It deviated from the free-enterprise capitalism or market capitalism of the West and could be named production-oriented capitalism, or industrial-policy-oriented capitalism. It contributed a great deal to the process of maximisation of allocative efficiency as well as production efficiency. Japan made optimal utilization of *wakon yosai*, that is, the Japanese spirit and

Western knowledge or technology during the pre- as well as post-appreciation periods. The macroeconomic managers of the Japanese economy were deft in making well-conceived and characteristically pragmatic policy moves on time. They made sure that they did not wake up a thousand miles astray. The Japanese economy has never attracted as much attention as it does today. In future the other countries will also look for the 'Japanese recipe' while formulating their own macroeconomic strategies.

The overarching objective of this book is to provide a clear and concise exposition of the process of yen appreciation, domestic economy's adjustment to it, how various sub-sectors of the international economy were influenced by the post-appreciation expansion of the Japanese economy and how, at the end of it all, Japan emerged as an economic superpower. The economic analysis and arguments are closely reasoned and statistically supported. The plan of the book is as follows: it tees off with the yen appreciation and its domestic impact and how the economy adjusted to such a steep appreciation. Apart from preparing the backdrop, Chapter 1 is also the logical beginning of the principal thematic strand of the book. Chapter 2 addresses the Japanese economy's international interaction with the other growth poles as well as with its globalisation efforts during the post-appreciation period. While the expansion of economic influence caused discomfiture in some countries – mostly for the wrong reasons – it benefited the others. The action and counteraction of economic forces thus produced is analysed in the second chapter. In the next chapter Japan's ascent in the international financial world and the new-found clout of the Japanese financial institutions has been traced. Chapter 4 follows the growth and changes in Japan's foreign direct investment. Several industrial and developing economies benefited from Japan's post-appreciation wave of foreign direct investment. It had decisive ramifications over the pattern of international trade. Japan also became increasingly important to developing countries and multilateral financial institutions. Chapter 5 gives a detailed account of Japan as the biggest donor country. Japan has had special ties with the East and South East Asian economies which came to acquire a new dynamism during the post-appreciation era. Their economic bond with Japan was further strengthened and possibilities of the formation of a yen bloc were seriously considered. The last chapter addresses this issue.

I wish to express my gratitude to Kenji Umetani of the OECD secretariat in Paris and Kazuo Fukuda of the Bank of Japan in Paris. I frequently took large swaths of their busy time and benefited from numerous discussions with them. I am also thankful to two of my MBA students, Shuji Yabe and Kiyoshi Sato, who translated various statistical tables for me. The first draft of this book was completed when I was a visiting professor at the *Ecole Supérieure des Sciences Economiques et Commerciales*, Paris. All the secretarial assistance was provided untiringly and efficiently by Annei Cvetic and Stephanie Dettling and the research assistance was provided by Natalie Ng. The current text is the product of several revisions. During this phase secretarial assistance was provided by J.P.S. Rawat and research assistance by Neerja Misra. I consider myself fortunate to have worked with these two efficacious and dedicated teams. But for their sedulous support, this book would have taken much longer to be completed.

Dilip K. Das

List of Acronyms and Abbreviations

ADB	Asian Development Bank
ADF	Asian Development Fund
AFDC	Asian Finance and Development Corporation
AFIC	Asian Finance and Investment Corporation
ANIEs	Asian Newly Industrialising Economies
APEC	Asia-Pacific Economic Co-operation
ASEAN	Association of South East Asian Nations
BA	bankers' acceptance
BIS	Bank for International Settlements
BOJ	Bank of Japan
CCFF	Compensatory and Contingency Financial Facility
CD	Certificate of Deposits
CP	commercial paper
DAC	Development Assistance Committee
DFIs	development finance institutions
EC	European Community
ECUs	European Currency Units
EFTA	European Free Trade Area
EPA	Economic Planning Agency
ESAF	Expanded Structural Adjustment Facility
FDI	foreign direct investment
Fed	Federal Reserve Board
FY	Financial Year
GATT	General Agreement on Tariffs and Trade
GDP	Gross Domestic Product
GIF	global infrastructure fund
GNP	Gross National Product
HICs	highly indebted countries
IBF	International Banking Facility
IBM	International Business Machines
IDA	International Development Association

IDS	International Development Strategy
IFC	International Finance Corporation
IMF	International Monetary Fund
JAIDO	Japan International Development Organisation
JETRO	Japanese External Trade Organisation
JOM	Japanese Offshore Market
LDCs	less developed countries
LLDCs	least developed countries
M&A	merger and acquisition
MFA	Ministry of Foreign Affairs
MITI	Ministry of International Trade and Industry
MoF	Ministry of Finance
NEEDS	Nikkei Economic Electronic Data System
NTBs	non-tariff barriers
ODA	overseas development assistance
ODR	official discount rate
OECD	Organisation for Economic Co-operation and Development
OECF	Overseas Economic Co-operation Fund
OMA	orderly marketing arrangements
OOF	other official flows
OPEC	Organisation of Petroleum Exporting Countries
PAFTAD	Pacific Trade and Development Conference
PBEC	Pacific Basin Economic Council
p/e	price-earning
PECC	Pacific Economic Co-operation Conference
PF	private flows
R&D	research and development
REER	real effective exchange rate
SAF	Structural Adjustment Facility
SDR	Special Drawing Rights
SIC	Standard Industrial Classification
SII	Structural Impediments Initiative
S&L	Savings and Loans
S&P	Standard and Poor
TSE	Tokyo Stock Exchange
UNCTAD	United Nations Conference on Trade and Development
UNDP	United Nations Development Programme
UNECAFE	United Nations Economic Commission for Asia and Far East

UNIDO	United Nations Industrial Development Organisation
VAN	value-added network
VERs	voluntary export restrictions
WIDER	World Institute for Development Economics Research

1 The Yen Appreciation and the Japanese Economy

THE BACKDROP

Following the collapse of the Bretton Woods regime, the economic and financial turmoils of the 1970s and the recession that set in in 1979, the international economy, particularly that of the industrialised countries, entered a palmy period of economic expansion in 1982. This was not to be a mere short-term upswing but a new phase of dynamic growth driven by technological innovation and bearish oil prices that continued uninterrupted for the rest of the decade. The level of oil prices is a significant variable because according to an estimate a 20 per cent decline in the oil prices raised the growth rate by 0.2 per cent in the industrialised economies during this period.[1] The flexible exchange rate regime, liberalised capital markets and freer capital movements had increased the interaction of economic policies – especially monetary policies – among the industrialised market economies as well as internationalised the capital markets. In such an economic milieu, which was becoming something approaching *laissez faire* and for a while Adam Smith seemed to be running the show, the exchange rates could well become dominated by capital flows and the natural operation of market forces could work to undermine the exchange rate and balance of payments adjustment mechanism which the neoclassical economists assume. The end result of it could be lasting distortions in the economic fundamentals. The prices of goods and services when translated using such a distorted exchange rate become out of line with those in the trade-partner economies. This made the world economy vulnerable. The international monetary system that evolved in the early 1980s was something of this nature and the exchange rates began to get out of line with underlying prices and economic performance comparisons.[2] Capital movements did overwhelm productivity, economic performance, purchasing power parity and even rational expectations. The yen/dollar exchange rate became a good illustration of divergence between a capital-flow-dominated exchange rate on one side and a free exchange rate reflecting the basic economic fundamentals on the other.

The story of the dollar's appreciation against the other four SDR currencies since early 1983 is well known. The pressure of government borrowings and private borrowings led to historically high interest rate spreads in the US and capital flowed persistently into the US. The flows were not limited to the US but extended to dollar accounts everywhere. The other four SDR currencies depreciated *vis-à-vis* the dollar at differing rates until the dollar peaked at the end of the first quarter of 1985, when for various reasons the other currencies, including the yen, began to rise, albeit the upsurge was not sharp. The new international economic milieu and high interest rate *inter alia* allowed the dollar to become overpriced – or 'strong' if you will.

Another relevant fact to be borne in mind in the context of the yen appreciation is that in 1981, the Japanese current account had a tiny surplus. It was hardly noticed because since the late 1960s Japan had a tradition of running small surpluses on its current account. The only exceptions were the two brief periods of 1973–75 and 1979–80 when the oil prices rose sharply. The build up of the current account surplus in the first half of the 1980s took place essentially against the background of improving Japanese economic competitiveness. It was given a helping hand by the currency value configuration of this period, that is, an overpriced dollar and underpriced yen. This pattern changed after the Plaza accord – as described below – when the yen started appreciating against the other SDR currencies in effective terms.

HOW THE YEN APPRECIATED

The imbalances generated due to distorted economic fundamentals in the international economy started reflecting in the current account imbalances of the three largest economies. In 1984 and 1985, they were set out in Table 1.1

Allegations that these current account imbalances were causing

Table 1.1   CURRENT ACCOUNT IMBALANCES, 1984–85
(IN BILLIONS OF $)

	1984	1985
1. Japan	35 (2.8)	50 (3.8)
2. West Germany	6 (1.0)	13 (2.1)
3. USA	–107 (2.8)	–119 (3.3)

SOURCE   Based on the IMF data from the International Financial
Statistics.
N.B.:   Figures in the parentheses stand for the ratio with the GNP.

worldwide disorder were made in no uncertain terms and there were loud calls for Japan to redress them. The commonest reaction to the imbalances was that either Japan exported too much or imported too little or it did both. The ratios of exports to GNP and imports to GNP for 1985, the year of the Plaza accord, disprove at least one of these hypotheses.

In Table 1.2 the ratios of exports of goods and nonfactor services to GNP for the industrialised economies show that Japan exported less than every other industrialised country except the US. This sets to rest one of the myths. Although Japan's economy survives through *kako-boeki* or export based on imported materials, its ratio of imports to GNP has remained conspicuously lower than those for the other industrialised economies. However, it cannot be taken for *the* reason behind its growing current account surpluses. Besides, various empirical studies have been made since the early 1980s to examine whether Japan's imports to GNP ratio is abnormally low.[3] A sub-set of these studies focused only on the manufactured imports. The structures of their models varied widely and depended upon the assumptions made and the methodology followed. In addition, there were serious divergences in the definitions of the variables. The common thread that seems to run through them is that they all believed that countries that are located far away from their trading partners, tended to trade less because of higher transport costs. But they all had their distinctive manner of calculating the transport costs. Some of them inferred that Japan's import behaviour is not significantly different from that in the other OECD economies when all the relevant explanatory variables are taken into account. These studies, however, did not take into consideration the formal and informal trade barriers.[4] The other studies reached the opposite

Table 1.2   EXPORT AND IMPORT RATIOS FOR SELECTED
INDUSTRIALISED ECONOMIES

		Export/GNP	Import/GNP
1.	Japan	14.6	11.2
2.	Australia	16.4	19.5
3.	Austria	40.8	40.6
4.	Belgium	76.1	73.7
5.	Canada	29.3	26.7
6.	Denmark	38.3	37.9
7.	Finland	29.7	28.7
8.	France	24.1	23.5
9.	Germany, FR	32.4	28.9
10.	Italy	23.2	23.5
11.	The Netherlands	63.7	58.8
12.	Norway	47.8	39.5
13.	Sweden	36.2	33.9
14.	Switzerland	36.9	36.5
15.	UK	29.2	28.2
16.	USA	7.5	10.0

SOURCE   The World Bank, *World Tables 1987*, Fourth Edition
(Washington DC: 1988).

conclusion. A recently concluded OECD study contended that while
Japan's merchandise imports are well explained, a significant negative factor lowering the manufactured imports was found which could
have been either due to (a) Japan's comparative advantage or (b)
trade barriers.[5] If one juxtaposes the results, one finds that these
empirical studies are inconclusive and that there is no consensus on
the answer to the question whether Japan is an underimporter.

For the real explanation behind the current account surpluses one
has to examine the macroeconomic variables. The Japanese current
account surplus has grown *pari passu* with the outflow of long-term
capital. Its total gross long-term outflows of resident funds reached
$131.5 billion in 1986 and was $130.9 billion in 1988.[6] The current
account surpluses for these two years were $85.8 billion and $79.6
billion, respectively. A widely, although not universally, accepted
explanation for this current account surplus is that it has grown
because of the Japanese tendency to 'oversave', that is, insofar as the
excess saving over investment in the private sector is not offset by a
fiscal deficit in the government sector, there should necessarily be an
ex post current account surplus in the balance of payments.[7] The

commonly held view of the Japanese current account surpluses was that because of a weak yen during the first half of the 1980s, a large current account surplus emerged, which in turn dictated that there should be a large capital outflow from Japan. One needs to pause and question which account has the driving force. It is likely that the emergence of long-term capital outflows depressed the value of the yen which in turn created the current account surpluses.

The Council of Economic Advisers in the US believed that the reason behind Japan's current account surpluses and export competitiveness in the first half of the 1980s was the undervalued yen and that American exports were losing market shares because of the over-priced dollar.[8] This logic was only partly correct because it ignored the macroeconomic factors and missed the whole point of how Japan transformed its industrial sector since the first oil price hike. The Japanese experience was a real supply-side miracle of investment enhancing the capital stock and ultimately resulting in augmented production. It was not the surrealistic supply-side fantasy of the US of the 1980s, which in fact was a demand-side reality. The contemporary reasons for Japan's superior performance lay more in its macro-economic planning by government and microeconomic planning by corporations. The days of Japan having a competitive edge over other industrialised economies due *only* to an undervalued currency and low labour costs had receded in the past. Also, the notion that Japan has been playing by different rules from other industrial nations is misguided. It has demonstrated more clearly than any other nation the incredible power of competition to foster dynamism.[9]

The Council's belief and advice ignored both macro- and micro-economic realities on the American side of the argument as well. For instance, the ramifications of the persistent budgetary deficits were paid inadequate attention. In addition, the low savings rate has remained a drag on domestic investment in the US. Despite large capital inflows the level of investment has remained low. For instance, the ratio of gross private investment in plant and equipment to GDP has remained close to 60 per cent of the level in Japan. Turning to the corporate level, quality defects in American manufacturing ran at 8 to 10 per cent of production versus 1 per cent in Japan. Also, at this point American business invested only $2600 per worker annually whereas the Japanese commitment to new equipment, training and improvements in the production process was two and a half times as large.[10] However, the yen/dollar Working Group at the G-2 (Japan and the US) level, which comprised economists and government officials of the two countries, began to have meetings to attack what was perceived as the villain of the piece, the yen/dollar exchange rate. The thinking of the Reagan administration had made a U-turn and they thought that letting the market forces take over, or a *laissez faire* policy on exchange rate, was not the best manner of treating the growing economic malaise.

The yen/dollar Working Group meetings achieved little more than working as precursors to the G-5 deputies (G-5D) meetings which took place in 1985 and laid the foundation of the Plaza accord. The new strategy was that a 'leaning with the wind' kind of *intervention* was needed. Although the latter term was assiduously avoided, the message was clear. C. Fred Bergsten was the first to publicly advocate this strategy in late 1984.[11] The US and Japan, after protracted negotiations, agreed on this strategy and the three European members of the G-5 subsequently acquiesced and prepared to participate in the package deal that was launched as the Plaza accord,[12] which is the next point of focus. If it sounded like a simple and smooth process, it was not. If anything, the process was fractious and full of discordance. It demanded an enormous amount of patience and negotiating skill from the G-5 deputies to finesse it.

The Plaza Accord

22 September 1985, was the beginning of a climacteric period when the Group of Five (G-5) finance ministers and central bankers met at the Plaza Hotel in New York to accord recognition to the view that 'recent shifts in fundamental economic conditions . . . together with policy commitments for the future . . . [had] not been reflected fully in exchange markets' and that economic fundamentals presented a disparate picture, albeit the international economic disparities at the time of accord were slowly giving way to a relatively more convergent performance.[13] The communiqué declared that in the international economic milieu 'some further orderly appreciation of the main non-dollar currencies is desirable' and that an exchange rate policy should play a role in place of the *laissez faire*. This should be taken to mean that the accord communiqué called for the appreciation of the yen and the Deutsche Mark, instead of the depreciation of the dollar.

In order to avoid igniting a fuse of currency speculation, details regarding the volume of foreign exchange reserves that each country was expected to use for intervention, the time horizon, and the extent of currency realignment were not disclosed. Meticulous details compiled by Funabashi from the conference papers indicate that a short-term target of downward adjustment of the dollar was kept at 10 to 12 per cent, that is, a drop to 214–18 from the erstwhile yen/dollar rate 237 and a drop to 2.54–2.59 from the erstwhile Deutsche Mark/dollar rate of 2.85. For the long term, however, a further downward adjustment was considered desirable 'without losing control of the market'. The strategy agreed was essentially to resist appreciation of the dollar; it was believed that a resistance to rise would lead to an eventual decline. The intervention was to be on a day-to-day basis so that currencies would not change direction on one hand and the dollar would not land hard on the other. The initial intervention period was established at six weeks with the total amount of intervention set at $18 billion, with maximum daily operations in each participant market in the region of $300 to $400 million. Although all the G-5 currencies were part of the operations, a greater role was to be played by the dollar, the yen and the Deutsche Mark. Of the three, the yen was to bear the brunt (30 per cent).[14]

The Plaza communiqué had a substantial short-run impact over the foreign exchange markets and the dollar went into a steep decline. After the first flush of activity, uncertainty hovered in the market for a short period, therefore, the Bank of Japan (BOJ) responded with a massive dollar sale and the Federal Reserve Board (Fed) intervened forcefully, so much so that they did not hesitate to intervene directly in the Tokyo market. By the end of October, the central banks had also entered the fray. Two things were obvious: first, the magnitude of collective intervention was impressive by any measure and despite initial differences in opinions and approaches the final stance taken by the G-5 countries appeared well orchestrated. Second, the impact of intervention exceeded the expectations of the G-5 participants without exhausting the $18 billion fund earmarked for the operation. This was the first half of the Plaza accord drama.

The Appreciation

The other half of it was enacted across the Pacific where a steady escalation in the value of the yen began. In February 1985 the yen was valued at 260 to the dollar in Tokyo and 237 in September. After the accord New Zealand's Wellington market was the first to open on Monday 23 September to find the yen at 234 to the dollar. With the Tokyo financial market on a holiday, the first currency operations took place in Europe. The Bundesbank started selling its dollars and

Table 1.3   MONTHLY YEN APPRECIATION AFTER THE
             PLAZA ACCORD (YEN PER DOLLAR)

1985	*September*	*October*	*November*	*December*			
	236.95	214.73	203.72	202.82			
1986	*January*	*February*	*March*	*April*	*May*	*June*	*July*
	200.07	184.64	178.93	175.62	166.83	167.95	158.60

SOURCE   The Bank of Japan, *Balance of Payments Monthly* (Tokyo,
         various issues).

by the time the New York market opened, the yen had climbed to 231
to the dollar. When the Fed ended their first operation of selling
dollars for yen and Deutsche Marks, the yen value had gone up to
225.5 yen to the dollar, proving that the US was still perceived as a
major financial power by the financial markets. The BOJ intervention
was substantial and Japan's foreign exchange reserve dropped by $1
billion during the month of September. To give an account of the
short-term developments, the month-to-month appreciations in the
yen valuation are tabulated in Table 1.3.

Table 1.4 gives a long-term, decadal, view of the value of the yen
against the dollar while Table 1.5 presents two of the most relevant
indicators, namely, the index numbers of nominal effective and real
effective exchange rates against a trade-weighted basket of currencies
of 15 other industrial countries. In nominal terms the yen was at its
peak in the last quarter of 1988, when its average value was 125.28 to
the dollar, which means a 92 per cent trough-to-crest rise in its
nominal value against the dollar since the Plaza accord.[15] The nominal effective exchange rate during 1985–88 escalated by 58 per cent
while the real effective exchange rate appreciated by 29 per cent
against the trade-weighted currency basket. The real effective exchange rate is calculated by adjusting the nominal trade-weighted
exchange rate for differences between inflation at home and that in
the trade-partner countries. The resulting index is a measure of
change in competitiveness due to exchange rate variations. A rise in
the index implies loss of competitiveness due to currency appreciation and a fall implies the opposite. Thus viewed, the competitiveness
of the Japanese exports fell compared to its trade partner countries
by 29 per cent due to yen appreciation. Although during the Louvre
accord (21 February 1987) the major currencies were seen within
ranges broadly consistent with underlying economic fundamentals

Table 1.4   YEN EXCHANGE RATE AGAINST THE US
DOLLAR, 1980–1990

	YEN/$	HIGHEST	LOWEST
	1	2	3
1980	226.74	202.95	264.00
1981	220.54	198.70	247.40
1982	249.08	217.70	278.50
1983	237.51	227.20	247.80
1984	237.52	220.00	251.76
1985	238.54	199.80	263.65
1986	168.52	152.55	203.30
1987	144.64	121.85	153.95
1988	128.15	120.80	134.30
1989	137.96	141.85	144.73
1990 I qtr.	147.90	158.85	142.85
II qtr	155.25	160.35	149.00

SOURCE   Column 1. International Monetary Fund, *International Financial
Statistics* (various issues). Columns 2 and 3 give the interbank
spot rates of the Tokyo forex market.

and the G-5 countries agreed to co-operate to foster the stability of
exchange rate 'around current levels', the stock market crash of
October 1987 pushed the dollar down and exerted upward pressure
on the yen. In 1989 and 1990, the yen depreciated somewhat from its
high perch (see graphs 1.1 and 1.2). In the beginning of 1990, its
nominal effective exchange rate was 168.0 yen to the dollar while the
real effective exchange rate was 111.8 yen to the dollar. The post-
Plaza appreciation was more than twice as large as that in 1970–73,
when the yen first emerged as a major international currency, and
also larger than that in 1975–78, when it recovered from the first oil
crisis. As is seen in Table 1.4, by 1988 the yen had stabilised and did
not show high variability. In fact, the range of variation was the
smallest in 1988 since the inception of the floating rate regime. The
highest value of the yen was attained on 25 November, when it was
120.80 to the dollar – the highest value since the Second World War.

A germane question is whether the yen appreciation was brought
about by monetary or fiscal measures. During the post-Plaza accord
period, Japanese monetary policy was determined largely by exchange rate considerations. The mechanism worked as follows: the
initial step that the BOJ took immediately after the Plaza accord was

Table 1.5   THE INDEX NUMBERS OF NOMINAL AND
REAL EFFECTIVE EXCHANGE RATES OF YEN AGAINST
15 OTHER INDUSTRIAL COUNTRIES' CURRENCIES

Year	Nominal Effective Exchange Rate	Real Effective Exchange Rate
1980	95.5	103.0
1981	105.8	104.8
1982	98.6	92.4
1983	107.8	96.8
1984	113.0	97.8
1985	115.9	96.9
1986	150.3	115.4
1987	164.3	119.5
1988	181.4	125.8
1989	172.7	118.3
1990	156.9	105.9
1991		
January	165.2	110.2
February	168.0	111.8

SOURCE   Morgan Guaranty Trust Company, *World Financial Markets*
(New York, various issues).

non-sterilised intervention in the exchange markets which implies an intervention that decreases the money supply and thus influences the domestic interest rates. In October the strategy was intensified pushing the interest rate further upward. The result was a sharp rise in interest rates from 6.4 per cent during mid-October to 9.1 per cent in mid-November. When the appreciation of the yen was found to be too brisk, the monetary policy went into reverse gear and the BOJ lowered the official discount rate from 5.0 per cent to 4.5 per cent on 30 January 1986. This was the first decline in two years. It was further lowered to 3.5 per cent on 21 April. Under usual circumstances lower interest rates in Japan would have led to depreciation of the yen but, since this was part of an internationally orchestrated move, nothing of the kind happened; instead the yen kept on going from one height to another. Relaxation of the monetary policy continued and the official discount rate continued to be reduced. During 1987 and 1988 it remained as low as 2.5 per cent, the lowest level during the post-war period. However, since then, with the strong recovery of domestic demand, the monetary policy has been more cautious.

FIGURE 1.1   *The Yen Exchange Rate Against the Dollar, 1980–90*

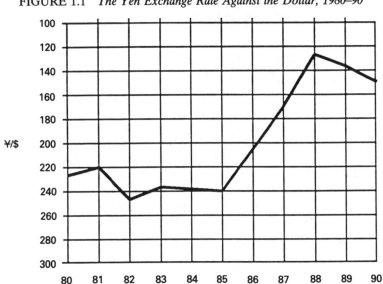

FIGURE 1.2   *The Index Numbers of Nominal and Real Effective Exchange Rates of the Yen Against 15 Other Industrial Countries' Currencies 1980–90 (1980–82 = 100)*

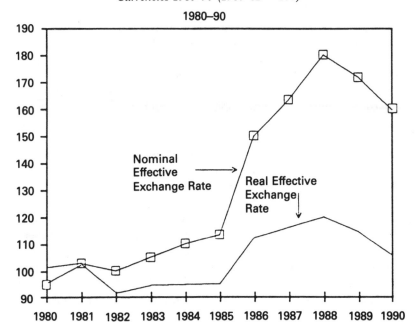

Monetary relaxation did not terminate until May 1989 when the official discount rate changed gear and began to climb.

MACROECONOMIC POLICY MANAGEMENT AND THE MAEKAWA COMMITTEE REPORT

During the G-5 D meetings there was pressure on Japan to revise its macroeconomic policies, albeit agreement on a specific macroeconomic policy package could not be reached. It was, however, clear that Japan (along with West Germany) needed to stimulate its economy either through an increase in the government expenditure or by boosting private investment and domestic demand. Also, the tax structure needed to be reformed and the capital markets needed to be deregulated and liberalised. Although the Japanese agreed, they made no commitments. An interesting custom has prevailed in Japan, namely, using external pressure to counter the domestic resistance towards economic policy management. In Japanese language there is a word for it, *gaiatsu*. It is usually a unidimensional force and is subliminally seen as the unrelenting and threatening foreign force of the black ships of Commodore Perry which opened Japan's doors for international trade in the middle of the last century. This international pressure is not always unwelcome in Japanese society because the Japanese use it as a tool in their own factional arguments. Perry's black ships served as a catalyst in easing the passage of the old order and advancing the Meiji cause. An indigenous movement for opening Japan had already existed. Presently various Japanese ministries use *gaiatsu* as a bureaucratic weapon against each other.

Accordingly an Advisory Group on Economic Structural Adjustment for International Harmony, popularly known as the Maekawa Committee after its chairman, was set up by Prime Minister Nakasone to study policy measures to help Japanese economy adapt to the changing realities of the international economy. The Committee's first report, published in April 1986, observed that (1) large current account imbalances have created strains in the international economy which were not only pernicious to the Japanese economic management but were also noxious for international economic harmony. Japan, therefore, should transform its macroeconomic management style as well as 'the national life style'. It observed that Japan needed to eradicate its image as a mercantilist nation and establish a medium-term national plan to reduce the current account imbalances to a level consistent with international economic harmony. (2) While the need for a more open domestic economy, improved market access for exporters abroad and encouragement of imports of manufactured goods was obvious, the Committee felt that more fundamental structural changes were required in the industrial sector and macro-economic policies for a significant reduction in the trade imbalances. There was an imperious need to change Japan's economic structure from an export-oriented one to a domestic-demand-oriented one by encouraging investment as well as private consumption. The final report, released in April 1987, said much the same and added that Japan's economic growth was not reflected in the quality of Japanese life, that housing standards were low, and that the prices and cost of living were high and working hours long. In absolute terms and objectively Japan had become a creditor nation but subjectively it still behaved and lived like a debtor nation. With such a no-nonsense world-view the report identified the following medium-term policy measures: (1) expansion of domestic demand by promoting construction and urban redevelopment, by easing building restrictions and strengthening tax incentives, and by stimulating private demand by wage hikes and tax reductions (2) transformation of the industrial structure by encouraging investment in manufacturing abroad and by easing restrictions on farm imports (3) improvement in market access by promoting greater imports of manufactured goods and streamlining the distribution system (4) further liberalisation of the capital and financial markets, and (5) expansion of international economic co-operation.

To be sure, the recommendations were perspicacious and were highly commended by the international community. However, the flip side of this coin was that most policy recommendations were abstract. Some doubted the ability of the government to implement them because the recommendations called for a sweeping reorientation of the economic goals and a radical change in macroeconomic management. Substantive policy initiatives were not slow to follow. The Maekawa report marked a turning point in the Japanese economic management. Meanwhile, the yen continued to appreciate and in addition exports suffered from protectionism in the US and increasingly in Europe. Clear prospects of a substantial decline in net foreign demand in future made the policy makers take the Maekawa recommendations more seriously. Hindsight reveals that this set of circumstances drove Japan away from the mercantilist notions of absolute advantage in international trade and came to grips with its comparative advantages. For restructuring of domestic economy a five-year Economic and Social Plan was announced in May 1988. It was consistent with the basic strategy outlined in the Maekawa report. It also included tax reforms to boost the domestic demand and deregulation in various sectors of the economy.

DYNAMISM OF INDUSTRIAL RESTRUCTURING

In the halcyon period of the Japanese economy manufacturing output, labour productivity, employment and export achievements were the building blocks of spectacular economic growth. Down to the first quinquennium of the 1980s net exports were responsible for almost 40 per cent of real GNP growth. While during the two post oil-shock periods manufacturing output suffered all over the industrialised world, it did not languish in Japan. If anything, its export-led growth pattern was firmly established after the first oil-shock and further strengthened during the export boom to the US market in the first half of the 1980s. From 1979 through 1984, the manufacturing sector grew by almost 8 per cent annually, contributing 61 per cent to overall GNP growth. Almost three fifths of the output growth was attributable to exports growth.[16] The European industrial sector virtually stagnated during this period and the US economy suffered from an overvalued dollar and was deindustrialising. However, the dollar made a turnaround in February 1985 and the Japanese economic management was marked by fiscal restraint, consequently the manufacturing output growth in Japan sagged to 2.1 per cent for 1985/6. Immediately before the Plaza accord and steep yen appreciation, the economy was grappling with the adjustment problems similar to those in Europe and the US. In addition, during the first quinquennium of the 1980s, when the yen was weak and the dollar was going from strength to strength, several export sectors, including low-technology ones, had expanded sharply in Japan. This success ironically made the economy vulnerable when the yen appreciation era began and substantial adjustment as well as restructuring became a pressing necessity.

The yen's appreciation affected the demand conditions in each industry. The Bank of Japan estimated the total demand for each industry using inducement coefficients derived from the input-output tables and found that (1) demand of the manufacturing industries slackened after the yen appreciated on account of weakened export demand, while (2) growth in demand in the non-manufacturing industries gained momentum reflecting a firm domestic demand, specially from the household sector. This resulted in growth of demand in the non-manufacturing sector outpacing that in the manufacturing sector.[17] An assumption can be made here that the manufacturing sector is export-oriented, or at least dominated by exports, while in contrast the non-manufacturing sector, which includes construction, utilities and services, is non-trade-oriented. Currency appreciation improves the profitability of the non-tradable goods sector compared to that in the tradable goods sector. In the domestic markets it makes indigenously produced goods less competitive than the imported goods. The appreciation of the yen influenced the relative prices in different industries and altered their relative profitability. The traded goods industries were adversely affected because output prices in yen declined as exporters did not wish to raise dollar prices sufficiently to maintain their profit margins. In the sixth section I shall return to this issue. In this section we shall also see that after the yen's appreciation export prices declined more than the domestic prices and that in the export sector the manufacturing goods prices recorded a marked fall. Little wonder that the traded goods industries contributed negatively to return on sales down to 1987 but the negative contribution gradually diminished as exporters raised their prices and reduced costs. Conversely, profitability improved in the non-traded goods sectors because, first, the output prices did not decline because there was not much international competition; second, several input prices had fallen; third, wage increases were restrained because of a fall in the price index from 100 in 1985 to 94 in 1988; and last, as noted in the second section, the interest rates had declined. In keeping with this trend, nominal value-added and operating profits declined substantially in the manufacturing sector while they soared in the non-manufacturing sector. We shall return to this point in the seventh section, while dealing with corporate level adjustments. This had a clear impact on the post-appreciation investment pattern and, in turn, on the industrial restructuring of the Japanese economy.

In the second quinquennium of the 1980s, unlike the first, external demand not only did not contribute to real GNP growth but its contributions were negative. It contributed −1.4 per cent to real growth rate in 1986, −1.0 per cent in 1987, −1.7 per cent in 1988 and

−0.7 per cent in 1989.[18] The domestic demand gained strength in 1986 and become stronger thereafter, which led to accelerated growth in 1987 (see Table 1.9) and import expansion. There was a complete reversal of the domestic economy during the post-appreciation period from a supply-oriented to a demand-oriented economy. For the first time excess demand was implanted in the system. The domestic sales activity expanded with increase in domestic demand which helped in switching of production structure from export-oriented to domestic-demand-oriented. It started contributing to a return on sales to a significant degree. The enterprises began to aim at achieving scale economies through expansion of sales volumes in the domestic markets rather than in export markets. Accordingly investment by export industries for capacity expansion declined from 28.8 per cent to 21.9 per cent between 1985 and 1987, while the domestic market-oriented industries showed an increase from 33.7 per cent to 34.9 per cent. A business investment survey of the Bank of Japan revealed that manufacturers were not only shifting away from exports and towards domestic markets but also from manufacturing to non-manufacturing. This readiness to enter the non-manufacturing industries increased in 1988.

Underpinning much of the post-appreciation surge in Japan's economic growth has been an extraordinary rebound in capital spending by industry. In the immediate aftermath of the yen appreciation the gross fixed capital formation rate fell to 3.9 per cent but it soon rebounded to 8.8 per cent in 1987 and a robust 12.2 per cent in 1988. In 1989, it stayed by and large at the same (12.0 per cent) level.[19] Likewise, although the private sector plant and equipment investment increased in real terms by a meagre 1 per cent in 1986, the subsequent increases were strong, with 1.5 per cent in 1987, 3.0 per cent in 1988 and 3.7 per cent in 1989, making the last two years the period of highest increase in such investment during the decade (see Table 1.9). Initially, outlays were devoted to shifting capacity offshore but subsequently they were devoted to upgrading domestic capacity and preparing for technological innovations. The domestic-demand-oriented industries increased their capital spendings as a result of the burgeoning demand. Overall manufacturing industries turned to increase after a slack of three years. In 1988 and 1989 their capital spendings grew by more than 10 per cent, the highest rate in 15 years. The investment surge was being spear-headed by high-tech industries, particularly industries like computers and communications technology, electronics, petroleum, pulp and paper.[20] In 1990, however, a whole range of industries were competing to boost investment and capacity but the Ministry of International Trade and Industry (MITI) restrained them, fearing that further investment would lead to a greater surge in exports causing more trade friction. The auto and chemicals industries were reined in and steel industry expansion plans were curbed.[21] Nevertheless, higher investment outlays for improving urban infrastructure continued. The new investment patterns went a long way in transforming the economic structure.

The industrial restructuring took place in an environment of declining interest rates and monetary relaxation. The monotonic fall in the official discount rate has already been mentioned in the second section. The three months *gensaki* rate also fell from 7.4 per cent in 1985 to 4.2 per cent in 1989.[22] Lowered interest rates helped in overcoming the initial deflationary impact of yen appreciation and softened its negative impact on the business enterprises. They also provided time for industry to refocus its orientation from exports to domestic markets. Thus, monetary policy helped the financial markets in not losing confidence, which could have threatened investment and precipitated recession.[23]

Currency appreciation adversely affects the unemployment situation because labour is less mobile than capital. Although employment was sensitive to relative price changes and transformation in the employment structure proceeded hand-in-hand with the changes in the investment structure, labour in the Japanese economy also was less mobile than capital, giving rise to frictional unemployment. A regional and occupational mismatch between demand for and supply of labour was created by structural changes. The unemployment rate reached 2.8 per cent during 1986/7, a level never reached in the post-war period. The situation began to improve in the latter half of 1987 because of brisk activity in the construction sector and the pent-up demand for fixed investment, and the level of unemployment declined to 2.5 per cent in 1988 and 2.3 per cent in 1989. Several labour-intensive sectors like textiles, and low-tech sectors like iron and steel, made a negative contribution to export expansion as well as to meeting the domestic demand.[24] The loss of comparative advantage by these sectors was obvious. Labour lobbies made pleas for protectionist policies to be adopted in textiles and other labour-intensive light manufacturing sectors to which the Japanese government responded stoically.

CHANGES IN THE IMPORT STRUCTURE

Japanese imports were traditionally dominated by raw materials, mineral fuels and other primary products, which made its trade composition different from that in other industrialised market economies. Its import dependence for natural resources is higher than that of the other industrialised economies. The comparative OECD statistics for import dependency for 1984, the year before appreciation, prove this point convincingly:

	Japan	US	Germany	UK
Oil	99.7	31.8	95.1	−60.3
Natural gas	92.4	5.2	66.3	22.7
Iron ore	99.8	33.4	97.8	97.3
Copper	96.8	46.7	99.9	99.8

Due to a lacklustre demand, the oil prices fell in the mid-1980s. The same was the case with several raw materials and primary goods. The weakness in the prices was magnified by the appreciation of the yen. Japan's oil bill fell from ¥ 9678 billion to ¥ 3307 billion between 1985 and 1988. Since oil was a large part of total Japanese imports, this fall had an inordinately large impact on overall Japanese import prices and the unit value of imports was almost halved and its index recorded a decline from 100.0 to 52.7 over this period.

The post-appreciation import volume growth rate was brisker and reflected the new strength of the yen as well as the lower prices of imported goods as compared to the domestic products. As Table 1.6 shows, they climbed steadily after 1986.

After the second quarter of 1986 Japan made a good deal of contribution to real import growth in the international economy. The large market made available for export expansion of the other economies worked towards stabilising the international economy. It is known as the 'locomotive' role and until recently it was performed only by the US economy. While the increases in imports took place in the context of a stronger yen, the fact that their growth continued even in 1989, when the yen had grown relatively weak, indicates that import expansion had taken roots as a stable trend in the economy.

Insofar as the value of manufactured goods imports in Japan had remained low, its trade structure was unusual. Compared to other

Table 1.6 IMPORT TREND (1985–89)

		1985	1986	1987	1988	1989
1.	Import value ($ billion)	129.5	126.4	149.5	187.4	210.8
2.	Growth rate over the previous year (per cent)	–5.1	–2.4	18.3	25.3	12.5
3.	Import volume index [1985 = 100]	100	109	119.7	139.7	150.6
4.	Volume growth rate over the previous year (per cent)	0.4	9.0	9.3	16.7	7.8

SOURCE   Ministry of International Trade and Industry, *White Paper on International Trade 1990* (Tokyo, June 1990).

industrial countries the Japanese manufactured imports were a small share of its domestic use of manufactured goods. In 1980, these imports accounted for only 5.8 per cent of Japanese expenditure on manufactured products. The comparable proportions for the US and the EC were 9.3 per cent and 13.9 per cent, respectively.[25] The two basic reasons that lay behind low imports of manufactures have already been alluded to, namely, Japan had a comparative advantage in producing manufactured goods and, secondly, because it was distant from its trading partners, the transport cost discouraged such imports and encouraged domestic production. It is alleged that imports to Japan often run into protectionist constraints and preferences and they manage to reduce the manufactured goods imports by as much as 40 per cent.[26] This trade structure began to alter and the domestic manufacturing industries saw their sales plummet in the domestic and export sectors as the yen began to appreciate.[27] As currency appreciation caused demand to shift from domestic to imported products, the proportion of manufactured imports to total imports rose in a steep curve. As seen in Table 1.7, the imports of manufactured goods doubled in volume terms between 1985 and 1989 and increased 2.6 times in dollar terms. In 1989 they crossed the $100 billion mark and as the ratio of imports of manufactured goods to total imports they passed the 50 per cent mark for the first time. The income elasticity of manufactured goods is higher than that of other goods by nature and in the Japanese economy the income elasticity to imports themselves rose from 0.3 to 3.0 over the 1986–89 period.[28] This is a structural change of far-reaching significance.

Table 1.7   IMPORTS OF MANUFACTURES (1985–89)

		1985	1986	1987	1988	1989
1.	Import value ($ billion)	40.16	52.78	65.96	91.84	106.11
2.	Growth rate over the previous year (per cent)	–1.1	31.4	25.0	39.2	15.5
3.	Volume index (1985 = 100)	100.0	122.6	137.9	180.0	202.1
4.	Growth rate over previous year (per cent)	1.8	22.6	12.5	30.5	12.3
5.	Ratio of manufactured imports to total imports	31.0	41.8	44.1	49.0	50.3

SOURCE   Ministry of International Trade and Industry, *White Paper on International Trade 1990* (Tokyo, June 1990).

These imports essentially comprised semi-finished and manufactured goods used by processing industries as well as final goods manufacturers. The shift from the imports of raw materials to that of manufactured goods was first noticed in a small way in 1980 when upgrading of technological levels and progress in industrialisation had created substantial supply capacity in the Asian Newly Industrialising Economies (ANIEs). The appreciation of the yen brought this shift to light and accelerated it. The domestic suppliers of several semi-finished goods were forced out of the market which gave warning of the transformation in the production structure. Lifting of import restrictions also assisted in this trend and helped in bringing about the metamorphosis of import structure in a short span of four years. The statistics below highlight the change in the structure:

		1985 per cent	1989 per cent	Percentage change-over 1985–89
1.	Industrial raw material imports	39.9	55.2	28.5
2.	Capital goods	8.9	12.6	130.8
3.	Durable goods	2.3	7.3	418.9
4.	Non-durable goods	2.6	6.5	309.9
5.	Others	13.1	25.1	86.7

A long or intermediate-term implication of rising imports could be lower prices. Japan has been known to be a country of high prices.

On a price index with Tokyo set at 100, in 1988 New York was 72 and Hamburg 68.[29] Also, taking into account the differences in per capita income, the Japanese prices were far above those in Canada and Luxembourg. Higher imports can drive Japan's prices down and bring them close to international level by intensifying competition. There are reasons to be optimistic on this count because when countries with similar levels of per capita income are compared, prices turn out to be lower where markets are more open.[30]

Another major macroeconomic implication of the transformation of the import structure was that Japanese trade shifted its axis from a vertical to horizontal international specialisation. Japan has become a large importer of durable and non-durable consumer goods and intermediate manufactured products and an exporter of capital goods and high-tech manufactured products.[31] Thus, the yen appreciation has ushered in a new era for Japan's trade structure. Interestingly, both pre- and post-appreciation trade structures remained loyal to the Heckscher-Ohlin-Samuelson model of international trade. The comparative advantage of the Japanese economy changed with the yen's appreciation and *pari passu* the trade structure was transformed. It is noteworthy that it happened in an incredibly short time span.

STRONG YEN AND CURRENT ACCOUNT SURPLUS: A PARADOX?

Variations in exchange rate influence the balance of payments in several ways from the demand side as well as the supply side. The primary channel of the demand side effect is the price effect on demand of exports and imports. In the textbook-argument fashion appreciation lowers the import prices in the local currency of the importing country and raises demand, that is, it would work towards increasing imports through price declines in yen terms. The second impact is through an increase in real domestic income brought about by terms-of-trade gains due to an appreciation which augments real purchasing power. The terms-of-trade improved from 100 in 1985 to 139.6 in 1988. With a depreciating yen they fell to 133.8 in 1989 and further to 125.7 in 1990.[32] The supply side impact – as noted in the fourth section – is brought about by switching demand from domestic to foreign products (see Figure 1.3). This adjustment works on real trade balances but not so readily – and not necessarily – on the

22

FIGURE 1.3 *The Principal Channels of Impact of Yen Appreciation on the Domestic Economy*

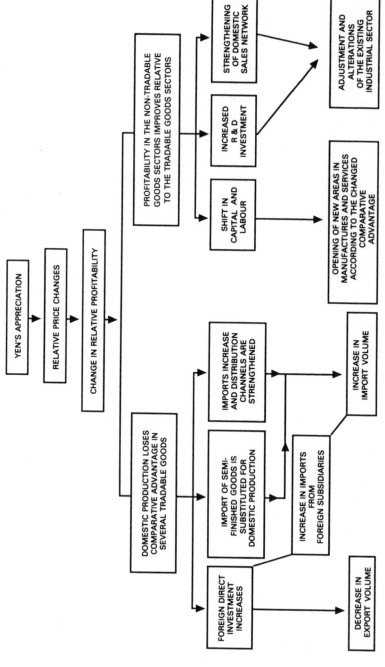

nominal ones, unless export and import elasticities change dramatically. The supply side effect of exchange rate realignment works by influencing relative profitability at home and in the trading partner countries and thereby triggers resource reallocation in the economy. It occurs in both tradable and non-tradable sectors, that is, from the former to the latter as well as within the former. The nature of these changes is such that they cannot take place in the short-term like the demand-side adjustments. Besides, the supply-side adjustments cast a longer shadow over the economy. The adjustment brought about by them remains a stable part of the new systemic equilibrium even after the stabilisation of exchange rate.

A small decline in the real surplus, albeit not in the nominal surplus, took place at the end of 1985. It was essentially due to the demand side reasons. A notable feature of this decline was that it was the result of smaller exports and greater imports, making it a more desirable pattern of adjustment than when exports and imports both go down. It implies that the 'locomotive' theory worked and that Japan's imports contributed to production abroad. As noted in the preceding paragraph, the terms-of-trade improvement together with bearish oil prices increased the real domestic income. The size of the terms-of-trade gain was estimated to have amounted to ¥ 12 trillion annually in 1986 and 1987, with the decline in oil prices in dollar terms and the yen's appreciation accounting for gains worth ¥ 2 trillion and ¥ 10 trillion, respectively.[33] Since there was an increase in the real purchasing power and the real income of the household sector expanded, the domestic demand increased in 1986 despite slowed economic growth due to the external drag on the economy. This was the income effect of yen appreciation. Part of the gain was offset by decline in export proceeds in yen terms but the net gain was ¥ 5 trillion or 1.4 per cent of real GNP.[34] The strong domestic demand of 1986 and thereafter was partly a consequence of the income effect.

Towards the end of this section I shall show that although in nominal terms the post-yen-appreciation current account surplus increased, in real terms, it began to plummet. This fall in real terms was the consequence of a 4.8 per cent rise in the volume of Japanese exports and 40 per cent rise in the volume of Japanese imports over the 1985–88 period. Such a large increase in the import volume resulted from increase in domestic demand which was noted earlier. The export volume growth was prompted by a cumulative 11 per cent growth in demand of the other industrialised economies during this period – demand growth being defined as growth in GNP plus imports minus exports. The strong foreign demand worked towards offsetting the negative impact of Japanese export prices due to appreciation on export volume.

Japan's strong nominal trade balance performance also reflected the starting bases of exports and imports. In nominal terms, exports in 1985 were 27 per cent higher than imports while in volume terms they were about one and a half times as large. These base period levels meant that imports had to grow roughly 50 per cent faster than exports just to keep Japan's trade surplus from rising.[35] Thus viewed, the rise in the nominal current account balance after 1985 reflected a starting base effect. There is also evidence of the dollar translation effect. The nominal trade balance measured in yen began to decline in 1987 and between 1986 and 1989 it contracted by ¥ 4881 billion. It was ¥ 13 739 billion in 1986, and fell to ¥ 8858 billion in 1989. Yet because the dollar value of the yen had increased, the dollar value of Japan's surplus rose despite this fall in yen terms. The opposite movements in trade balance in yen terms and in dollar terms has a great deal of significance for economic adjustment. The former is more fundamental to the economy because the labour payments and profits are both measured in yen terms. In addition, savings and investment are economically determined in yen terms.[36]

The quantitative impact on exports of increasing world demand and declining export prices, while the currency is appreciating, will depend upon relative price elasticity. The long-term price elasticity of Japanese export demand has been found to be low; it was estimated at −1.1. The export volume elasticity with respect to foreign demand was estimated at 1.8.[37] With such a fortuitous combination of elasticities, even an 11 per cent rise in foreign demand would mean a substantial impetus to export volumes.

Hysteresis and Pass-through in Export Prices

Such a large rise in the nominal effective exchange rate would reasonably have a significant adverse affect on Japanese trade balances unless the raw materials and the input prices and the profit margins were to act as a buffer. The former has already been dealt with, therefore let us turn to the latter. Varying the exchange rate affects the prices of traded goods and the concept of pass-through relates the two, namely, the traded goods prices and the changes in the exchange rate. If the exporter does not adjust prices in his domestic currency and allows the exchange rate variation to be entirely reflected in the import prices abroad, it is said that the pass-through into export prices is complete. As opposed to this, if the import prices abroad remain stable despite the rise in currency value and the price received by the exporter is adjusted to the exchange rate shocks, the pass-through is said to be zero.[38] The extent of pass-through is determined by the existence of hysteresis and the corporate planning horizon. In the case of the yen it was one way currency value change but in a floating exchange rate regime hysteresis can cause frequent problems for currencies and economies. The concept of hysteresis has been taken by economists like Krugman[39] and Baldwin[40] from the jargon of physics to express a certain nonlinearity between two or more variables, whereby the relationship between them is determined by the circumstances in the past. It essentially denotes resistance to change from the *status quo*. This stickiness can be generated by both the supply-side and the demand-side.

Taking the supply-side reasons first, increasing returns to scale can cause market inertia. Firms that have already succeeded in capturing large market shares are better placed with regard to cost than those that have small market shares and are trying to grow. Besides, given the static advantages of large-scale production or the dynamic advantages of learning effect, the mere fact of a set of firms being the first to dominate the market ensures their cost advantage over the follower firms, thus perpetuating their leading position. On the demand-side, brand loyalties causes market stickiness. Products that Japan sells at a commanding competitive advantage include durable consumer products like autos, cameras, stereos, video, etc., as well as investment goods like machinery and equipment. A certain amount of human and non-human capital becomes associated with the use of the brand. For instance, a computer user would surely choose to use the peripherals from the same producer.[41] In markets where hysteresis exists, the competing firms have to incur additional expenditure to overcome the market inertia. Some economists explain away why the yen/dollar exchange rate change failed to bring down the nominal trade imbalances with the help of hysteresis.[42]

Export prices may respond differently to large and small changes in the exchange rate. The behaviour of output and prices can go through three potential phases as exchange rate appreciation proceeds. First, when the degree of appreciation is insignificant or low, firms do not respond and the output and prices remain constant over time, largely because potential gains from output adjustment are more or less equal to the potential cost. Second, as the appreciation becomes sufficiently large, the firms begin to adjust output and prices. Finally, as appreciation becomes even larger the firms make a retreat from the export market. Thus, the planning horizon matters and determines the time points at which these changes as well as pass-through take place.[43] Initially insufficient pass-through was considered a short-term phenomenon resulting from factors like trade contracts and delivery lags. It was believed that the more fundamental factors like markets did not have an impact in the short-term. This perception, however, changed and current thinking deals more with the fundamental factors. The pass-through has been found to be strongly influenced by the trade composition of an individual country. In general, economies having a high proportion of final goods in their exports tended to have a higher pass-through ratio than countries where raw material exports predominate. Japan turned out to be an exception to this generalisation and initially had low, even less than 50 per cent, pass-through.[44] The IFS data corroborate this and show a fall in the unit value of Japanese exports from 100.0 in 1985 to 77.7 in 1988.

Although the change in the yen/dollar exchange rate influenced the relative production cost of the Japanese and the US firms, as noted above, the Japanese firms managed to keep the dollar prices of their exports low. A comparative study of pass-through using price data disaggregated to two-digit and four-digit SIC (Standard Industrial Classification) was done by Ohno. He inferred that for the US manufactured exports the pass-through was almost complete whereas the Japanese estimates were lower. On an average, the United States had a pass-through coefficient of 0.95 while that for Japan was 0.72.[45] Lower pass-through in Japan reduced profits of the tradable goods sector substantially. The periodic survey of the business enterprises done by the Bank of Japan bears out this observation and shows that until the first half of 1989 Japan's export prices fell in the manufactured goods sector.[46] This happened against the background of stable prices worldwide. An important distinction to be made here is between the domestic and export prices of the manufactured goods. On a cumulative basis while the domestic prices fell by 8.1 per cent during 1985–88, the export prices fell by 21.2 per cent.[47] Prices did not, however, fall in the non-tradable goods sector and the profit margins remained at their pre-appreciation level resulting in a profit differential in the tradable and non-tradable goods sectors.[48] The profit decline in the tradable goods sector was facilitated by decline in the prices of raw material inputs which has been noted before. Another factor easing the profit decline was the fall in the unit labour cost after 1985; due to strong productivity growth the labour cost declined by 4 per cent between 1985 and 1988. Over these years manufacturing unit labour costs in the other industrialised economies rose by 2 per cent.[49] Consequently, Japan gained by 6 per cent in relative labour cost competitiveness.

An additional reason why the normal J-curve theory did not apply to Japanese export volumes after the yen appreciation was a certain structural characteristic of exports. Several areas of Japanese exports consisted of products of strong non-price competitiveness. Their sales volumes did not decline even after the dollar prices were readjusted and the pass-through was complete. Thus, their exports in value terms increased. In this process, the usual inverted J-curve was replaced by an unusual horizontal L-curve. Several of the Japanese export lines were L-curve goods, like the capital goods, which allowed high yen to coexist with trade balance surpluses.[50] Such exports to the middle income developing countries did not flag after the yen appreciation.

The cumulative impact of lower pass-through rates, existence of L-curve goods in exports, declining raw material input prices and falling unit labour costs was enough to maintain Japan's price-competitiveness, in spite of a large nominal currency appreciation. Thus, hysteresis was supported by these price movements which contributed strength to the economy and its trade performance failed to weaken. This implies that the currency appreciation was over-whelmed by the above factors. They sufficiently explain the seem-ingly paradoxical rise in the current account surplus in the wake of yen appreciation. However, two simulation exercises tried to reckon the external surplus in the absence of yen appreciation. A non-realignment assumption was made which implies that there is no change in both the yen and the dollar effective exchange rates and that they remained at their third quarter 1985 levels. The simulation estimates were made over the quarterly data sample for 1975–87 so that the tracking error of the components of the current account remained small, especially in relation to the size of the simulated changes. Corker's (1989) simulation results show that Japan's current account surplus measured in yen would have been substantially larger – as much as 2 per cent of the GNP in 1987 – if the yen had not appreciated. He found that in real terms by 1987 Japanese exports would have been 19 per cent higher and real imports 10 per cent lower than actually observed and the real trade balance would have been 6 per cent instead of 4 per cent of Japanese GNP. This estimate is by and large in agreement with the results reached by a similar exercise done by the Economic Planning Agency World Model.[51] Thus viewed, the yen appreciation did exert a significant corrective influence on the external imbalance in the international economy.

	1985	1986	1987	1988
1. Nominal current account balance [billion of $]	49.14	85.83	87.00	79.63
2. Real current account balance at 1985 prices and exchange rate billions of $]		58.38	3.48	−11.15

As alluded to earlier in this section, although in nominal terms the post-appreciation current account surplus increased, in real terms, at 1985 prices and exchange rate, it began to dip in 1987. We also saw that the current account surplus began to decline in 1988 in dollar terms but in yen terms it had begun to fall a year earlier. Measured as a percentage of GNP, the surplus declined monotonically from 4.4 per cent in 1986 to 1.7 per cent in 1990. Performance on this count must have heartened the managers of the Japanese economy because it implied attainment of one more objective of the Maekawa committee and the Plaza accord. In 1989, the export volume growth of Japan was 4 per cent – about half the world average. This marked the fifth consecutive year of export expansion below the world average.

STREAMLINING AND RATIONALISATION AT THE CORPORATE LEVEL

The yen appreciation polarised Japanese business activity. On the one hand, a deflationary impact was created by adjustments in export and import volumes which in turn created downward pressure on stock figures in the manufacturing sector in such areas as inventories and equipment and some firms had to accept temporary losses. On the other hand, it has also had an expansionary effect through the steady growth of household expenditure and fixed investment by non-manufacturers and domestic-demand-oriented industries, a point which has been amply discussed. The nominal corporate profits plummeted in 1986 due to reduction in sales reflecting appreciation in the yen and a transitory increase in valuation losses on inventories. However, price stability brought about by a strong yen and corporate efforts to improve their costs-and-profits structures worked together to improve the subsequent profits. Therefore, as set out earlier, the deflationary impact of the yen's appreciation was significant in 1986, but we saw how the economic activity recorded a gradual recovery led by domestic demand and high investment rates. Although industries posted an 11.4 per cent year-to-year drop in profits in 1986, there was a clear contrast between industries favourably affected by the appreciated yen and those adversely affected. Principal manufacturers, excluding oil refineries, incurred their first profit decline in three years in fiscal year 1985 due to the deflationary impact of yen appreciation. In 1986, these industries posted a greater profit decrease of 26.8 per cent, the largest since the first oil crisis. As opposed to this, the profits of the non-manufacturers firmed significantly and were up 14.5 per cent in fiscal year 1986.[52]

The stability in the domestic prices was brought about by a sharp drop in the cost of imported materials in yen terms and exerted a favourable impact on corporate profits through improvements in the terms-of-trade. The general price index stood at 99.7 in 1989 and that for the manufactured goods at 94.2 (1985 = 100). Besides, the declining interest rates favourably influenced the financial accounts of business enterprises and largely absorbed the upward pressure on the ratio of fixed cost to sales, reflecting the drop in sales. On the micro side, firms reacted by rationalisation through retooling from top to bottom for crunching down costs, dropping unprofitable product lines and increasing the output of high value-added products, starting new enterprises, cultivating interbusiness fields and stepping up R&D to improve costs-and-profits structures. The result was that the fixed costs of manufacturers decreased by 1.6 per cent in 1986, the first such drop since 1975. The export-related manufacturers recorded a steeper, 3.7 per cent drop, which indicated that the business firms had rapidly begun to establish an improved costs-and-profits structure, enabling them to secure profitability without a large increase in sales.[53] Efforts to improve the profitability were assisted by the preference shown by business firms for imported parts and finished goods over the costly domestic production. Imports of parts increased by 40 per cent in 1986 and further by 20 per cent in 1987.[54] Imports by Japanese firms from foreign subsidiaries also increased substantially.

Both profits and sales of industrial enterprises registered a firm

Table 1.8   SALES AND CURRENT PROFITS OF
INDUSTRIAL ENTERPRISES, 1984–90 (IN PER CENT)

		1984	1985	1986	1987	1988	1989	1990
1. Manufacturers	Sales	7.9	1.9	−7.3	3.1	9.6	7.8	6.6
	Profits	33.9	−9.2	−26.8	36.0	39.3	11.3	5.3
2. Non-manufacturers	Sales	8.2	4.4	−11.9	7.3	8.0	21.6	0.0
	Profits	4.6	17.7	14.5	−4.1	8.7	4.6	0.9
3. All Industries	Sales	8.1	3.4	−10.1	5.6	8.6	16.0	2.5
	Profits	23.0	−0.7	−11.4	16.7	27.3	8.9	3.0

SOURCE   The Bank of Japan, *Tankan*: *Short-Term Economic Survey of
Principal Enterprises* (Tokyo, August 1990).

growth trend after a poor showing in 1986 (Table 1.8). Profits in the
manufacturing industries showed double digit growth for the three
years 1987–89. For the non-manufacturers the profits and sales
growth was lower because of (1) the electric utilities industry which
suffered from a sharp drop in profit because of the yen's depreciation
in 1989, (2) the hike in crude oil prices in the late 1980s and (3)
addition of communications and leasing industries to this sector. If
the electric utilities industry is excluded, the non-manufacturers show
seven straight years of increasing profits.

While on the one hand, domestic markets became increasingly
important for the Japanese corporations, on the other they pushed
manufacturing facilities offshore in third countries. For giant *sogo
shoshas* like Mitsubishi and Marubeni, tapping the domestic markets
was not easy because they were traditionally geared to large-scale,
wholesale dealings. It meant taking a fresh look at the product mix,
adding more consumer and high-tech goods and services to it and
studying ways of getting into the retail distribution system. Retail
marketing was an area of notable weakness for the large Japanese
corporations. An important post-appreciation change in the corporate behaviour was a nearly universal increase in the advertisement
expenditure. This was aimed at developing the domestic markets and
retaining the export markets.

The other noteworthy microeconomic measure that was adopted
by corporations was shifting from tradable goods to high-value-added
goods. Developments of new electronics-related areas and new materials and products drew a great deal of attention and resources.

Enterprises made active R&D investments in terms of men and money in order to develop new business areas. They were spurred on by economic restructuring and fear of losing international economic competitiveness due to the yen's strength against other major currencies. A strong across-the-board increase was observed in R&D investment by the industrial sector, it increased from 21.8 per cent to 26.0 per cent between 1985 and 1987.[55] This future-oriented investment moderately enhanced the fixed costs of the firms. A note of caution is needed here, that is, not all the heightened investment and movement of labour in R&D can be attributed to yen appreciation. During the late 1970s and early 1980s, the comparative advantage was shifting in Japan from low-tech heavy industries to high-tech industries. The government and the private sector firms attempted to expand the latter sector and, to this end, the government provided a package of incentives and conducted various programmes. The R&D efforts were intensified after the second oil price hike and the annual reports of corporations clearly showed a substantial increase in the R&D expenditure. The Ratio of R&D expenses to sales had increased from 0.6 per cent in 1979 to 1.8 per cent in 1986 and at this point Japan had a higher proportion of its population engaged in R&D than the US.[56] Nevertheless, the yen's appreciation provided a definite impetus to the R&D investment trend and the private sector accounted for the lion's share of annual increases. As opposed to this, research spendings by universities and research laboratories recorded anaemic gains. According to an Economic Planning Agency (EPA) survey, the manufacturing sector had plans to spend in excess of ¥ 3 trillion on R&D in the year ending March 1990. This achievement was to cap a quinquennium in which manufacturers' R&D outlays rose at an average annual rate of more than 10 per cent.[57] Consequently, according to a US National Science Foundation study, Japan had achieved parity in semiconductor technology, silicon product technology and high-definition television by 1989 and was pulling ahead in superconductivity research.[58]

THE *ENDAKA* RECESSION

The Japanese word *endaka* has the characters of both high and yen. The question is often asked whether the appreciating yen created recession in the economy. Table 1.9 provides a clear and convincing answer.

Table 1.9 THE DECADAL ECONOMIC TREND, 1980–89

	1980	81	82	83	84	85	86	87	88	89
1. Real economic growth rate	4.3	3.7	3.1	3.2	5.1	4.9	2.5	4.6	5.7	4.9
2. Domestic demand growth rate	0.9	2.2	2.8	1.7	3.7	3.8	3.9	5.2	7.4	5.9
3. Growth rate of plant and equipment investment by private sector	1.2	0.8	0.4	0.4	1.8	2.1	1.0	1.5	3.0	3.7

SOURCE Economic Planning Agency, *Annual Report on National Accounts* (Tokyo, various issues).

In the first post-appreciation year (1986) the negative effects were strong and the economy showed a sharp deceleration. The real economic growth rate made a nose dive and plant and equipment investment rate fell to half its pre-appreciation level. The gross fixed capital formation declined by 32 per cent from its previous year's level. It has been noted that the nominal corporate profits also plunged in 1986. The economy absorbed the deflationary impact of the high yen by mid-1986 and the bottom of the *endaka* recession was reached in June 1986, thereafter, *vide ut supra* the economic activity displayed a gradual and sustained recovery led by domestic demand. An extraordinary rebound in capital spending was the other propelling factor. This upswing of the business cycle continued unabated during 1990 and according to the Ministry of Finance the nominal GNP growth rate was 7.6 per cent while in real terms it was 5.6 per cent.[59] This is after the real economic growth rates of 5.7 per cent in 1988 and 4.9 per cent in 1989. During 1990, when the UK and the US were showing signs of sliding into recession, the Japanese economy was cruising at a healthy pace. The survey results of the Industrial Bank of Japan show that the following major industries recorded favourable and high earning trends during the fiscal 1989 and 1990: electronics, motor vehicles, general machinery, shipping, steel, synthetic fibres, paper and pulp, nonferrous smelting, departmental stores and superstores, shipping and construction.[60] Although economic growth slowed during the closing months of 1990, there was little concern about a recession setting in. On the contrary, in non-government economists and banking circles there was an anxiety about overheating. It was hardly irrelevant because the economy demonstrated remarkable vigour in the face of recession abroad and high interest rates at home and grew at an astonishing annual rate of 11.2 per cent in the first quarter of 1991.[61] By mid-1990, the current upswing had surpassed the *Iwato* boom of the late 1950s which had lasted for 42 months to become the second longest economic upturn in the post-war period after the *Izanagi* boom in the latter half of the 1960s, which had lasted for 57 months. The current boom has exceeded even the *Izanagi* boom and become the longest lasting upswing of the business cycle in the post-war period. This boom has been named *Izanami* by some, after the goddess *Izanami*, the wife of god *Izanagi* and co-creator of the Japanese Archipelago. The reason for choosing the goddess' name was that this boom is based on domestic demand and led by personal spending which is largely controlled by housewives.[62] Thus, Japan's macro- and microeconomic management and its economic resilience shrugged off a steep currency appreciation that could have been fatal to most other economies. Vigorous rationalisation efforts by the industrial sector enabled the economy to turn the *endaka* recession on its head.

The expansion of domestic demand, that pulled the economy out of the *endaka* recession, has already been alluded to in a different context. It was initially based on construction and public investment and subsequently on private consumption and fixed investment. Supported by rising household disposable incomes, private consumption growth rate recorded rapid increases from 3.1 per cent in 1987, to 4.2 per cent in 1987 and to 5.0 per cent in 1988. The saving rates accordingly dropped to 15.1 per cent of the household disposable income in 1987 to 14.8 per cent in 1988. This was the lowest rate in 22 years. The personal income tax was reduced in 1988 which contributed to consumption increases. They were broadly based and spread from the self-employed to employee households and from higher-income to lower-income households. Gross fixed investment also steadily increased from its trough in the second half of 1986 to its highest level since the early 1970s (see pp. 16–17 above).

The *endaka* induced perceptible changes in domestic demand and influenced the Japanese life style. The dominant change in demand was its growing sophistication, which was discernible in its diversity. Expenditure has been rising on leisure-related activities and higher class products. This demand pattern stimulated corporate activities substantially in the areas of high value-added products and promoted information intensification and diversification of business activity.

The post-yen-appreciation economic expansion entailed constantly expanding personal consumption. A bullish trend is easy to see in the post-1985 statistics: the real personal consumption growth was 3.4 per cent in 1986 over the previous year. It then increased by 4.5 per cent in 1987 and further by 4.7 per cent in 1988, exhibiting a steady rise. The gain in 1988 was the highest in ten years. A family income and expenditure survey revealed that the increase in consumption spending by households was irrespective of income class.[63] The breakdown of increased spending shows that it centred on (1) durable consumer goods like automobiles and household electrical appliances, and (2) services like travel, education and health-related services.

SUMMING UP

When the US Council of Economic Advisers suggested that an appreciation of the yen would be a necessary and sufficient condition for correcting the international current account imbalances, they were only partly correct because they ignored the macroeconomic rationale behind them. In the aftermath of the Plaza accord, the yen began to appreciate at a steep rate and before the end of 1988 its nominal value against the dollar doubled. If the real effective exchange rate is taken as an indicator, this appreciation caused a loss of competitiveness for the Japanese exports by as much as 30 per cent.

That a major restructuring of the economy is needed was apparent to the managers of the Japanese economy and the radical measures suggested by the Maekawa committee did not surprise anyone. The proposed strategy called for such a fundamental economic restructuring that most doubted the ability of the Government to perform. However, the yen appreciation became a propelling force and managed to bring about many of the proposed changes. For instance, traditionally external demand contributed a great deal to the economic growth. Currency appreciation improved the profitability of the non-traded goods sector and strengthened the domestic demand leading to a switch in the production structure from export-oriented to domestic-demand-oriented. Some of the finer changes included a slackening in the demand for the manufacturing industries and continuing growth in the non-manufacturing industries. Firms became domestic-market-oriented. Capital investment recorded extraordinary increases and business enterprises made a great deal of investment in the domestic-demand-oriented industries and high-tech manufacturing. The investment activity was so effervescent in the late 1980s that the Ministry of International Trade and Industry had to restrain firms in 1990. The higher investment outlays went a long way in bringing about the structural changes suggested by the Maekawa committee. Many of its objectives, which initially had seemed implausible and unattainable, were achieved by the end of the decade.

Imports recorded steep growth rates and the economy became more open after the yen appreciation. The import structure changed from raw-material-dominated to manufactured-goods-dominated. The imports of manufactured products doubled in the short span of five years. Currency appreciation caused a demand shift from domestic to imported products in durable consumer goods and several manufactured products, consequently several domestic production lines and many low-tech producers were driven out of the market. It eventually shifted the axis of international trade from vertical to horizontal specialization. The increased imports of the Japanese economy contributed to production growth abroad and the Japanese economy began to play 'locomotive' role in the international economy. The yen appreciation contributed to price stability on the domestic front and decline on the export front.

Somewhat paradoxically the trade surpluses in volume terms as well as nominal current account surpluses co-existed with the appreciated yen for a long time. This seeming incongruity could be explained by the following factors: (1) terms of trade improvement leading to real income effect, (2) continued growth in demand of the other industrialised countries, (3) capital goods exports behaving like L-curve goods, (4) wide difference in the starting bases of exports and imports, (5) the pass-through coefficient in Japan was low, (6) oil and raw material prices declined and the yen appreciation magnified this decline, and (7) unit labour costs fell in the post appreciation period. Yet, at 1985 prices and exchange rate as well as in terms of the yen, the current account surpluses had began to fall in 1987 and after 1988 they began to record a decline even in nominal terms.

Currency appreciation polarised the Japanese firms into those benefiting from the strong domestic demand and those suffering from the deflationary impact created by adjustment in import and export volumes. Profits improved for the former category of firms while they suffered a decline in the latter group. In general, the price stabilising effect of yen appreciation had a favourable impact on corporate finances. The export-related manufacturers brought down their fixed cost and succeeded in re-establishing an improved profit structure, allowing them to secure profitability without large increases in sales. These efforts were assisted by the preference shown by firms for imported parts and finished goods over the expensive domestic production. Another noteworthy microeconomic shift that was adopted by firms was moving from tradable goods to high-value-added goods. Also firms increased their R&D and advertising budgets across the board.

An honest answer to the question of whether a strong yen created conditions of recession in the Japanese economy, will have to be in the affirmative. It is visible in the macroeconomic indicators for 1986. But the *endaka* recession was only a passing phase of the Japanese economy and in 1987 it entered into a sustained upswing of the business cycle which was showing no signs of a down-turn even in 1991, despite high interest rates. The economy was propelled out of recession by a strong expansion in capital investment and domestic demand.

2 Interaction with the International Economy

INTRODUCTION

During a major part of the 1960s and 1970s the Japanese economy outperformed the other industrial economies in terms of total factor productivity growth, that is, the combined productivity of labour and capital inputs. The 1980s were an eventful decade for the international economy and a momentous one for Japan. Ebullient growth rates and the yen appreciation made it the second largest economy in the world after the United States. The conventional method of comparing the nominal GNP of different countries is to convert the GNP figures in current prices into a common currency using market exchange rates. Accordingly, measured in the European Currency Unit (Ecu) the GNP of the US in 1990 was Ecu 4288 billion and it was the largest economy in the world. Japan stood second with a GNP of Ecu 2335 billion and Germany came next with Ecu 1190 billion.[1] However, when measured in constant prices some surprising developments may come to the fore. For instance, the Japanese GNP contracted in 1990 (see above) from Ecu 2625 billion in 1989, thus reducing Japan's share in the total output of the six largest industrialised countries (the US, Japan, Germany, France, Italy and the UK) from 24.2 per cent in 1989 to 22.5 per cent in 1990. Yet at constant prices Japan's growth rate, at 5.6 per cent, was the highest of the six countries in 1990. This apparent contraction is explained by the yen's 21 per cent depreciation against the Ecu between 1989 and 1990.[2]

Japan was the third largest exporter in the world in 1989 and it held the same position in imports. During the latter quinquennium of the 1980s, the role of Japanese financial institutions grew dramatically in the world of international finance. In terms of assets, several Japanese banks appear at the top of the list of major banks in the world. The assets held by the Bank of Japan surpassed even those of the Federal Reserve Board in 1989 – this achievement is only partly attributable to the appreciation of the yen. Japan's net external assets amounted to $29.2 billion at the end of 1988, making it the largest creditor country in the world.[3] It has become the single most important supplier of liquidity to the international financial markets. According to the OECD data, with a total disbursement of official development assistance (ODA) of $8965 million in 1989, Japan became the largest donor country in the world in absolute terms.[4] During the same year Japan's foreign direct investment outflows became the highest in the world. A large number of Japanese corporations were making their presence felt in the international business world. In the *Fortune's* unique list of the world's 500 biggest industrial corporations, the US stood at the top in 1990 with 164 companies, followed by Japan with 111 corporations. Britain and France ranked third and fourth, respectively, with 43 and 30 corporations.[5] Due to high rates of investment in R&D during the latter half of the 1980s and the post-appreciation economic restructuring, the Japanese industrial sector has become among the most sophisticated in the world. An interesting indicator of this trend is that while in dollar terms commodity trade expanded, in physical volume terms it actually decreased. This was the consequence of Japanese industries moving towards the so-called 'higher, thinner, shorter and smaller' industries, or the downsizing of economic output. At the end of 1989, the industrial robot population of Japan was 219 667, the highest in the world. The corresponding statistics for the United States and Germany were 36 977 and 22 395, respectively. The GDPs of the US, Western Europe and Japan are now roughly in the ratio of 5:5:3 and the Japanese economy is showing every sign of growing faster than most of the other industrialised economies.[6]

After Japan became an economic superpower, international expectations began to rise and it was expected to move to the centre-stage and play an international role commensurate with its new status. Although this new status and financial leverage is strong enough to block any hostile policy initiative abroad, its economic and financial prowess has given it only a limited one-dimensional power base. Without geopolitical and military dimensions Japan cannot acquire a fully-fledged world-class superpower status and there are no indications that the two missing dimensions are anywhere near realisation. In addition, so far Japan has frustrated international expectations and displayed reluctance to move to centre-stage. The maximum it has done in this direction is to offer a tentative plan to play a more active regional security role, which alarms the Asia-Pacific countries.[7] At times, Japan gives an impression that it does not have a clear vision of its international role and that its sporadic *beaux gestes* are reluctant attempts to shore up its relations with other countries rather than statesmanlike acts of generosity. One of the reasons behind this reluctance is that Japan's Peace Constitution forced it to de-emphasise foreign policy and concentrate on economic relations. Besides, for a long time during the post-war period, international relations for Japan meant its relationship with the US because this bond was indispensable for Japan's well-being. The rest of the world had a peripheral significance for it. At this point Japan was wrapped up in itself and all its energy was focused on rebuilding its economy.

Japan being a one-dimensional superpower is not the same as Japan being an inconsequential superpower, because from the vantage point of the early 1990s it is easy to see that the world of the immediate future will be led not so much by military strength as by economic prowess and technological capabilities. In addition, the international economic community is far more interdependent than it was a couple of decades ago. The essential aspect of this interdependence is the accelerating flow of goods, services, capital and information, and, to be sure, the locus of international interdependence lies in the principles of economics which are rational and universal. Therefore, despite being a one-dimensional power Japan is bound to play a much larger role in the emerging international economic order. The two missing dimensions need not necessarily reduce Japan's international status to naught. The importance of this new role cannot be overemphasised because Japan's own continued growth and prosperity are *inter alia* premised upon a stable and smoothly functioning international economy.

PAX JAPONICA?

Notwithstanding the unidimensionality of the power base, being one of the two largest economies, one of the three largest traders and the largest creditor in the world gives a country a significant status in the international economy and enables it to cast longer shadows in the geopolitical, strategic and cultural affairs of the world. There has been a close correlation between the country that dominates world finances and the one that has the maximum international influence in other ways, namely, geopolitically, technologically, and industrially. The leading creditor country has generally been equated with the leading global power in the past in a somewhat mechanical manner. This mechanical equality applied squarely to the United Kingdom in the past century when it grew into the world's largest creditor country by continuing to run large trade surpluses.

At the end of the First World War the torch was passed on to the United States and *Pax* Britannica changed to *Pax* Americana.[8] In the Bretton Woods Conference, which was to lay the foundation of the post-war monetary system, the Keynesian plan lost to the White plan and the dollar became the key currency instead of the pound. Another historical turning point came in the latter half of the 1980s when the United States turned from the largest creditor nation to the largest debtor and the baton was passed from the United States to Japan. Does this imply the beginning of *Pax* Japonica? Although the United States does not have the same domineering presence on the international economic stage as it did until the mid-1980s, it still is the largest economy and the dollar is still the key currency. Strong indications are that the international economy of the 1990s will be a multipolar or, more precisely, a tripolar economy, with Japan and the four Asian newly industrialising economies (ANIEs) working as a strong growth pole. The yen's appreciation and that of the major European currencies as well as macroeconomic policy coordination among industrialised countries have improved the competitiveness of the ANIEs, which in turn, together with expansion of domestic demand in Japan, accelerated growth in these economies (cf. Chapter 6). That they, along with Japan, will play a role of growing significance is no longer a matter of conjecture. We shall return to this point on pp. 56–63, below.

The growth in Japan's stature in the international economy has not been free of friction. It is difficult for an economy not to have problems while internationalising its operations and status. As trade penetrates or when direct investment is made, the host countries may feel the pinch of market domination or over-presence of foreign enterprises. The resulting economic frictions may express themselves in diverse ways such as trade friction, investment friction, the problems of market access and the like. Expansion of free trade leads to or intensifies competition. The trade tensions emerge when sometimes some industries that were not exposed to competition in the past, lose to more competitive foreign exporters. When these industries are forced to move or shed factors of production, trade related tensions are born. Although from a neoclassical economic viewpoint economic adjustment has costs and these costs are unavoidable in a growing economy, sound economic ideas are politically unsellable. Positive economics is often negative politics. Therefore, throughout the 1970s and the first half of the 1980s, Japan had to face economic discord with other industrial economies. As time passed, friction increased. By the mid-1980s, trade imbalances between Japan and the United States had widened significantly. Trade surpluses also existed in Japan's trade with the European Community (EC) but they were not as large and grew slowly. The trade partners, therefore, demanded better access to the Japanese markets and decline or removal of non-tariff barriers. Since Japan benefited enormously from the easy market access to the United States and the EC during its growth phase, it was thought that it would be morally obliged to react positively and graciously to the demands of its trading partners.

In the mid-1980s, Japan became the butt of acrimonious criticism of the other industrialised economies for not opening its markets wide enough for their exports. Not all of this criticism could stand the scrutiny of probing economists. The basic and oft-repeated gripe was that Japan's visible trade barriers were higher than those of its competitors. Statistics for 1985 show that its tariffs were among the world's lowest; the tariff burden on imports in Japan was 2.6 per cent compared to 3.3 per cent for the United States and 2.7 per cent for the EC.[9] When this became obvious, the criticism shifted to the charge that the Ministry of International Trade and Industry (MITI) was managing to prevent an increase in imports despite lower trade barriers. When empirical scrutiny failed to sustain this charge as well, the argument shifted from the efficiency of the visible, import-restraining hand of MITI to the inefficiency of Adam Smith's invisible import-enhancing hand. It was not an economic but a cultural argument and contended that in its economic organisation Japan was so exotic that its markets did not function as they normally do in the West.[10] Coarse accusations that it was trying to become a mercantilistic power and thereby seeking national supremacy were made against Japan. All this went against the grain of the Japanese concept of *chowa*, seeking harmony in all vital spheres of life.

The culturalists have had a field day predicting the advent of Japan's hegemony and determining its nature. Nester related it to the historical an psycho-cultural norms and asserted that the Japanese hegemony would be of a neo-mercantilist nature: before 1945, Japan pursued classical mercantilist policies and since then, neo-mercantilist policies. A casual look at the trade statistics supported his contention. In his scheme of things, Japan's traditions of international isolation, centralised rule, and a close business–government alliance fed its neo-mercantilist urges. Neo-mercantilism is more than an economic strategy, it is a manifestation of the national culture. Therefore, Japan will probably remain neo-mercantilist even if it achieves global economic hegemony. Under Japan's group-oriented ethical system, it is the group's subjective interpretation of its needs, rather than any objective standard of behaviour, that determines right and wrong. Since Japanese people will continue to view Japan as their ultimate group, they will remain insensitive to the economic hardships and negative effects of their neo-mercantilist policies in other countries.[11] According to this view, Japan has denied and will continue to deny its international responsibilities as an economic superpower.

Culturalists or not, if one were to take a long-term view, the three principal channels through which Japan influences the international economy, and can further this influence, are as follows: first, by supporting and promoting a new pragmatic international economic order which would conform with the erosion of economic boundaries and globalisation of business activity, by actively assuming its share in the burden of providing international public goods and by encouraging macroeconomic policy coordination among the industrialised countries. In specific terms it implies (a) becoming a principal supporter of the collective management system of the international economy and fully throwing its weight behind multilateral trade negotiations like the Uruguay Round which restarted after a collapse, helping to devise new liberal rules of overseas investment, technology transfer, and intellectual property rights, (b) co-operating with the United States and the European Community through economic summit meetings, quadrilateral conferences, OECD and other similar fora, (c) stabilising the exchange rate through continued international financial policy co-ordination, and (d) participating more actively in the multilateral financial institutions.[12]

Several of the influences enumerated above are already being exerted by Japan. For instance, in the World Bank and the International Monetary Fund, Japan is being seen as the country that will wield considerably larger influence in the 1990s.[13] Both in the World Bank and the International Development Association (IDA), the Japanese shareholding and voting power is next to that of the US.

According to the 1990 annual report it was 8.88 per cent in the World Bank and 9.73 per cent in the IDA.[14] Japan provides a substantial amount of financial resources to the latter and a growing amount to the Asian Development Fund (ADF). Although Japan and the United States both own 16.4 per cent of shares, the Japanese have virtually taken over the Asian Development Bank. In the IMF Japan is the joint second-biggest quota holder along with Germany. The intellectual or policy input from Japan in the multilateral institutions is presently more in keeping with its economic and financial status (cf. Chapter 5). For instance, in 1992 Japan insisted on an enhanced significance of the 'visible hand' in development strategy and succeeded in persuading the new World Bank president to internally circulate a study on it. In the IMF Japan constantly presses for reforming the international monetary system. However, the Japanese physical presence in these organisations is so small as to belie its faith in, and commitment to, multilateralism. Second, the size and attractiveness of Japan's domestic market has grown in importance for the other economies and it is considered one of the megamarkets of the 1990s. Consequently, during the late 1980s there was a constant pressure on Japan from its trading partners to liberalise its domestic markets in both the goods and services sectors. To be sure, Japan was slow to open its markets to foreign products and enterprises. However, as we shall see, in the post-appreciation period the Japanese economy has progressively internationalised and market access for non-Japanese firms has improved. A related endeavour is implementing domestic institutional reforms to conform to international standards because some of the long-standing legal, institutional and business practices in Japan are regarded by the non-Japanese as disguised forms of trade barriers. They need to be modified and made acceptable to the international community. Some progress on this count has already been made. Third, promotion of trade and investment activities around the world is taking its natural market-led course but Japan needs to do so with an objective to strengthen the fibres of the international economy. The specific measures that have been taken in this regard include (a) reducing current account imbalances, (b) infusion of new liquidity in the heavily debt-ridden developing economies, and (c) expansion of foreign direct investment. The ODA and recycling of surplus to developing economies through the private sector has reached a high pitch which needs to be sustained. Be it noted that none of these three conduits of impact over the international economy need to make the Japanese economy hegemonic.

While no one seriously disputes Japan's status as an economic superpower, it seems implausible to believe that Japan would squander its energy in establishing a *Pax* Japonica. However, Japan has been active in the above-named spheres of the international economy and it has succeeded in defusing a good deal of the economic tensions of the mid-1980s. This has enabled Japan to become a dynamic growth pole of the international economy in company with the four ANIEs. To be sure, Japan's influence would be much greater than what it was in the past but in the multipolar world of the immediate future it is difficult to see any nation having a hegemonic status. One can, therefore, conclude that although the chances of *Pax* Japonica reigning supreme are slender or non-existent, Japan would work as a strong and dynamic economic pole of the international economy without dominating it. Japan is ready for a soft-edged international economic leadership in a world of several equals. In the 1980s, particularly after the yen's appreciation, there has been a variation in the intensity of its influence over the international economy. Expansion in Japan's economic and financial influence created knotty snags as well as opportunities. The following exposition addresses the pattern and process of mutation in Japan's interaction with its principal economic partners.

THE JAPAN–US ECONOMIC ASYMMETRY

There has been a long-standing symbiotic relationship between the two largest economies of the world. According to the latest (1989) available statistics, the US is the largest trading partner of Japan, accounting for 34.2 per cent of its total exports and 23.0 per cent of its total imports. In turn, Japan is the second largest trading partner of the US after Canada, accounting for 12.2 per cent of its total exports and 19.7 per cent of its total imports. This nexus has existed for a substantial time span. The US has not only provided Japan's exports with their best markets but also attractive investment opportunities for its surplus savings, which in turn became the much-needed capital base for the American industries. Japan has had comparative advantage in consumer products and has supplied American consumers with reasonably-priced and high-quality consumer goods. Both economies have traded in high-tech products and advanced technology with each other for a long time. Despite the closeness of the link, the economic relationship between the two countries has soured and in some quarters, notably Capitol Hill, Japan is being branded as a public enemy responsible for all American economic problems. Although there were two brief periods of trade friction between Japan and the US during the late 1960s and the late 1970s, the current wave was created due to Japanese exports of steel, colour televisions, automobiles, machine tools and semiconductors. The US complains of Japanese overpresence in these areas. The friction has been exacerbated by the problems related to the US exports of beef, oranges, tobacco, rice, Japan's domestic distribution system, the so-called *keiretsu*[15] links among corporations and tendering procedures for public construction projects. These issues, despite efforts from both the trade partners, have defied resolution.

In view of the growing current account deficit of the US since 1983, the discordant issues have taken a larger dimension. Unsavoury expressions like 'Japan bashing' and 'Japanese invasion' have become a part of common parlance.[16] American pique has *inter alia* found expression in Section 301 and the related section of the Omnibus Trade Act of 1988. The Japanese are beginning to hit back and a celebrated sign of their irritation was a book called *'No' to ieru Nihon*, or *The Japan That Can Say No*. One of its two authors is the illustrious Akio Morita, which gives the book its bite. The hub of controversy is the trade imbalances between the two economies, the US deficits stood at $40.6 billion in 1985, on the eve of the Plaza accord. Notwithstanding the steep appreciation in the value of the yen, it soared until 1987. However, it began to decline the next year (Table 2.1). In 1990, the annual deficit of the US contracted further to $36 593 million. During the pre-appreciation period US exports to Japan were approximately half of its exports to the EC, although the US imports from Japan and the EC were not very different. The unprecedented trade imbalances that resulted exceeded the political tolerance of the US and galvanised a movement for trade protectionism. The protectionist calls of the US Congress became increasingly strident, causing serious strains in the politics of economic policy.

The polemic was premised on the belief that the trade imbalance has obstinately persisted because the Japanese markets are not open, the Japanese trade practices are unfair and that Japan's economic agenda places higher priority on industrial strategy than commitment to the principles of free trade, comparative advantage and *laissez faire*. The protagonists of this heresy argued that since Japan's economy worked in a different way from that in the other industrial countries, it must be dealt with differently from that of the other

Table 2.1   JAPAN–US TRADE 1982–89

Year	Japan's Export to the US		Japan's Import from the US		Trade Balance millions of $	Percentage change over the preceding year
	Value in millions of $	Percentage change over the preceding year	Value in millions of $	Percentage change over the preceding year		
1982	36 546		24 185		12 361	
1983	43 339	+81.6	24 795	+2.5	18 544	+50.0
1984	60 429	+39.4	26 887	+8.4	33 542	+80.9
1985	66 684	+10.3	26 099	−2.9	40 585	+20.9
1986	81 926	+22.8	29 410	+12.7	52 516	+29.4
1987	85 017	+10.4	31 957	+8.6	53 060	+1.0
1988	90 245	+6.1	42 265	+32.3	47 980	−9.6
1989	93 954	+4.1	48 253	+14.2	45 701	−4.7
1990 (September)	66 111		38 656		27 455	

SOURCE   International Monetary Fund, *Direction of Trade Statistics Yearbook 1990* and *Direction of Trade Statistics Monthly, August 1991* (Washington DC: 1990 and 1991).

trading partners. All these arguments became more piquant after the early 1980s when the US developed a homegrown gap in its economy: savings. Federal budget deficits, allowed the US to consistently save less than it invested. Given these facts, let us scrutinise the veracity of the above allegations. As for Japan's market not being open, it has been set forth in the first section that Japan's tariffs on imports were lower than those in the EC and the US and that it has a low level of import quotas on manufactured goods in comparison to the other OECD economies. Although the series of market-opening measures that Japan has carried out were dismissed as *tatem* by some, an image or a certain version of truth for a particular audience, imports of manufactured goods have steadily increased over the 1980s. Over the 1980–85 period their growth rate was not so high but after the yen's appreciation they increased at a steep rate. They were 31.0 per cent of the total Japanese imports in 1985, but their proportion soared to 50.3 per cent in 1989 (cf. Chapter 1). Thus, the macroeconomic indicators suggest that with the exception of some agricultural products, Japan's domestic market is one of the most open among the industrialised countries.

Those who argue from the other side cite very specific examples of selective setting of tariffs to protect certain domestic industries. They also refer to the *jimae shugi* principle of the Japanese corporations which implies 'make, do not buy whenever possible'. Japan has been liberalising and deregulating its industries but the American exporters feel that it is being done excessively carefully and slowly.[17] Those who wag an accusing finger forget that selective protection of infant industries is done all over the world and even the trade theory allows it. Second, the charge of *jimae shugi* was correct for the decade of the 1960s, or in a mild manner for the 1970s, but the statistics of manufactured imports for the 1980s, cited in the preceding paragraph, prove it wrong. Lastly, those who contend that comparative advantage is not a part of Japanese economic thinking, strain credulity because it does not stand to logic that the Japanese economy became so competitive in a broad range of high-value-added products without its managers paying attention to its comparative advantage as well as constant changes in it.

Japan is indeed protectionist in an unreasonable manner in farm products like rice and beef and in areas like telecommunications, satellites, fibre-optics and construction services, and bilateral or multilateral pressure to dismantle barriers in these areas is correct. However, seriously proposing promotion of 'managed trade', or voluntary export restrictions (VERs), or sector by sector bilateral negotiations is as absurd as Rudigar Donbusch's *quid pro quo* prescription of a tariff hike on all Japanese imports into the US if Japan does not increase the imports of American manufactures by 10 per cent.[18] All such economic-defying solutions are artificial, short-term, short-sighted, and retrograde. If American exports are the victim of the so-called 'structural impediments' in Japan, one has to judge their performance in the world markets which is a level playing field. This is where the Japanese economic prowess is felt *a fortiori*.

The Rationale Behind Trade Imbalances

Long-term trade imbalances need not necessarily be created by unfair trade practices. The mechanics of the increase in Japan's trade surplus with the US during the 1980s is partly explained by structural factors. Japan mainly exports manufactured products like autos, computers, integrated circuits, VCRs, scientific and precision instruments, semiconductors and other electronic devices. A large proportion of Japan's imports from the US comprises primary products, that is, foods and raw materials like timber, corn, soyabean, coal and seafood. The industrial and high-tech products that Japan exports have had a strong demand in the US whereas the US exports to Japan, specially the agricultural products, suffered from demand as well as price stagnation. From a structuralist viewpoint it is apparent that Japanese exports to the US are mainly composed of commodities having high income elasticity, while its imports from the US are mostly low income elasticity products. This situation has been conducive to the gradual enlargement of the trade imbalances between the two economies.[19] Japan's exports also had a strong correlation with the US GNP growth rate. For instance, in 1984 the growth rate of GNP was 6.5 per cent, the highest in the last three decades. As seen in Table 2.1, the trade surplus of Japan leapt by 81 per cent in 1984.

The economic policies of the Reagan administration contributed substantially to the increase in the US fiscal deficit as well as the Japanese trade surpluses *vis-à-vis* the US. The chain of policy actions began in the last quarter of 1979 when the Federal Reserve Board (Fed) shifted its operational instrument from interest rates to high powered money. That is, in view of the high inflationary rates after the second oil shock, the US adopted a monetarist approach and tried to rein in the money supply. This was intended to be a disinflationary measure. This move sent the interest rates soaring which, in turn, went a long way in appreciating the dollar. Subsequently, the supply-side policies of the Reagan administration, in their endeavour to revitalise the economy, reduced taxes to increase savings and investment. The supply-side programme raised the general confidence in the fundamentals of the US economy, and coupled with high interest rates, it increased foreign investment. The supply-side policies like lowering income and corporate taxes resulted in a steady rise in fiscal deficits. Several econometric analyses of this scenario have concluded that the US fiscal expansion has had a large and growing effect on the deterioration of the US current account balances and that it has forced the Japanese current account in the opposite direction, that is, towards surplus.[20] Sachs and Roubini have successfully used the Mundell-Fleming model to explain the courses of the Japanese and the US economies during the 1980s.[21] The model attributes a great deal to domestic fiscal expansion and infers that a fiscal contraction can improve the current account mainly through exchange rate depreciation. The major reason for the Japanese current account surplus was the high growth of absorption in the US. It largely means great consumption growth because the growth rate of investment in the US has remained low. The absorption approach tells us that the trade balance turns into a deficit when domestic absorption exceeds a nation's GNP, or when domestic investment exceeds savings. About two-thirds of the increase in total Japanese exports between 1980 and 1986 can be explained by the increase in exports to the US.[22] Using the vector autoregression technique to model the bilateral current account balances and taking exchange rate, budget deficits and national incomes as endogenous variables, a simulation exercise was conducted under a variety of fiscal policy scenarios. The simulation results indicated that without any change in the fiscal policy stance of either country, the trade deficit would continue to grow. Reduction of fiscal deficits in the US reduces the trade deficit, but the cost is lower national incomes in the US as well as Japan.[23] These results corroborate the inferences arrived at by the studies mentioned above.

Another set of stimulation used a dynamic model to point to the complementarity of expenditure-reducing and expenditure-switching policies in analysing the US trade deficits. The current account balance is both S-I and X-M. Therefore, an adjustment plan cannot be narrowed by attacking only one front. The job requires the closing of two gaps, that is, that of savings and investments on one hand and of exports and imports on the other. The model supports the expansion of domestic demand in Japan and the reserve in the US for controlling the deficits. But their results also emphasised real depreciation of the dollar against the yen and the Deutsche Mark.[24]

In trying to explain that imbalance does not have to be merely a function of unfair trade practices, Bergsten and Cline concluded that protection can explain at most a modest part of the bilateral trade imbalance or even its growth in recent years.[25] They contended that virtually the entire increase in the bilateral trade deficit until late 1985 was caused by macroeconomic factors, particularly the 'overvaluation of the dollar', which they and others attributed to the fiscal policies in the US.[26] Casual empiricism supports this contention because there was a discernible increase in the trade imbalances after 1982. Since it did not follow a massive increase in the Japanese trade barriers or a large liberalisation by the US, the soaring dollar keeps coming in focus as the prime causal factor. Lagged effects of the strong dollar continued to be a major source of trade deficit even after the 1980–85 rise of the dollar was reversed. It is established by the simple model used by Krugman and Baldwin.[27] Besides, it is a commonly accepted view that substantial lags existed in the adjustment of both prices and quantities to exchange rate, probably reflecting a tendency of firms to commit themselves to suppliers for extended periods of time. The impact of the lag became so pronounced because the dollar had appreciated steeply before it began to fall and firms were still adjusting to the strength of the dollar and shifting to foreign suppliers even as the dollar fell. Many of them had started making this adjustment belatedly. There are two related macroeconomic tendencies of the Japanese economy that are often ignored: First, since the early 1970s investment relative to GNP decreased more sharply than savings, which resulted in a large excess of savings over investment. Second, the large budget deficit in the 1970s, which had offset the net private savings, gradually disappeared in the 1980s. As we saw above, the behaviour of investment and savings is crucial for the movements in the current account. Taking the Japanese data, Ueda (1988) established that the decline in the Japanese budget deficit during the 1980s was partly a result of expansion in the US economy and partly due to the slow growth of expenditure in Japan.

Admittedly there are some peculiarities like higher market concentration and higher barriers to entry, but as some would like to believe, Japan is not immune to market discipline. If anything, its post-war economic performance shows that the market forces work in a reasonably healthy manner. There are indeed some differences from other industrial countries. For all appearances the American democratic, free-market and free-enterprise kind of capitalism has not been able to compete with Japan's authoritarian, industrial policy-led, strategically-targeted, pragmatic mutant of capitalism.[28] But the Japanese economy is not so different that it has repealed the laws of economics. Besides, the yen's appreciation has worked towards easing some of the peculiarities of the Japanese economy because the GNP growth since then has come entirely from growth in domestic demand. In addition, in the Structural Impediments Initiative (SII) talks, efforts were made to shift bilateral tensions from particular problems to a broader framework of structural obstacles. The negotiations claim several successes. For instance, Japan has agreed to strengthen the enforcement of the antimonopoly act against exclusive business practices.[29] Other notable achievements include Japan's agreeing to ease some restrictions in the distribution system for retail goods, and taking some measures to address the *keiretsu* related problems such as introduction of internationally accepted standards of accountancy with an element of transparency in them. Once implemented these measures should make the Japanese economy appear less peculiar to onlookers and bring dynamism to the frayed Japan–US relationship.[30]

As indicated, after a lag, the Japanese export growth rate plummeted and the same trend was noticed in exports to the US. Similarly, American exports to Japan have responded, albeit with a lag, to the yen's appreciation and during the three years 1987–89, the average annual growth rate of Japanese imports from the US was much higher (18.4 per cent) than that of exports to the US (6.8 per cent). Instead of working at contrived solutions which could create future economic distortions, the managers of the American economy should restore its manufacturing competitiveness by making the necessary macroeconomic and industrial structural changes. No economy can afford to ignore for long that its industrial structure needs to sway with the dynamics of its comparative advantage. Structural adjustments have their costs and there can be little soft-pedalling on this count. But, to be sure, adjustments have their benefits which far outweigh the costs. The adjustments would enable the American industrialists to squarely face the Japanese competition in their domestic market, in Japan and globally. The salvation lies in the market solution, that is, in becoming a global competitor of Japan.

A recent study of the structure of comparative advantage in the US and Japan estimated econometrically that comparative advantage is a function of interindustry differences in factor intensities. The study was conducted with the time series data for 167 manufacturing product categories in the two economies. The impact of factor endowment on the US and the Japanese patterns of specialisation in manufactured goods was estimated by regressing net exports on industry factor usage. The study concluded that the pattern of specialisation in manufactures has changed dramatically. The econometric estimates revealed the transformation of Japan's comparative advantage from unskilled labour-intensive to human capital and R&D-intensive manufactured goods, while its position in regard to physical capital-intensive products has been approximately maintained over time. The principal change in the US involved increased specialisation in R&D intensive products, whereas the strong US disadvantage in unskilled labour-intensive products did not change significantly over time. Another scrutiny of data for high-tech and R&D-intensive product groups confirmed these conclusions and provided evidence that the two countries specialised in different industries in the high-tech sector.[31] With its strong industrial base, the US can in future work on its comparative advantage in physical capital-intensive and R&D-intensive industries and compete in these markets internationally.

Paul Krugman's simple and succinct statement had a great deal of sagacity when he advocated that the US must sell more goods to Japan or buy fewer goods as a part of the process of deficit reduction, which can only be accomplished by making US goods and services relatively better and cheaper – or more competitive. Translated into an economist's parlance it implies that reducing the deficit needs both a reduction in overall domestic demand and depreciation of the dollar. Exchange rate adjustment and expenditure adjustment are not alternatives, they necessarily go together. This process has been poorly understood because there are those who believe that a lower US budget deficit will somehow translate itself into a lower trade deficit, without any need for the currency depreciation. Conversely, there are those who believe that the dollar depreciation would resolve the trade deficit problem, without any need for domestic belt-tightening.[32] Both of these stands reflect half truths.

THE JAPAN–EC DISCORDANCE

The European Community (EC) as a group is the next most important partner of the Japanese economy and large economies like Germany, the UK and France are significant traders with Japan as well as recipients of its foreign investment. According to the latest (1989) available statistics, the EC accounted for 17.5 per cent of Japan's exports and 13.4 per cent of its imports. Both the proportions were about half that of the US. However, for the EC, unlike for the US, Japan does not count for much because of its strong regional economic ties. Its intratrade looms large and accounts for more than half of its exports (59 per cent) as well as imports (57 per cent). The Community's economic ties with the European Free Trade Area (EFTA) and East European countries including the former Soviet Union are also close. Japan accounted for a mere 2.0 per cent of its exports and 4.5 per cent of its total imports.

Before analysing the pre- and post-appreciation periods, it would be pertinent to take note of the recent economic history and the causes of mutual distrust between the EC and Japan. First, the memories of aggressive Japanese trade practices of the pre-war years and inexpensive Japanese goods have lingered in Western Europe and the Japanese image of a country that relentlessly dumps goods and harms indigenous industries has persisted. Second, while the US supported Japan's entry into the General Agreement on Tariffs and Trade (GATT) as early as 1952, European countries did not allow Japan an entry until 1955. Having allowed entry, they invoked Article 35, which provides for 'non-application of GATT rules between particular members' under certain circumstances. Third, Japan was made to cool its heels for several years before its membership to the OECD was accepted in 1963. Fourth, Japan manifested anxiety when the EC was created in 1957 because it feared that integration would sharpen the EC's competitive edge as well as adversely affect Japan's exports to the EC. In addition, it would be outcompeted in the third country markets. Fifth, in the 1960s, the EC protected their textiles and clothing industries so vigorously that they became a net exporter of upmarket textiles. Sectors like ball-bearings, steel, motorcycle, optics, camera and electronics also became areas of dispute in the 1970s and the Community successfully protected the majority of these industries using voluntary export restraints (VERs) agreements. Subsequently, Japanese exports of automobiles, colour televisions, VCRs and machine tools were also controlled in a similar manner.[33] Sixth, rapid penetration of Japan in industries like cameras and motorcycles had rung the death knell of these industries in Germany and the UK, respectively. Although these disputes were never blown out of proportion, they created an environment of sustained disharmonious disagreement between the EC and Japan. One commentator compared them to the lingering prolonged drizzle that characterises the rainy season of Japan.[34]

The Lingering Drizzle

After 1968, the EC never enjoyed a trade surplus and the deficit grew over the 1970s to come close to $10 billion in the early 1980s (Table 2.2). Unlike the US, it did not grow at an alarming pace in the first quinquennium of the 1980s and remained by and large at the same level, making the 'lingering drizzle' analogy a meaningful one. Yet the pre-appreciation deficits were enough to create pressure on Japan to dismantle its non-tariff barriers (NTBs) and open its markets more for the EC exports. They helped in making Japan accept the VERs in many areas. With such a widespread use of VERs in almost all major

Table 2.2   JAPAN–EC TRADE 1982–89

Year	Japan's Export to the EC		Japan's Import from the EC		Trade Balance in millions of $	Percentage change over the preceding year
	Value in millions of $	Percentage change over the preceding year	Value in millions of $	Percentage change over the preceding year		
1982	18 105		7 946		10 159	
1983	19 457	+10.7	8 577	+7.9	10 880	+7.1
1984	20 163	+3.6	9 800	+14.3	10 363	−4.8
1985	21 128	+4.8	9 371	−4.4	11 757	+13.4
1986	31 123	+47.3	14 173	+51.2	16 950	+44.2
1987	38 305	+23.1	17 862	+26.0	20 443	+20.6
1988	47 172	+23.1	24 163	+35.3	23 009	+12.6
1989	47 989	+1.7	28 137	+16.4	19 852	−13.7
1990 (September)	39 010		25 735		13 275	

SOURCE   International Monetary Fund, *Direction of Trade Statistics Yearbook 1990* and *Direction of Trade Statistics Monthly, August 1991* (Washington DC: 1990 and 1991).

sectors, Japan–EC trade has a striking resemblance to what has come to be known as the managed trade. Little wonder that Table 2.2 shows no effects of the steep yen-appreciation. If anything, the value of Japan's exports recorded the highest average growth rate (31.2 per cent) during the three post-appreciation years (1986–88).

Other than the managed trade practices, the trade surplus is attributable to the presence of L-curve goods in Japan's export. These are non-price competitive goods and currency appreciation only ends up raising the value of exports instead of bringing down their volume (see Chapter 1). The Japanese auto exports to the EC is perhaps the best illustration of an L-curve product. The average import growth rate for the 1986–88 period was also the highest ever (37.5 per cent) and is attributable to the expansion of domestic demand in Japan and the efforts made to encourage imports after the Maekawa committee report. The *nouveau riche* Japanese society freely spent on high quality, luxury European products. The net result on the trade balance front was high but declining trade deficits between the EC and Japan. In 1989, however, the export value growth rate fell to a tiny

1.7 per cent but imports from the EC kept on booming at a rate of 16.4 per cent, consequently the trade balance contracted by 13.7 per cent. In 1990, on an annualised basis, it further contracted to $17 700 million.

Japan's investment in the EC has recorded a dramatic rise over 1985–88, from $2 billion to $9 billion. It was supported by Japan's enhanced economic prowess and inspired by the EC's 1992-unification strategy. Between 1985 and 1989, the highest increase was recorded by the banking and insurance sectors. Investment in the manufacturing sector also recorded a high growth rate. There was a growing spread in the range of industries that were picked up for investment. Due to trade restrictions, the electrical equipment and electronics sectors absorbed a great deal of Japanese investment. During this period, Japanese M&A deals in the EC recorded a three-fold increase. This will be taken up for a detailed treatment in Chapter 4.

After years of Eurosclerosis, the EC region has been undergoing a high level of economic vitalisation since 1985. The economic growth since then has been led by domestic demand and high investment. As the EC moves closer to market integration the optimism is on the increase and the Cecchini Report has forecast that economic growth in the EC will rise to between 4.5 per cent to 7.0 per cent.[35] While on one hand the single-market programme has created hopes for additional opportunities for Japan, it has on the other hand created fears that Europe may emerge as a protectionist 'Fortress Europe'.[36] In June 1989, the EC and Japan agreed to set up a joint panel of experts to discuss economic links as the EC moves towards 1992. The challenge of 1992, however, is being met at the micro level, and sensing that entering the EC markets may be difficult after 1992, many Japanese enterprises have established manufacturing facilities in EC countries. According to a survey carried out by the Japanese External Trade Organization (JETRO), the number of Japanese manufacturing enterprises in Europe tripled from 1983 to 1987.[37] Also, the Japanese merger and acquisition (M&A) activity has accelerated. A Yamaichi securities survey reported 103 M&A deals between Japanese and European companies in 1989, more than double the number a year ago.[38]

Inasmuch as the discord was sector specific, endeavours have been made to come to sector-specific solutions. For instance, the long standing issue of high taxes in Japan on imported alcoholic beverages (champagne and Scotch) has been settled by a downward revision. A three-year-old price dispute over Japanese pricing of two types of integrated circuits, namely, DRAMs and EPROMs was settled in October 1990. A long-simmering and acrimonious dispute over the Japanese auto exports and production in the EC was settled in July 1991. Under the accord Japan will limit its auto sales and production in the EC to 16 per cent of the EC market, up from a limit of 11 per cent in 1990. The increase will be affected gradually but by the year 2000 the Japanese auto makers will have free access to the EC market.[39] Although this accord is being claimed as a victory for both sides, it is yet another classic example of managed trade and will be abhorred by trade economists because it has deferred full competition in the auto market until the year 2000. Several mundane disputes have, however, persisted. For instance, the dispute over the semiconductor industry is still simmering and the EC, in early 1991, decided to slap anti-dumping duty on Japanese halogen bulbs. In a somewhat curious development in 1990, the European currency traders accused Japan of artificially depressing the value of the yen against the principal European currencies. While such a caper may make Japanese exports more competitive, it would also raise the cost of investing in Europe, making the ploy of questionable value.

The tenor of the Japan–US relationship changed considerably over the 1980s. A decade of discord has not only frozen the friendship but also created a fissure of distrust between the two. Partly motivated by the ire for the US carpings, Japan has been trying to cultivate close economic ties with the EC. During the early 1990s, the two sides made considerable progress in easing mutual trade friction as well as expanding the Euro-Japanese dialogue to economic issues other than mutual trade. Japan's relations with major individual European countries like Britain and Germany were good while they faced a mixture of fear, hauteur and le défi Japonais in France. Recognising their growing economic entanglement the EC and Japan signed a charter upgrading mutual relations in July 1991. It provided for consultations on a wide range of issues like joint action in the developing countries, efforts to reduce trade conflicts and co-operation in science and technology.[40]

THE JAPAN–ASIA SYNERGISM

The third set of economies that interacted with and were influenced by – albeit to differing degrees – the post-appreciation expansion in

Japan's economic influence were the Asian economies. Japan's interaction and ability to sway these economies worked on three tiers. At the top were the ANIEs (South Korea, Taiwan, Hong Kong and Singapore) whose process of intertwining with the Japanese economy began before the yen's appreciation. The second tier was that of the economies of the ASEAN[41] countries (Thailand, Malaysia, Indonesia and the Philippines), which benefited immensely, although less than those of the ANIEs. Third, the south Asian economies that benefited little from the Japanese economic expansion and could not, or did not, integrate with the Japanese economy. The dimensions of Japan's economic interaction with the ANIEs and the ASEAN groups were of significant degree and Japan's trade and investment binge, along with massive infusions of high-technology and manufacturing know-how, helped transform these surging economies. In a short time a substantive degree of structural transformation came about in the ANIEs and the ASEAN economies and they have been drawn closer into the Japanese economic ambit. Until the late 1980s the US was the largest 'absorber' of exports from these countries while Japan was their second largest trading partner. Between 1985 and 1989, total annual trade between Japan and these country groups doubled to reach $118 billion.[42] If, in line with the Krugman formula, the US demand shrinks in future and the Japanese demand keeps growing, Japan may become as close an economic partner of these two country groups as the US. The intra-regional trade will grow faster if individual countries avoid creating directly competing industrial structures and an industry-wide division of labour is planned.

The ANIEs' Acumen

The ANIEs recorded extremely high GNP growth rates during the 1960s and 1970s, 9.0 per cent and 9.1 per cent, respectively. They continued booming ahead in the 1980s as well with an average (1980–88) growth rate of 8.4 per cent. During the last two decades their average growth rates were higher than Japan's, a super performer in its own right. Their exceptional performance attracted attention and they began to be customarily counted in as the Asian 'growth pole' with Japan. Until 1983, the ANIEs recorded trade deficits. A small surplus ($2.3 billion) appeared in 1984 and, thereafter, it continued to widen. Their export growth accounted for one quarter of the growth of total world exports in 1986 and 1987 and their trade surplus reached $25.9 billion in the latter year. Impressive as this performance was, it also caused some consternation. The growth in their imports was equally remarkable since 1987, accounting for one quarter of the growth of total world imports. Their proportion in total world imports has been rising rapidly and in this respect they are not far behind Japan. In 1988 their total imports stood at $179.86 billion against $187.38 billion for Japan and in 1989 they inched closer with $208.27 billion against $209.72 billion for Japan.[43] Thus, this tiny group of countries has been making its presence felt on the international economic scene.

Among the ANIEs, Japan has enjoyed closer economic ties with the Republic of Korea, the most important member in the group – although these ties were never free of friction and ironies. Japan is Korea's chief source of imports and, after the US, Korea's largest export market. The relationship is not one-sided and Korea is the second largest importer country of Japanese products as well as the second largest source of Japanese imports. When the Japanese exports in certain high-tech product lines faltered during the post-appreciation period, Korea was quick to pick up the slack. Korea has had the tradition of importing capital and intermediate products and components from Japan and exporting Japanese-style products to the US, the EC and, after the yen-appreciation, back to Japan. It has been acting as a downmarket second source for the Japanese-style product lines. Therefore, the import content of the Korean exports during late 1980s was as high as 43 per cent.[44]

The currencies of the ANIEs were pegged to the dollar. After the Plaza accord when the yen started appreciating and the dollar began to depreciate *vis-à-vis* the other SDR currencies, the competitiveness of the ANIEs products improved significantly in the international markets. The reason, apparently, was that the exchange rates of the ANIEs currencies began to depreciate substantially *vis-à-vis* the yen and major European currencies. After 1986, however, the exchange rates of the ANIEs showed a divergent trend. For instance, the Hong Kong dollar maintained a one-to-one parity with the dollar, the Singapore dollar appreciated a little while the Korean won and the New Taiwan (NT) dollar appreciated considerably. Thus, between 1986 and 1989, the Singapore dollar appreciated by 12 per cent, the Korean won by 24 per cent and the NT dollar by 31 per cent *vis-à-vis* the dollar. Over this period, the real effective exchange rate (REER) depreciated by 8 per cent in Singapore and 5 per cent in Hong Kong whereas it appreciated by 20 per cent in Korea and 21 per cent in Taiwan.[45] This exchange rate dynamics rendered ANIEs' exports

Table 2.3   JAPAN–ANIEs TRADE 1982–89

Year	Japan's Export to the ANIEs		Japan's Import from the ANIEs		Trade Balance in millions of $	Percentage change over the preceding year
	Value in millions of $	Percentage change over the preceding year	Value in millions of $	Percentage change over the preceding year		
1982	18 117		8 150		10 027	
1983	20 834	+14.6	8 165	+0.2	12 669	+26.3
1984	24 335	+16.8	10 014	+22.6	14 321	+11.3
1985	22 666	−6.9	10 341	+3.3	12 325	−13.9
1986	30 285	+33.6	12 609	+21.9	17 676	+43.4
1987	39 803	+31.4	19 001	+50.7	20 802	+17.7
1988	49 819	+25.2	25 115	+31.7	24 804	+19.2
1989	52 511	+5.4	26 988	**+7.9**	25 523	+2.9
1990 [September]	35 474		15 309		20 164	

SOURCE   International Monetary Fund, *Direction of Trade Statistics Yearbook 1990* (Washington DC: 1990).

more price-competitive against those from Japan and the other European countries, raising their share in total world exports. In addition, since the yen's appreciation began, the Japanese market became the most attractive market for the ANIEs' exporters. As shown in Table 2.3, in the three post-appreciation years (1986–88) imports from ANIEs recorded an extremely high (38.4 per cent) average growth rate. The reality behind these high statistics were the Japanese consumers who responded favourably to the availability of reasonably-priced imports. Their response was not limited to high-quality, luxury goods from Europe but extended to inexpensive clothing, electrical appliances and consumer electronics from the ANIEs. Along with the post-appreciation domestic demand expansion, consumerism caught on in Japan and gradually a new merchandising boom developed, complete with the institution of the *bahgen say-ru*, or the discount chain stores like Jusco and Daiei. As the Japanese economy adjusted and the industrial structure underwent transformation, imports of manufactured goods from the ANIEs also soared. During this period, Japan's exports to ANIEs also recorded an extremely high average annual growth rate (30.0 per cent), although it was lower than the rate of imports from them. The reason for this growth was that the markets that the ANIEs succeeded in capturing in the US and elsewhere were in products that required Japanese capital and intermediate goods and components. As set forth in the preceding paragraph, this trading pattern already existed for Korea. It resulted in a steady rise in Japan's trade surplus *vis-à-vis* the ANIEs. It reached $25.5 billion in 1989 and at this level it was 29 per cent larger than Japan's surplus with the EC. On an annualised basis, it will be $26 885 million in 1990. So far the trade surplus has not created any discord or tension between Japan and the ANIEs.

As stated earlier, the relative alterations in the valuation of the major currencies assisted ANIEs in slicing away Japan's market share in the third country markets in industries like integrated circuits, TV picture tubes, pocket calculators, VCRs, steel, machine tools, bolts and nuts, etc.[46] The Japanese exporters suffered a tangible setback not only because of ANIEs' price advantage but also because of a change in Japan's export strategy. The major export companies, particularly in areas like ICs and electronics, stepped up offshore production in the ASEAN countries, decreasing the Japanese export volumes. Soon the ANIEs' exporters became credible, even tough, rivals for firms like Sony, Hitachi and Namiki. A breakdown of the trade data shows that ANIEs' exports destined for Japan grew faster than those destined for the US. Japan's imports from the ANIEs were 13.8 per cent of the total in 1980, but they crossed the 20 per cent mark in 1987.[47] This delineates the growing importance of the Japanese market for the ANIEs. Nevertheless, the US Department of the Treasury was convinced that the ANIEs 'manipulated' their exchange rates for the purpose of gaining unfair competitive advantage in international trade.[48] The charge did not stand up to economic scrutiny because a close analysis showed that the surpluses did not emerge due to unfair currency manipulations but from a variety of more basic macroeconomic factors. Sachs and Sunderberg show that the basic reasons behind them were: rising saving rates in the ANIEs, a sharp fall in Taiwanese investment rates since the early 1980s, high productivity of investment in Korea and Taiwan which led to a spurt in real output in the mid-1980s and favourable terms of trade shocks in the mid-1980s.[49] The allegation of the US Treasury was *a fortiori* unsound because, *vide ut supra* except Hong Kong, the currencies of the ANIEs did appreciate *vis-à-vis* the dollar during the late 1980s.

The Asean Group

The ASEAN economies did reasonably well during the 1960s and much better in the 1970s. Their average growth rate of GNP was only 5.3 per cent in the 1960s but rose to 7.5 per cent in the 1970s. The average annual growth rate of the ASEAN-4 for the 1981–90 period was 8.0 per cent.[50] Such a performance, although not outstanding like that of the ANIEs, is considered respectable by any measure. Led by export-orientation and supported by foreign direct investment, these economies embarked on a path of rapid industrialisation. They managed to sustain their growth rates for long spells – the Philippines was an exception – and adjusted successfully to external shocks. In 1988 their growth rate was higher than that of Japan and in 1989 they outpaced the ANIEs. Other than the rapid GNP growth, these economies are characterised by low inflation rates and steadily rising per capita income levels. They also managed to steer clear of the debt crisis of the 1980s. Their performance is more laudable in that they suffered severely from the commodity price declines of the 1980s. With the help of Japanese technology, manufacturing know-how and capital goods they are fast emerging as manufacturing economies in their own right.

Since the trade surpluses in the ASEAN economies were small and of very recent vintage, they did not attract international attention. Besides, only Malaysia has gone into a significant current account surplus since 1987; the other three members are still in the red. With expansion of domestic demand in Japan and economic adjustments in Japan, the United States and the ANIEs provided the ASEAN countries an opportunity to increase exports of manufactures, which in turn proved to be an extra impetus to their economic growth in the late 1980s. Their latest growth spurt can be attributed to (a) an increased labour cost advantage *vis-à-vis* Japan, the EC and the ANIEs, and (b) a marked increase in foreign direct investment from exporting firms in Japan and the ANIEs. The wage differential between Japan and the ASEAN countries was large and the yen's appreciation made it wider. Similarly, appreciation of the won and the New Taiwan dollar further widened the wage differential. The labour productivity in the ASEAN economies has steadily risen because of the improved quality of the labour force and infrastructure. They are evidenced by rising literacy rates as well as the diffusion rate of telephones, power generation capacity, and the number of commercial vehicles, which are all essential parts of an industrial infrastructure.

These factors motivated an increase in Japanese investment in the ASEAN countries after 1986. According to an estimate it doubled over 1986–89, to reach $50 billion in 1989.[51] The currency appreciation and the other factors indicated in the preceding paragraph led to a pouring in of capital into the ASEAN countries by the cash-rich regional economies like Korea and Taiwan. The same factors also compelled the labour-intensive industries from Japan and the ANIEs to move to the ASEAN countries. Initially, when large capital- and technology-intensive Japanese companies like Matsushita, Sony, JVC and Hitachi established themselves in the ASEAN region, they had not gone into full-fledged manufacturing and used components supplied by their factories in Japan, Korea and Taiwan. But the soaring value of the yen, and later the won and the New Taiwan dollar, made imports of components an uneconomic proposition. This trend ensured a second tier shift of ancillary and component-manufacturing industries from Japan and the ANIEs to the ASEAN region.[52] We shall return to a detailed analysis of this issue in Chapter 4. Thus, production bases in many industries have moved to this region. Inasmuch as there is a technology gap between Japan and the ANIEs and the ASEAN countries (cf. Chapter 6) and also Japan's ratio of R&D investment has increased steadily since the early 1980s, it seems likely that in the foreseeable future Japan will specialize in the high-tech and R&D-intensive products while the ANIEs and the ASEAN economies specialize in the standard technology products.

The ASEAN region was also a large recipient of Japanese overseas development assistance (ODA) in the form of grants, developmental loans and technical assistance. Two-thirds of Japan's total ODA to Asia was poured into this region and there are plans to maintain this proportion during the 1990s.[53] Much of it goes into the development of infrastructure. The official capital flows are accompanied by private capital. Its impact is being felt in the banking and capital markets of the ASEAN economies. Japanese capital is also stimulating privatisation programmes in these countries and, thereby, favourably affecting the resource allocation pattern.

The South Asians

The third group of economies failed to profit as much from the post-appreciation economic expansion of Japan as the first two. The

rapidly since 1984. Continental Europe was the prototype for the post-war Japanese financial system. It was built around the banks and served the economy well. While reconstructing their financial system the Japanese authorities, namely the Ministry of Finance and the Ministry of International Trade and Industry (MITI), had rejected the Anglo-Saxon belief in the ability of private capital markets to allocate financial resources efficiently. It was done for pragmatic, rather than ideological, reasons. Therefore, the Japanese financial system differed considerably from the Anglo-Saxon system which is still characterised by the pivotal role of open markets.

The financial authorities had kept control over interest rates which were fixed well below the market clearing level. Credit was allocated or 'rationed' through the banking system and specialised government financial institutions. This turned commercial banks and the financial institutions into arbiters of credit and placed them in a strong position. The monetary policy in Japan was implemented through the use of both interest-rates and quantitative controls.[18] The financial authorities also emphasised functional separation, for instance, banks and securities companies had to be separate entities, somewhat on the lines of the US Glass-Steagall Act. Its Japanese parallel was called Article 65. Clear lines were drawn between banks that lent to larger corporations and the financial institutions meant for small business, as well as between ordinary banks that could take only short-term deposits and trust banks and long-term credit banks that could hold long-term liabilities, like trust funds and debentures. The functions of each type of financial institution were rigidly specified and there was little transfer of resources between them. A stringent foreign exchange control law reinforced the domestic regulations and controls. These controls were such that they even hindered current account transactions towards the end of the period of the fixed exchange rate regime.

The need for an interest rate control-based system existed *a fortiori* because there was no efficient bond market and the foreign exchange transactions were rigidly controlled. The development of a corporate bond market was constrained by extensive regulations on issuing conditions and collateral requirements for the issuing firms in the primary market. Much of the corporate bond business that existed was between financial institutions and the issuing firms. It was based on long-term relationships between the two and in reality worked as a form of bank lending. It was a legacy of the *keiretsu* system, according to which a group of firms centred around a bank and developed a high degree of mutual interdependence. Besides, the government sector either remained in surplus or recorded minor deficits because of a rapidly expanding tax base during the period of high economic growth. Therefore, until 1975, the volume of government bonds outstanding was negligible.[19] The ones that were issued were purchased by a cartel, or a 'captive syndicate', of banks and securities companies in a predetermined proportion at above-market prices. These institutions were prohibited from selling the bonds, except to the Bank of Japan, which in turn restricted the development of a secondary market for government bonds. The international economic environment of the early and mid-1970s, and a fall in the rate of growth of tax revenue deteriorated the fiscal and financial position of the government in 1975, and a pressing need to change the system arose. Thus, catalysts for financial reforms emerged from the real sector of the economy. Additionally, the abandonment of the fixed exchange rate regime placed no less a pressure on Japan to liberalise. Its growing stature in international trade and a flexible exchange rate regime were incompatible with a rigidly-regulated domestic financial structure and the absence of open money and capital markets.[20] That apart, since the international financial systemic norms were dominated by the Anglo-Saxon regime, and since the Japanese financial community was eager to keep in step with the international trend to internationalise, it was logical to deregulate, liberalise and assimilate the Anglo-Saxon financial norms.

The December 1980 revision of the Foreign Exchange and Foreign Trade Control Law was the first significant step. It entailed a drastic liberalisation of all foreign exchange transactions and abolition of the approval requirement for investment in foreign securities. However, a system of monitoring capital transactions was retained. The basic principle behind the revised law was changed from 'prohibition of foreign transactions with exceptions' to 'freedom of transaction with exceptions'. The old principle not only created an impression that Japan's legal framework was not transparent but also was not in keeping with Japan's status as a developed and industrialised economy. If 1980 is taken as the time point when financial regulation started, Japan was a decade behind the US. However, to be sure, minor deregulation and liberalisation of the capital account had taken place even in the 1970s. Since economic growth had slowed after the 1973 oil shock – in the background of the phenomenal double-digit growth of the 1960s it appeared extra pale – Japanese investors sought to widen their opportunities abroad by diversifying their assets. The objective was to improve their returns on investments. The Japanese authorities, therefore, had to relent and relax controls on international capital transactions, albeit at a gradual pace. When deregulation began in full swing in 1984, the first moves were related to the liberalisation of interest rates, followed by abolition of formally prescribed business boundaries. Next to come were the deregulation of new products and opening of financial business to non-financial firms.[21] These developments, with the exception of non-financial firms' market entry, progressed almost simultaneously. The result was that (a) the financial cost structures responded to deregulation of interest rates and changed, (b) relaxation of business boundaries enabled firms to forge ties with other firms and set up bankers' banks, and (c) new functional areas were developed by firms. The drive in the early 1990s was toward reforming the Article 65 by allowing banks and securities firms to enter each others' business through wholly-owned subsidiaries.[22]

Although an absence of a significant amount of government securities was a traditional characteristic of the Japanese financial markets, things began to change after 1975. It has been indicated that the economy had entered a contractionary phase after the first oil-price hike which led to a government budget deficit. The transformation of government into a deficit sector during the mid-1970s had a great deal of sway on the Japanese financial system. There were few alternatives but to devise a means of diverting personal savings from financing industrial investments to financing the budget deficit. The amount of government bonds, therefore, expanded dramatically. The outstanding amount rose almost eight-fold between fiscal year 1974 and 1982 from ¥ 1920 billion to ¥ 14 831 billion or from the equivalent of 7 per cent of GNP to 32 per cent of GNP.[23] The authorities had to encourage the development of a secondary market in government bonds by first allowing (in 1977) the banks to sell the accumulated bonds and then progressively easing the conditions imposed on their secondary sales. This process contributed to a rapid growth of primary and secondary bond markets. Open market transactions gradually became the norm in the secondary markets for government bonds and the *gensaki* market[24] expanded rapidly. So did the CD and commercial paper markets. Since there are common participants in all these markets, deregulation facilitated arbitrage between Euroyen markets and the *gensaki* and CD markets. Likewise, changes came about in the long-term end of the financial markets. Traditionally banks had provided the bulk of long-term funds to industry and they had dominated long-term lending. The cartelised control over the government bond markets changed with deregulation and between 1984 and 1990 they expanded with a healthy rate and the outstanding amount doubled, to reach ¥ 36 278 billion in 1990.[25] Successful measures were taken to develop full-fledged private bond markets along with the government bond market. The banks' importance in long-term lending, therefore, has dwindled. Firms have increasingly taken to offering securities in the domestic and overseas markets. This trend is more prevalent among large firms than medium-sized or small firms. The same is likely to happen in the short-term end of the market because with the growing proliferation of open market operations firms will prefer instruments like commercial paper (CP). Endeavours to establish a commercial paper market were made in 1987.

Several steps were taken, particularly after 1986, to liberalise international yen transactions. Foreign private corporations which met certain minimum standards of creditworthiness were made eligible to issue Euroyen bonds and conversion of foreign currencies into the yen was completely decontrolled. The maximum maturity of Euroyen CDs was extended in 1986 and restrictions on the recycling of Euroyen were relaxed. Foreign banks were allowed to issue Euroyen bonds. Next year, the medium-term Euroyen bonds and Euroyen commercial paper issuance by non-residents was decontrolled. In 1989, Euroyen loans to residents were relaxed. These liberalisation measures were taken to increase the use of the yen in international financial markets. Reforms were made to facilitate large Japanese firms to issue CPs in overseas markets, and several measures were implemented to provide the non-Japanese financial institutions easier access to the Japanese market. The number of foreign banks and securities firms operating in Japan rose sharply after 1985, while the number of Japanese financial institutions operating abroad rose more rapidly. Towards the end of the decade steps were taken to start and promote financial futures trading, which included the establishment of futures markets for the yen-dollar exchange rate and Euroyen and Eurodollar interest rates. Patterned largely after the International Banking Facility (IBF) in New York, the Japan Offshore Market (JOM) was established in December 1986. The offshore market was separated from the domestic market, yet the JOM was adapted to accommodate the special features of the Japanese financial system.

The deregulation also spread to the giant public sector financial institutions that controlled large volumes of liquidity but were restricted from investing in foreign securities. *Kempo* or the postal life insurance organisation was allowed to purchase foreign securities in 1983, and the next year controls on holdings of foreign securities by special money and fund trusts were relaxed, which led to a dramatic increase in their purchase of foreign securities. The postal saving system or *yubin chokin* and the Trust Fund Bureau run by the Ministry of Finance were given permission to invest in foreign securities in 1987. Reacting to the steep appreciation of the yen, the Ministry of Finance with an unaccustomed alacrity raised the ceiling of investment in foreign securities from 10 per cent to 30 per cent of the assets by August 1986 for life and non-life insurance companies. Similar relaxations were made for non-bank financial institutions. This was an important move and, as we shall see in the following section, it had a large impact over the capital outflows. All these measures were intended to increase the international use of the yen and develop Tokyo as a centre for international transactions in the yen. The policy makers saw in them the possibility of internationalisation of the yen as well as expansion of Euroyen transactions. By the late 1980s, Tokyo had established itself as one of the three major financial centres of the world. New York's strength lay in the geopolitical prowess and economic acumen of the US. In addition, the dollar is the key and vehicle currency. Despite the low profile of its domestic market, London will continue to be an important financial centre because of its large unregulated Euromarket. Tokyo acquired its due financial importance after Japan became the largest creditor nation. The Tokyo capital market has been far more active than in the past. Apart from its international role, with the fast growing Pacific region economies, Tokyo is expected to play an increasingly important role in the region's finance and commerce in the future. As the internationalisation of the yen progresses, it can be expected to play a supplementary role to the dollar in the Pacific region, or work as a quasi-key currency.

Deregulation, liberalisation and efforts to internationalise have affected so many areas and functions that the financial markets appear to have undergone a fundamental transformation which, in turn, has enabled the Japanese financial structure to adapt a good deal to the international norms. The deregulation and internationalisation of financial transactions made parallel progress because the former facilitated international capital mobility. The end result of interaction of these two processes was that the Japanese economy made a significant niche for itself in the world financial markets. The

statistics in the following section will show that financial internationalisation gained momentum in the latter half of the 1980s and that
there was a phenomenal increase in the amount of funds flowing into
and out of Japan. By the late 1980s, deregulation had reached a point
of no return and the internationalisation of finance became a self-
propelling force and was exerting its own pressure and dictating its
own pace of movement. It pushed to reinforce the securitisation of
the domestic market. It also exerted increasing pressure to establish
an open short-term government securities market. Such a market is
considered an important means for assuring a free flow of funds in
and out of Japan. In an endeavour to create a short-term securities
market, the Ministry of Finance started issuing six-month treasury
bills in 1987. The pace with which this market grew was exceedingly
slow, despite an active role played by the Bank of Japan.[26] Despite
the progress, a great deal remains to be done. The deregulation is
likely to be completed by 1995 and financial internationalisation will
advance with it.[27]

MOVEMENTS IN LONG-TERM
CAPITAL ACCOUNTS

The process of Japanese financial institutions dominating the international financial and banking markets is clearly visible in the assets
and liabilities sides of the long-term capital account. The long-term
assets comprise securities, loans, direct investment, trade credits and
the like, while the short-term liabilities largely consist of the financial
account of the private sector, like the Eurobond issues of Japanese
companies. Table 3.2 shows the steady rise in the current account
surplus until 1987 and then a sharp decline to $36 billion in 1990. A
more significant story is told by the times series for the long-term
capital account which shows a monotonic increase in the capital
outflows after 1980. This expansion was fuelled by the expanding
current account surplus and a widening gap between domestic and
foreign interest rates. A dramatic rise was recorded after the appreciation of the yen and between 1985 and 1986 the dollar value of
capital outflows more than doubled. In 1986, they had crossed the
$130 billion mark and the following two years hovered around the
same level, before beginning an equally dramatic decline in 1989. In
1990, long-term capital outflows fell to $43 billion, which is a third of
the 1988 level. We shall see the reasons behind this fall below,

Table 3.2 JAPAN'S CAPITAL ACCOUNT, 1980–90 (IN BILLIONS OF $)

	1980	1981	1982	1983	1984	1985	1986	1987	1988	1989	1990 (P)
Current Account	-10.746	4.770	6.850	20.799	35.003	49.169	85.845	87.015	79.631	57.157	35.792
Long-term Capital Account	2.324	-9.672	-14.969	-17.700	-49.651	-64.542	-131.461	-129.126	-130.930	-89.246	-43.455
Direct Investments	-2.107	-4.705	-4.101	-3.196	-5.975	-5.810	-14.254	-18.345	-33.725	-43.076	-46.191
Trade Credits	-0.733	-2.746	-3.245	-2.581	-4.934	-2.788	-1.876	-0.536	-6.957	-4.011	-5.304
Loans	-2.784	-5.269	-8.083	-8.462	-11.999	-10.502	-9.315	-16.309	-15.293	-4.682	-16.922
Securities	9.360	4.443	2.117	-1.876	-23.601	-43.032	-101.432	-93.838	-66.651	-28.032	-5.028
Others	-1.412	-1.395	-1.657	-1.585	-3.142	-2.410	-4.584	-1.383	-7.334	-7.335	-9.900
Short-term Capital Account	3.141	2.265	-1.579	0.023	-4.295	-0.936	-1.609	23.865	19.521	20.811	21.367
Changes in Foreign Exchange Reserves	4.905	3.171	-5.141	1.234	1.817	0.197	15.729	39.240	16.183	-12.767	-7.842

NB. The minus signs imply capital outflows.
P stands for preliminary.

SOURCE The Bank of Japan, *Balance of Payments Monthly* (various issues).

pp. 106–13. Another interesting revelation is made by the data on investments in securities. Until 1982, the Japanese economy was a net recipient of foreign capital on this account. Foreign investment in Japanese stock and bonds peaked in 1980, when it had reached $9 billion. It fell to $2 billion in 1982 and became negative, though small, the next year. Negative investment means Japanese assets were larger than liabilities and that the Japanese were investing more abroad than they were receiving from abroad. The outflow on this count continued to rise until it reached $101 billion in 1986. Between 1984 and 1988, more than half the long-term capital outflow was in the form of investment in foreign securities. This proportion declined along with the total volume of long-term capital outflows in 1989 and 1990; for these two years it was recorded at 31 per cent and 12 per cent of the total long-term capital outflows, respectively. A large part of the decline in the long-term capital outflows in 1989 and 1990 is explained by the steep fall in net investment in foreign securities by Japanese investors during these two years.

Table 3.3 shows further break up of Japanese securities investment abroad, foreign investment in the Japanese securities and the net situation. Foreign bonds have traditionally been the favourite instrument of the Japanese investors. Investment in stocks was always far behind that in bonds. The yen-denominated external bonds came third in the order of significance. The October 1987 crash of stock prices undercut the interest of Japanese investors in foreign securities, pushing investment down to $87.75 billions in 1987. It declined further the next year as the after effects of the crash persisted. The investment in foreign securities swelled in 1989 due to a widening gap between the domestic and foreign interest rates under a stable but declining movement of the yen/dollar exchange rate. US securities, especially Treasury bonds, were the most attractive investments for the Japanese investors during the pre-appreciation period. But when the yen began to appreciate this situation reversed.[28] The Japanese fund managers became more flexible and rate of return conscious and turned increasingly to short-term trading. Foreign investment in Japanese securities shows no trends. It had dramatically declined in 1986 and the next year it slipped into the negative quadrant, that is, the Japanese securities bought by foreigners were less than those sold. However, after 1988 foreign investment in Japan remained at a much higher level than in the past. The deregulation and liberalisation opened opportunities for the non-Japanese investors in the Japanese markets which led to an increase in the inflow of funds into

Table 3.3 JAPAN'S AND FOREIGN INVESTORS' INVESTMENT IN SECURITIES, 1980–90
(IN BILLIONS OF $)

	1980	1981	1982	1983	1984	1985	1986	1987	1988	1989	1990(P)
1. Japan Investment in Foreign Securities	-3.573	-8.777	-9.473	-16.024	-30.795	-59.773	-101.977	-87.757	-86.949	-113.178	-39.681
Stocks & Shares	0.213	-0.240	-0.151	-0.661	-0.051	-0.995	-7.048	-16.874	-2.993	-17.887	-6.256
Bonds	-2.996	-5.810	-6.076	-12.505	-26.773	-53.479	-93.024	-72.885	-85.812	-94.083	-28.961
Yen-denominated External Bonds, etc.	-0.970	-2.727	-3.516	-2.858	-3.971	-5.299	-1.905	-2.002	-1.856	-1.208	-4.464
2. Foreign Investment in Japanese Securities	13.113	13.220	11.860	14.148	7.194	16.741	0.545	-6.081	20.298	85.144	34.653
Stocks & Shares	6.546	5.916	2.549	6.126	-3.610	-0.673	-15.758	-42.835	6.810	6.998	-13.276
Bonds	5.331	5.936	5.030	2.359	3.454	4.524	-2.109	6.675	-21.628	2.400	16.991
External Bonds	1.236	1.386	4.281	5.663	7.350	12.890	18.412	30.079	35.116	75.746	30.938
3. Net Investment in Securities	9.360	4.443	2.117	-1.876	-23.601	-43.032	-101.432	-93.838	-66.651	-28.032	-5.028

NB. The minus signs implies capital outflows.
P stands for preliminary.

SOURCE The Bank of Japan, *Balance of Payment Monthly* (various issues).

Japan. Between Japanese stocks and bonds, there are no favourites among foreign investors.

By the standard balance of payments identity we understand that the net capital outflows equal the current account surpluses. However, the capital accounts statistics show that after 1984, the long-term capital outflows were larger in volume than the current account surpluses for the respective years. Over the 1986–88 period the outflows were large *inter alia* because Japan intervened in the currency markets to buy dollars to support the dollar, which again implies capital outflows. This suggests two possibilities. First, that there was an increased degree of financial intermediation and Japan borrowed short-term to lend long-term. Much of the short-term capital inflows, that is, increase in dollar borrowings, came through the Eurobond issues of Japanese companies and the foreign branches of the Japanese banks. Second, that the Japanese have a propensity to 'oversave'. This may go part of the way to explaining why Japanese investers bought dollar securities while the dollar fell. A part of the bond buying was by Japanese banks which had borrowed dollars and thus were hedging against currency risk while accepting interest rate risk.

The argument regarding oversaving needs to be embellished. Individual monetary assets in CDs, pension funds, and other forms of saving instruments have continued to expand, resulting in a high rate of household savings. They clearly were the mainspring of Japan's large stock of savings. Although the rate of saving has declined somewhat since the mid-1970s, it remained as high as 16 per cent in the recent past. This compares with approximately 5 per cent for the US and 7 per cent for the UK. High domestic savings do not become excess funds unless a substantial amount of savings are left unabsorbed by borrowings from domestic deficit units, namely, the public and corporate sectors. In Japan, the domestic deficit units were not able to deploy the accumulated funds of the household sector, making it necessary for the remaining funds to be lent abroad. Thus, the personal sector's surplus minus the domestic deficits of the public and corporate sectors nearly equal Japan's current account surplus.

Japan's current account surplus and long-term capital account deficit have begun to shrink but the deficit in the long-term capital account continues to overwhelm the surplus in the current account. As seen in the preceeding two paragraphs, the contraction in the long-term capital account deficit, that is, reduction in the capital

Table 3.4   JAPAN'S LONG-TERM CAPITAL OUTFLOWS:
BROKEN UP INTO TYPES OF FLOWS: USA, 1980–89
(IN BILLIONS OF $)

YEAR	Total	Direct Investment	Trade Credits	Loans Extended	Investment in Securities	Others
1980	−0.309	0.833	−0.026	0.281	−1.609	0.212
1986	59.186	7.973	0.342	0.612	49.395	0.864
1987	61.030	9.018	0.449	1.663	48.223	1.637
1988	59.260	19.568	1.024	2.830	33.320	2.518
1989	53.861	22.768	1.255	4.761	22.074	3.003

SOURCE   The Bank of Japan, *Balance of Payments Monthly* (various
issues).

Table 3.5   JAPAN'S LONG-TERM CAPITAL OUTFLOWS:
BROKEN UP INTO TYPES OF FLOWS; EC, 1980–89
(IN BILLIONS OF $)

Year	Total	Direct investment	Trade credits	Loans extended	Investment in securities	Others
1980	2.402	0.262	−0.013	−0.012	2.035	0.106
1986	46.117	2.748	1.088	1.102	40.624	0.555
1987	34.327	3.476	1.066	2.091	26.434	1.260
1988	34.114	5.693	4.507	1.768	21.229	0.917
1989	−13.245	9.419	1.625	−1.431	−24.562	1.713

SOURCE   The Bank of Japan, *Balance of Payments Monthly* (various
issues).

outflows, was made up of a fall in the net investment in foreign
securities by the Japanese investors and an increase in the inflow of
funds into Japan.

As Tables 3.4 and 3.5 indicate, other than the US the EC is a large
destination of Japanese capital outflows. It has been stated that the
former absorbed a large amount of Japanese capital in the form of
securities, including the Treasury bonds to offset its budget deficit. In
the EC, investment in securities was large but it was largely business
and M&A related investment, made as a prelude to 1992. The UK
gilts and Australian bonds also attracted funds, but to a much lesser

extent. One reason why the Japanese investors have shown relatively less interest in continental European currencies was because the movement of these currencies and their interest rates were not very significantly different from those found in the Japanese financial markets. This left little motive to diversify out of the yen into the European currencies.[29] The US and the EC together attracted an overwhelmingly large proportion because they had the most favourable investment climate, the lowest country risk and large capital markets in terms of size, diversification and liquidity. These markets also promised the highest yields. As the deregulation progressed, foreign securities began to gain importance in the portfolio of financial institutions. Their share in total securities of all financial institutions expanded from 3 per cent in 1980 to 9 per cent in 1984 and to 17 per cent at the end of September 1987.[30] The swift rise in the proportion of foreign securities held by financial institutions was the direct outcome of absolute and relative growth of the contractual-type saving institutions like insurance companies, trust banks and investment trusts in all financial institutions. The deregulation allowed the contractual-type savings institutions to hold a higher proportion of foreign securities than depository-type savings institutions.

There was a virtual explosion of capital outflow from the banks and non-bank financial intermediaries. Other than the regulatory factors noted above, these institutional investors had higher propensities to hold foreign securities which resulted in a decline in average degree of risk aversion and, therefore, increase in capital outflows. They invested large amounts in high grade long-term bonds. Table 3.6 shows the outstanding amounts of foreign securities investment for major institutional investors during 1980–90; the figures are for the end of each calendar year. The nine institutions for which the statistics are given in the table account for over three-quarters of the total foreign securities holdings of Japan. Of these, banking accounts of all banks, as opposed to trust accounts, accounted for the largest amount of foreign securities holdings in 1990, totalling over ¥ 18 trillion. All of this was hedged through foreign currency borrowings because of prudential regulations on the foreign exchange positions of the banks. The next largest holders were the life insurance companies, which are known for their massive financial power, which held over ¥ 17 trillion. A major part of this investment was not hedged. The large life insurance companies like Nippon Life. Meiji Life and Sumitomo Life are the leviathans of the Japanese financial system. As we saw, they are among the leading institutional investors and have a great

Table 3.6 FOREIGN SECURITIES INVESTMENTS BY
INSTITUTIONAL INVESTORS
(OUTSTANDING FOREIGN SECURITIES INVESTMENTS,
1980–90, IN BILLIONS OF YEN)

	1980	1981	1982	1983	1984	1985	1986	1987	1988	1989	1990
Banking accounts of all banks	1062	1430	2119	2722	4414	7327	9516	10620	11083	15207	18390
Trust accounts of all banks	173	332	560	944	1436	3461	6213	7872	8169	10306	11146
The Norinchukin Bank	239	313	322	283	380	955	1624	1608	2032	2376	2500
Life insurance companies	682	1123	1902	2927	3842	4772	7306	10343	13086	17162	17239
Casualty insurance companies	193	236	336	571	820	1022	1375	1745	2045	2667	3088
Securities investment trusts	116	203	174	240	843	1635	3909	4146	4784	4829	3620
Sogo banks	22	56	86	112	165	548	888	907	887	1083	1107
Shinkin banks	189	291	295	363	495	721	783	746	734	986	1758
Postal life insurance	0	1	4	194	558	946	1465	1968	2240	2480	2827
Total	2676	3985	5798	8356	12953	21387	33079	39955	45060	57096	61675

SHARES OF FOREIGN SECURITIES IN TOTAL ASSETS (IN PER CENT)

	1980	1981	1982	1983	1984	1985	1986	1987	1988	1989	1990
Banking accounts of all banks	0.46	0.57	0.78	0.91	1.33	1.95	2.24	2.23	2.10	2.24	2.52
Trust accounts of all banks	0.48	0.95	1.36	2.01	2.65	5.40	7.53	7.94	7.14	7.74	5.83
The Norinchukin Bank	2.00	2.20	2.00	1.50	1.90	4.40	6.30	5.59	6.61	7.44	2.82
Life insurance companies	2.70	3.90	5.70	7.70	8.80	9.30	11.70	13.73	14.15	15.43	13.67
Casualty insurance companies	2.80	3.00	3.90	6.00	7.80	8.70	11.20	10.38	10.42	11.59	12.22
Securities investment trusts	1.90	2.80	1.90	1.70	4.70	8.30	12.50	9.25	9.08	8.45	8.99
Sogo banks	0.07	0.16	0.22	0.27	0.40	1.25	1.92	1.76	1.60	1.73	1.62
Shinkin banks	0.46	0.65	0.61	0.71	0.89	1.22	1.23	1.06	1.96	1.13	1.84
Postal life insurance	0.00	0.01	0.02	0.87	2.24	3.38	4.68	5.57	5.61	5.54	5.66

NOTE   Assets and liabilities of the trust accounts of all banks are
calculated after subtracting securities investment trusts.

SOURCE   Bank of Japan, *Economics Statistics Monthly* (various issues).

deal of influence over the trend in the direction of investible flows. As seen in Table 3.6, the proportion of foreign terms, the proportion of total portfolio investment in foreign securities either increased only marginally in 1990 or it declined. While the average annual increase in total investment in foreign securities by institutional investors was 41.75 per cent between 1985 and 1989, it increased by a mere 8.07 per cent during 1989–90. The stock market plunge and the tightening of the monetary policy since May 1989 to curb 'asset inflation' were behind this lacklustre performance.[31] Yet, with over ¥ 57 trillion worth of investment in foreign securities in 1989 and over ¥ 61 trillion worth in 1990, Japanese financial institutions were a substantial force in the international capital markets. The short-term prospects are that the virtual stagnation in participation in foreign securities markets is likely to continue, particularly by large investors like the life insurance companies. There has been a rise in the domestic demand of capital to meet the Bank of International Settlements (BIS) capital adequacy ratio, therefore the Japanese banks have become captive borrowers of large funds from the life insurance companies. In addition, the credit-tightening policies noted above have caused the yield differentials between the US and Japanese lending rates to narrow considerably, reducing the incentives to invest in the US securities.[32]

While investing in foreign securities, the institutional investors suffered some of the world's most spectacular currency losses due to the depreciation of the dollar after the Plaza accord. They lacked foreign exchange know-how and needed to have better knowledge of hedging their currency exposures. Between 1985 and 1987, the dollar fell by 21 per cent each year. According to estimates made by Salomon Brothers, this meant a cumulative loss of 24.5 per cent in yen terms on investments in US bonds over this period and 25.5 per cent on investments in US equities.[33] However, at the end of the decade as much as 40 per cent of the portfolios of the institutional investors comprised US bonds, notably the treasury securities. During 1990, they curbed their investment in US bonds and increased their holdings of Eurobonds. The high cost of the dollar was a deterrent. Besides, they were lured by the jump in European yields. Debt securities denominated in the pound, the French franc and the European Currency Units (ECUs) drew a great deal of Japanese institutional liquidity.[34] In the near term, institutional investors are expected to pay relatively more attention to securities markets in other countries than the US, particularly, Luxembourg, Britain, Germany, France, Canada and the Asia-Pacific economies.[35]

Foreign branches of the Japanese banks and the international dealings of the domestic offices of Japanese banks both participated in the growth of short-, medium and long-term transactions in foreign securities and lending in the yen and foreign currencies. Another impetus to the expansion of foreign assets was given by the establishment of the Japan Offshore Market (JOM). In this market the foreign exchange banks can engage in 'foreign-foreign transactions', that is, like Euromarkets funds are raised from non-residents and lent to non-residents. This is entrepôt trade in finance. Since this market is offshore, by definition the interest rate controls, deposit insurance and reserve requirements of the domestic market do not apply to it. These transactions have grown over the years and have led to the growth of capital inflows and outflows through foreign exchange banks. By 1989, the volume of operations in the JOM had become equal to that in other neighbouring offshore markets like Hong Kong and Singapore. Since all long-term capital outflows are recorded in the long-term category above the line in the balance of payments, these transactions showed through in the financial statistics.[36]

The macroeconomic interpretation of such a large investment in long-term foreign securities can be made with the help of variables like wealth effect, international interest rate differentials, exchange rate expectations and exchange rate risk. The effect of high US interest rates and expectation of exchange rate depreciation were important and a positive correlation between the nominal interest rate differential and long-term capital outflows was found for the period between 1979 and 1984. The exchange rate expectations were slightly more important and explained about 50 per cent of the capital outflows during the 1980–85 period.[37] But these variables failed to explain the whole story because the US–Japan interest rate differential and exchange rate expectation moved in the direction of decreasing capital outflows after 1985. Sharp increases in the stock of wealth in Japan have exerted significant positive effects on capital outflows throughout the 1980s. This variable explained about one third of total outflows. The other important factor was the very rapid growth of institutional investors with a high propensity to hold foreign assets. As we saw, deregulation and relaxation of controls on holdings of foreign assets helped these institutions build on their holdings rapidly. Thus, while increased wealth became available for the purchase of the foreign assets, the average risk aversion declined, increasing the demand for risky foreign assets in the mid- and late-1980s, even though there was no increase in yield differentials. A low degree of risk aversion of the large institutional investors has been noted. In addition, the revision of the foreign exchange law also decreased transaction costs, which encouraged the demand for foreign assets by smaller investors as well. The newest trend is that since 1989, individuals have become an important source of capital outflows from Japan. Their horizons were typically long-term and their actions were typically not sensitive to changes in economic indicators.

A question that is often posed is why the capital outflow continued despite large losses by the institutional investors following the sharp appreciation of the yen. Was this a case of irrational behaviour by economic agents? The foregoing analysis has indicated that a major force behind the rise in capital outflows in 1986 and immediately thereafter was the deregulation and relaxation of controls on the portfolios of institutional investors and the wealth effect. In addition, the appreciation of the yen and depreciation of the dollar were a part of an internationally co-ordinated macroeconomic endeavour. The need to support the dollar made the yen outflow and investment in the dollar securities a necessity. In the absence of these institutional factors, capital outflows would have been much lower and the yen would have appreciated even more than it did.

Several Asian countries opened their capital markets to the outside world over the 1980s. The attention of the institutional investors and the Big Four was barely drawn towards these 'emerging' Asian equity markets until 1987. Although by international standards Asian securities markets were small and somewhat liquid, they manifested strong growth potential and had efficient execution and settlement systems. The amounts invested in Asian equities were tiny by Japanese standards, but they constantly swelled. Beginning from a standing start two years ago, the fresh investment made in the fiscal year 1989/90 was $1 billion – three times the previous year's investment.[38] The twelve major institutional investors increased the proportion of foreign equity capital allocated to Asia by an average of 6 per cent during 1989/90.[39] The life insurance companies played a leading and active role in establishing this new trend. The Big Four were working on plans for new branches and looking for seats on stock exchanges in Bangkok, Manila and Kuala Lumpur. All four had ambitions for future country funds. They were also eager to replicate in Asia the success with which they had lead-managed Japanese equity-linked Euro-issues. Despite modest success, Nomura has been particularly active in this field. There are several cogent underlying reasons behind the recent diversion of investment towards Asia. First, due to a change in the tax law on capital gains, the portfolios of life insurance companies moved in a conspicuous manner towards equity. In an endeavour to maintain their diversification, these funds spilt into Asian equity. Second, on the one hand, the 'emerging' markets have been deepening, while on the other, the perception regarding the US equity markets was that earnings per share have matured. Therefore, a shift from US equity was logical. Asia and Europe became the beneficiaries of the move away from US equity. Third, for equity investment the most important variable is economic growth potential. The ASEAN countries were singled out for their high growth potential by the Japanese investors; this should go a long way in helping the merging markets like Indonesia, Thailand and Malaysia to emerge. Initially, investment related research was confined to macroeconomic analysis rather than sector or company research. Investors soon acquired more expertise on Asian securities markets and gained sophistication. Also, the p/e ratios in Asia became relatively stable. Therefore, they did not have to pick country or blue chips to record high capital gains as they did in the past.

MODEST INTERNATIONALISATION OF THE YEN

Despite Japan's status as the largest creditor nation, its marathon efforts to deregulate and liberalise its financial markets, the establishment of the JOM, taking definitive measures to facilitate non-residents' use of the Euroyen sector, and despite internationalisation of the financial system, yen internationalisation has made delayed and modest progress so far. The yen has not displaced the Deutsche Mark as the second most important international currency. Notwithstanding the recent travails of the American economy, the dollar continues to be the most international currency because (a) it is a vehicle currency and the medium of exchange in the forex markets and large amounts in any pairs of currencies can be traded by going through the dollar, (b) central banks the world over use it as the intervention currency to manage exchange rates and the largest proportion of official international reserves are held in the dollar, and (c) in general when neither party to the contract is American, commercial contracts are denominated in the dollar.

The set of variables that facilitate and promote the international use of a currency are: first, confidence in the value of the currency supported by the economic strength and the political stability of the issuing country. High and variable relative inflation rates render a currency unfit for international use. Second, the domestic financial markets of the issuing country should possess a broad assortment of financial instruments and they should be deep. These markets should be well-developed, if internationalisation is their objective, and must not be regulated and controlled. Well-developed markets are necessary to support the supply and demand for such a currency. Existence of instruments like bankers' acceptance (BA) markets facilitates trade financing in that currency and leads to expansion in trade invoicing in it.[40] It is axiomatic that the larger the volume of transactions conducted in a currency, the lower will be the transaction cost of using it. The other variable that impinges upon the transaction cost is its exchange rate volatility, and therefore the exchange risk. From these perspectives, the dollar has had impeccable qualifications to be the leading international currency and little wonder that it maintained its supremacy, although its international role contracted over the 1980s. Conversely, internationalisation of the yen grew – albeit gradually – since 1980.

On the inflation front, due to a medium-term anti-inflationary monetary policy stance, Japan did well, but for a bad patch in the first quinquennium of the 1970s. In absolute terms, the average inflation rate for the 1970s was higher than that for the 1980s. The average for the former period was 9.3 per cent while for the latter it was 2.5 per cent. Comparative data for 1970–89 indicate that Japan experienced the third lowest inflationary rate in the industrial world. Switzerland and Germany were the two better performers. However, if the inflationary rates are compared only for the 1980–89 sub-period, Japan turns out to be the best performer with the lowest average. The average for 1985–89 is as low as 1.0 per cent, which is partly attributable to the price-steadying effect of the yen appreciation. These numbers silently speak for themselves and convey that the monetary policy succeeded in maintaining the internal value of the yen. This established its credibility which in turn contributed to internationalisation of the yen. Endeavours to deregulate and liberalise the financial markets and establishment of the JOM have been dealt with at length above, p. 93.

The current account transactions of Japan and the currency invoicing pattern of its trade are an important pointer to the yen internationalisation. Table 3.7 shows that the yen-denominated trade transactions have grown over the years in an unbalanced manner.

Table 3.7   YEN INVOICING OF JAPANESE TRADE, 1975–89
(IN PER CENT)

	1975	1980	1983	1985	1986	1987	1988	1989
1. Yen-denominated Exports	17.5	29.4	40.5	35.9	35.5	34.6	34.3	34.7
2. Yen-denominated Imports	0.9	2.4	3.0	7.3	9.7	11.6	13.6	14.1

SOURCE   Ministry of Finance, *Kokusai Kin'yukyoku nenpo*, Annual Report of the International Finance Bureau (Tokyo, various issues).

While they abounded in the case of exports, their growth has been slow in the case of imports. The 1983 levels are as far apart as 41 per cent and 3 per cent for exports and imports, respectively. During the latter half of the 1980s, the share of export transactions in yen declined and remained around 35 per cent. There are several reasons behind the lack of progress on this count. First, Japan's imports of primary goods and industrial raw materials are traditionally invoiced in the dollar and sterling. Second, a substantial proportion of Japanese exports go to the US and are dollar denominated. Third, although the market for bankers' acceptance (BA) was created in June 1985, it has remained depressed and the transactions costs are still considered high, which has proved to be an effective drag. This is a classic case of the egg-and-chicken riddle. The BA market is not growing because there is little growth in the yen invoicing of Japanese trade which, in turn, has been retarded because of the low volume of the BA market. About a third of the BAs had to be financed in the dollar in New York because of the market constraints in Tokyo. Fourth, many Japanese firms prefer invoicing their exports in foreign currencies to enable them to absorb the initial shock of the currency appreciation, that is to control their pass-through in export prices. It helped them in maintaining the export prices, and hence the demand, at the pre-appreciation level.

Unlike exports, the proportion of import transactions in the yen has recorded a steady increase and doubled over the 1985–89 period. This reflects a rise in the share of manufactured imports from the East Asian and South-East Asian developing countries, following the yen appreciation. Since Japan's trade structure has changed its axis from vertical to horizontal, the international division of labour will continue and so will the yen's share of import trade. The use of the yen in trade between third countries is negligible. The yen's share of total world trade was calculated at 4.2 per cent in 1988.[41] In 1989, it inched up to 4.3 per cent which shows the unattractiveness of the yen as an instrument of international trade. As opposed to the yen, the level of internationalisation of the Deutsche Mark is much higher. More than 80 per cent of Germany's (FRG) exports and over 40 per cent of its imports are invoiced in the Deutsche Mark.[42] The Deutsche Mark's share of total world trade, in 1988, was estimated at 14 per cent.[43] Thus, it may be inferred that the role of the yen as an invoicing currency has not become significant as yet.

The volume of the yen traded on the forex market is another indicator of its relative importance as the unit of account and vehicle or medium of exchange currency. Data relating to the currency turnover in the interbank markets in New York, London and Tokyo show a sharp rise in the share of the yen in the New York market. The market share for the yen increased from 5.8 per cent to 12.5 per cent over 1980–89. In London, it chalked up only a marginal increase, from 7.0 per cent to 7.5 per cent. The Tokyo market recorded a marginal decline in the yen's share over this period. As opposed to the yen, the market shares of the Deutsche Mark remained steady in New York and Tokyo but fell marginally in London. The interbank markets continue to be overwhelmingly dominated by dollar transactions. The large capital outflows that enabled the Japanese economy to dominate the international financial markets, somewhat paradoxically, had a negative effect on the process of yen internationalisation. The outflows required Japanese investors to sell the yen in the forex markets in order to obtain dollars and other currencies to make foreign investments. This created a yen-selling pressure in the markets which in turn weakened the position of the yen *vis-à-vis* the other Special Drawing Rights (SDR) currencies.

The forex markets are the 24-hour markets and London, Tokyo and New York together account for over two-thirds of total foreign exchange business. The three dominate dealings in their own eight-hour time slots. London is the major centre in the European time zone, Tokyo in the Asia–Pacific time zone and New York in North America. Competition among them is intense. According to the last official forex markets survey, conducted by the Bank for International Settlements in 1989,[44] the global net daily turnover was $640 billion, of which London accounted for $187 billion, New York for $129 billion and Tokyo for $115 billion. The remainder was divided between 11 other centres with Switzerland, Singapore and Hong Kong taking significant parts of the forex business. Since then, London has maintained its dominance and remained the largest market for both interbank and corporate forex business. But Tokyo has caught up with and possibly overtaken New York as the second largest centre. The next survey is likely to confirm New York's relegation to third place.[45] Foreign exchange traders develop a range of different currency rates to deal in and since the dollar has impeccable qualifications, the dollar exchange rates of the other SDR currencies overwhelmingly dominate the market. The dollar/mark rate is the busiest exchange rate, closely followed by the dollar/yen rate. The dollar/sterling, the dollar/Swiss franc and the yen/mark rates take third, fourth and fifth banks. The importance of the dollar/yen rate and the growth of the yen/mark rate has helped in the progress of internationalisation of the yen and added to the importance of Tokyo.

Likewise in terms of the currency composition of international banks' assets, the yen is presently positioned after the dollar and the Deutsche Mark. According to the statistics published by the Bank for International Settlements (BIS), the volume of yen-denominated assets is far smaller than those denominated in the dollar. Although the difference between the volume of assets in the yen and the Deutsche Mark is not large, the yen comes after the Deutsche Mark. Of the total international bank assets at the end of September 1990, 49.9 per cent were dollar-denominated, 14.3 per cent were in the Deutsche Mark and 11.6 per cent in the yen.[46]

Use of a currency as a reserve currency is considered another barometer of its accepted international significance. In the early 1970s, use of the yen in foreign exchange reserves of countries was negligible. During the major part of the 1970s, over 75 per cent of the reserves were held in the dollar. The pound sterling was the second most important reserve currency in the first half of the decade but it was displaced by the Deutsche Mark in the latter half. Diversification of exchange reserves out of the dollar into other currencies was modest until 1977. The sharp depreciation of the dollar over 1977–80 was accompanied by a decline in the share of the dollar in total foreign exchange reserves from 79 per cent at the end of 1977 to 69 per cent at the end of 1980. This was a logical reaction of the central bankers the world over. There was a weak reversal in the diversification away from the dollar in the early 1980s when the dollar appreciated strongly relative to the other SDR currencies, the share of the

Table 3.8   CURRENCY BREAKDOWN OF EXCHANGE
RESERVES, 1980–89 (IN PER CENT)

	1980	1981	1982	1983	1984	1985	1986	1987	1988	1989
All countries										
US dollar	68.6	71.5	70.5	71.4	70.1	64.9	67.1	67.2	64.9	60.2
Pound sterling	2.9	2.1	2.3	2.5	2.9	3.0	2.6	2.4	2.8	2.7
Deutsche mark	14.9	12.8	12.4	11.8	12.7	15.2	14.6	14.4	15.7	19.3
French franc	1.7	1.3	1.0	0.8	0.8	0.9	0.8	0.8	1.0	1.3
Swiss franc	3.2	2.7	2.7	2.4	2.0	2.3	2.0	2.0	1.9	1.7
Netherlands guilder	1.3	1.1	1.1	0.8	0.7	1.0	1.1	1.2	1.1	1.1
Yen	4.4	4.2	4.7	5.0	5.8	8.0	7.9	7.5	7.7	7.9
Unspecified currencies	3.0	4.2	5.2	5.3	5.0	4.6	3.9	4.4	4.9	5.7
Industrial countries										
US dollar	77.2	78.4	76.6	77.1	73.5	65.0	69.4	70.3	67.8	59.4
Pound sterling	0.8	0.7	0.7	0.7	1.4	1.9	1.3	1.1	1.6	1.4
Deutsche mark	14.3	13.0	12.5	13.0	15.2	19.5	16.8	15.9	17.4	22.9
French franc	0.7	0.5	0.1	0.1	0.1	0.1	0.1	0.4	0.7	1.1
Swiss franc	1.7	1.7	1.7	1.5	1.5	2.1	1.7	1.6	1.7	1.5
Netherlands guilder	0.7	0.8	0.7	0.5	0.6	1.0	1.1	1.3	1.1	1.2
Yen	3.3	3.6	4.5	5.1	6.3	8.9	8.3	7.1	7.0	8.2
Unspecified currencies	1.3	1.3	3.2	2.1	1.4	1.5	1.4	2.3	2.7	4.4
Developing countries										
US dollar	59.9	64.4	64.2	65.4	66.6	64.8	63.5	60.4	58.1	62.1
Pound sterling	5.1	3.5	4.0	4.4	4.4	4.3	4.6	5.2	5.6	5.7
Deutsche mark	15.4	12.7	12.3	10.5	10.0	10.2	11.1	11.1	11.7	11.4
French franc	2.7	2.1	2.0	1.7	1.5	1.9	2.0	1.8	1.7	1.8
Swiss franc	4.8	3.8	3.8	3.4	2.6	2.7	2.6	2.7	2.6	2.4
Netherlands guilder	1.9	1.4	1.5	1.1	0.8	0.9	1.1	1.1	0.9	0.8
Yen	5.4	4.9	4.9	4.8	5.2	7.0	7.1	8.6	9.4	7.1
Unspecified currencies	4.8	7.3	7.3	8.7	8.8	8.3	7.9	9.0	9.9	8.7

SOURCE   International Monetary Fund, *Annual Report 1990*
(Washington DC).

dollar rose to 71 per cent in 1983 (Table 3.8). However, by 1985 it
declined by 7 percentage points as monetary authorities again diversified the currency composition of their exchange reserves and the
proportion of reserves denominated in the Deutsche Mark, the yen
and, to a smaller extent, sterling increased. The extensive foreign
exchange market intervention by Japan, Germany and the US after
the Plaza accord forced a rise in the proportion of reserves held as
dollar-denominated assets during 1986 and 1987. However, the share

of the dollar fell sharply thereafter to 60 per cent at the end of 1989. The counterpart of this fall was a sharp increase in the share of the Deutsche Mark, which increased from 14 per cent to 19 per cent over 1987–89. Thus, almost a fifth of the total exchange reserves were denominated in the Deutsche Mark at the end of the decade. Relatively, they increased from twice the volume of the yen reserves in 1985 to two-and-a-half times in 1989. The yen denominated reserves did not expand after 1980 when they were 8.0 per cent of the total. They ended the decade virtually at the same level.

The industrialised economies evinced a clear preference for the Deutsche Mark over the yen. Close to a quarter of their total foreign exchange reserves were denominated in the Deutsche Mark. Also, their proportion had increased by 8.6 per cent over the 1980–89 period. The corresponding increase of the yen reserves was only 4.9 per cent. The situation for the developing countries was the reverse. The Deutsche Mark was not their favoured reserve currency and its proportion recorded a decline over this period. The yen's share of their reserves increased to 9.4 per cent of the total in 1988 but declined somewhat in the next year. This differential behaviour may perhaps be explained by (a) the differences in the relative exposure to yen liabilities of the two country groups and (b) the differences in the trade partners of the two sets of economies.

The weight of the yen has gone on increasing in the SDR currency basket since its inception. Yet, in the current SDR valuation basket it stands third after the dollar and the deutsche mark. The percentage weight of the yen was 7.5 at the time of inception of the SDR in 1974. At the time of the 1981 recomposition of the SDR basket, the yen's weight increased to 13 per cent. When it was revised in January 1986, the yen's weight was further increased to 15 per cent. It gained by 1 per cent each at the expense of the French franc and the pound sterling. The proportional weights of different currencies in the current SDR basket are given in Table 3.9.

International Bonds Markets

Raising of funds through foreign and international bonds by non-residents in the Japanese capital markets increased somewhat after 1980. All the early expansion was concentrated in syndicated loans and sales of yen-denominated foreign bonds. The instruments used included (1) *Samurai* bonds or yen-denominated public placements by non-residents, (2) *Shibosai* bonds or the yen-denominated private

Table 3.9   CURRENT VALUATION OF THE SDR BASKET

Currency	Percentage weight	Currency unit
1. Dollar	42	0.452
2. Deutsche mark	19	0.527
3. Yen	15	33.400
4. French franc	12	1.020
5. Pound sterling	12	0.089

SOURCE   International Monetary Fund, *International Financial Statistics 1990 Handbook* (Washington DC, 1991).

placements by non-residents and (3) the Euroyen bonds. As shown in Table 3.10, between the *Samurai* and the *Shibosai* markets, the former was more active in the 1980s while the latter stabilised at a relatively low level. The *Samurai* market was exclusively dominated by sovereign borrowers and supranational institutions like the Asian Development Bank and the World Bank and government agencies. The *Samurai* market has been important to Asian borrowers like China, India and Korea. These borrowers would have faced problems if they had tried to tap the Euromarkets. By the late 1980s, it was obvious that both these markets had reached their plateaux.

The *Shogun* bonds or foreign-currency-denominated foreign bonds were born in August 1985. This was another attempt to internationalise Japanese bonds markets. Like the first two, this market also stagnated despite the low coupon rate. The yen-denominated syndicate loans fell steeply after 1985. Their weak performances are ascribed to the following market drawbacks: first, the secondary market for this type of bonds was considered underdeveloped. Although the Big Four securities firms undertook to maintain a secondary market in these issues in a bid to improve the liquidity, the move failed to improve the situation appreciably and a lack of liquidity is still considered a frailty of these markets. Second, the issuing procedures were cumbersome and included onerous rigmarole like advance notification to the Ministry of Finance, and the decision-making process for underwriters' issuing terms was a long-drawn-out one. Besides, the limit of smallest acceptable issue of ¥ 10 billion was too high for a developing country borrower. Third, participants who tried to make quick use of currency swaps and interest rate swaps faced several obstacles. Fourth, *Shibosai* bonds

Table 3.10 YEN AND FOREIGN CURRENCY
DENOMINATED FUNDS RAISED BY NON-RESIDENTS
(AMOUNT IN BILLIONS OF YEN)

	Samurai bonds		*Shibosai bonds*		*Shogun bonds*		*Euroyen bonds*	
	$N°$	*Amount*	$N°$	*Amount*	$N°$	*Amount (in millions of $)*	$N°$	*Amount*
1970	1	6	–	–	–	–	–	–
1971	3	33	–	–	–	–	–	–
1972	6	85	1	10.69	–	–	–	–
1973	–	–	6	40.05	–	–	–	–
1974	–	–	–	–	–	–	–	–
1975	2	20	–	–	–	–	–	–
1976	6	65	–	–	–	–	–	–
1977	15	294	3	30.00	–	–	2	30
1978	29	722	11	105.00	–	–	1	15
1979	16	333	6	67.00	–	–	2	25
1980	14	261	–	–	–	–	4	55
1981	27	495	13	117.50	–	–	5	80
1982	37	663	30	193.00	–	–	6	95
1983	41	720	32	179.00	–	–	4	70
1984	37	915	34	199.50	–	–	13	227
1985	35	1115	24	157.50	8	932.36	66	1445.7
1986	21	590	21	195.00	10	956.39	141	2551.5
1987	15	420	10	77.50	8	847.80	151	2993.9
1988	22	635	19	162.20	1	100.00	224	2213.0

SOURCE Ministry of Finance, Kokusai Kin'yukyoku nenpo, Annual
Report of the International of the International Finance
Bureau (Tokyo, 1989–90).

were strictly controlled and the amount raised through them was
limited to one-third of *Samurai* bonds. Fifth, these markets were
adversely influenced by the appreciation of the yen which more than
offset the low coupon incentive for most borrowers. Consequently,
all the three markets remained insignificant in size.

The Euroyen markets operated in all large financial centres, London being the most important in this respect. The Japanese banks
have had the largest share in the Euroyen transactions, they cover
over a half of the total market. The remainder is dealt with by foreign
banks, foreign monetary authorities and non-financial institutions.

These markets also remained thin until March 1985 when the Foreign Exchange Council advocated the promotion of Euroyen transactions as another important step towards the internationalisation of the yen. To this end, several measures were recommended and implemented to facilitate the issuance of Euroyen bonds, medium- and long-term Euroyen loans for non-residents, short-term Euroyen loans to residents and short-term Euroyen CDs. The issuing controls were made less burdensome, the issuing procedure was streamlined and the terms of issue were made flexible. The Euroyen bond market had enormous liquidity and depth in terms of secondary market, which according to an estimate enabled the coupon for Euroyen issues to be cut by around 0.5 per cent compared with the new issues coming in the *Samurai* market.[47] Consequently, the Euroyen bond issues became more popular than the *Samurai* bonds and recorded strong growth after 1985. It is generally believed that the Euroyen markets took the growth away from the *Samurai* bond market. They soon overtook the *Samurai* bonds in terms of number and volume of issue. The associated swap dealings were made easier by allowing the Japanese and foreign securities firms to step in. It added a flavour of competition to this business. It was important because as much as 80 per cent of Euroyen issues were swapped for other currencies.[48] The recent expansion of the Euroyen bond market is expected to lead to wider use of the yen by non-residents both for raising capital and investment purposes. Of late, these bonds have found acceptance among international investors seeking to diversify their portfolio in terms of currencies. The diversity of borrowing participants has expanded with the growth in the volume of the market. The US residents are the largest group of borrowers in the Euroyen markets. Others include Australians, Canadians, French and Swedes. The majority of borrowing entities are corporations from these countries or the multinational corporations.

The international bond market has been dominated by the following three currency sectors: the dollar, the pound sterling and the yen. The statistics in Table 3.11 give a comparative picture of the fixed rate issues over 1986–90. Comparative data reveal that yen-denominated issues have not gained consistently relative to their dollar-denominated counterparts. They ranked second to dollar issues in each year except 1987 when they were the largest. Although comparable figures are not available for years before 1986, the yen's share more than doubled between 1983 and 1986.[49] Taking another dimension of international assets, namely, the composition of foreign

Table 3.11 CURRENCY STRUCTURE OF INTERNATIONAL BOND ISSUES, 1986–90 (IN PER CENT)

	Dollars	Yen	Pound Sterling	Total (In Billions of $)
1986	42.3	17.4	4.5	108.6
1987	15.5	26.7	11.9	68.9
1988	26.8	12.0	10.5	99.4
1989	29.1	16.2	12.4	89.0
1990 (September)	32.2	15.8	5.8	119.9

SOURCE Bank for International Settlements, *International Banking and Financial Market Development* (Basle, February 1991).

Table 3.12 CURRENCY COMPOSITION OF FOREIGN CURRENCY HOLDINGS OF THE BIS REPORTING BANKS (IN BILLIONS OF $)

Currencies	1985 Dec.	1986 Dec.	1987 Dec.	1988 Dec.	1989 Dec.	1990 Sept.
US dollars	401.6	444.7	459.9	491.1	535.7	493.2
Other currencies of which	287.2	453.7	703.5	737.0	831.8	942.9
Belgian francs	6.8	9.8	13.0	12.1	13.4	18.4
Deutsche Mark	69.9	116.4	147.9	145.4	188.1	224.5
French francs	26.5	34.5	46.7	42.5	50.9	59.5
Guilders	15.6	19.8	23.5	21.4	29.5	34.1
Italian Lire	2.7	5.9	4.7	3.4	12.8	9.6
Sterling	40.0	49.5	72.2	77.0	73.8	92.4
Swiss francs	35.4	59.5	80.0	66.1	58.4	69.2
Yen	73.8	137.9	288.5	344.4	372.7	399.3
Other	16.4	20.2	26.9	24.7	32.1	35.9

SOURCE Bank for International Settlements, *International Banking and Financial Market Developments* (Basle, February 1991).

currency holdings of banks reporting to the BIS, Table 3.12 shows a continuous swing towards the yen in the recent past. The yen's share recorded a sharp rise from 10.7 per cent in 1985 to 28.0 per cent in 1988. This increase was at the cost of both the dollar and Deutsche Mark. After 1988, the yen's share stabilised and it stayed around its

1988 level in 1990, when it was 27.8 per cent. These two considerations are a pointer to the realisation and recognition of the growing importance of the yen by the international banking community.

Thus, it is apparent from the foregoing exposition and statistics that the yen is more widely used in capital account transactions than in current account transactions and that its internationalisation has occurred faster in the long-term transactions than in the short-term ones. The statistical analysis relating to the capital accounts revealed that Japan's long-term capital outflows were predominantly in the form of securities. The composition of debt instruments and the direction of international capital flows had an undesirable impact on the internationalisation of the yen. A good part of these flows were dollar-denominated and went into the US Treasury securities. The EC was a relatively smaller destination while the East Asian developing countries were even smaller. Due to this skewed pattern of capital flows, a large number of countries did not have any incentive or necessity to accumulate yen-denominated assets or balances to pay for their yen-invoiced imports or service yen-denominated loans. This has proved to be detrimental to the yen internationalisation process. In addition, when the pound sterling and the dollar became international currencies, London and New York had highly developed financial markets which, in turn, was conducive to financial intermediation in terms of the pound sterling and the dollar respectively. As opposed to this scenario, Japan had tightly regulated financial markets until recently and its financial intermediation was not predominantly yen-denominated.[50] Further, some segments of the Japanese financial market are still considered narrow and thin instead of broad and deep. The Euroyen markets are still not totally deregulated. This state of affairs is a disincentive to those willing to hold short-term, yen-denominated assets. It may, therefore, be concluded that although the yen has internationalised slowly, particularly after the appreciation, it is and is likely to remain the third international currency in the foreseeable future. This ranking is not incompatible with a high degree of internationalisation of the Japanese financial system.

THE CONTRACTIONAL PHASE

Another area which reflected Japan's economic might was Kabutocho, the stock market district of Tokyo. During the 1980s, the stock market grew five-fold. The Nikkei index of 225 selected first-section stocks, Tokyo's most widely-watched financial indicator, soared from an average of 6870.16 for 1980 to 34 042.79 for 1989.[51] Over the 1984–89 period Nikkei-225 more than tripled. A dollar-based investor could have got back his initial investment nearly six times over. The index reached a dizzying 38 915.87 on 29 December 1989. Although in terms of GNP Japan was the second largest economy, the value of Japanese companies far exceeded those of the US – it was $4.2 trillion in 1989 against $3.0 trillion for the American companies. Non-residents, however, were the net sellers in the booming Tokyo Stock Exchange (TSE), which became the biggest of the world's main stockmarkets. Their share of trading steadily declined over the 1980s. Non-residents' stockholding as a percentage of market capitalisation slipped from 7.4 per cent in 1984 to 4.1 per cent in 1987. In 1989, it was virtually at the same (4.2 per cent) level.[52] Other than the rapid economic growth, the golden era for Japanese equities was created by falling interest and inflation rates, a dramatic drop in the oil prices, and a steeply appreciating yen. The *Keiretsu* arrangement was another causal factor. Under this arrangement companies form blood brotherhood by cross-shareholdings. About three-quarters of the TSE's capitalisation is accounted for by *Keiretsu* members. That is, only about a quarter of shares quoted on the TSE are available for purchase by ordinary investors, leading to scarcity of securities and a sharp rise in prices. This unusually powerful combination of economic events underpinned the meteoric rise of the TSE, which in turn was magnified by high price-earning (p/e) ratios. During the latter half of the 1980s high ratios were commonplace at the TSE. In 1989, the Japanese issues commanded astronomic p/e ratios. Major Tokyo stock exchange issues sold for an average of 60 p/e, more than four times the 13.8 p/e for the Standard and Poor's (S&P) 500 in the US.[53]

Another noteworthy market trait of the TSE was the abysmally low rate of dividend. Since the market was rising relentlessly, investors saw their profits only in the form of capital gains. The tax laws encouraged this tendency. Dividend yields had been falling for a long time. They came down from 11.9 per cent in 1951 to 0.54 per cent in 1990.[54] Investors did not resent it because total returns over 1980–89 period were spectacular. Total return (dividends + capital gains) on the TSE were a compound 28 per cent a year in dollar terms, compared to 17.5 per cent at the New York Stock Exchange.[55] Thus, firms and financial institutions were funding themselves through the equity market at almost zero cost and the TSE became an equity market that provided capital gains instead of yields. This changed the corporate financing pattern and in 1984/85 Japanese corporations, especially the large ones, virtually deserted the banks, their traditional source of long-term finance because money was so cheap in the security market. As a consequence, the average debt-equity ratio changed from 64 per cent in 1981 to 30 or below in 1990.[56]

To be sure, cheap money injected an element of surrealism at the TSE. The existence of speculative bubble was obvious and was estimated to be larger than that for the US stock market.[57] The additional causal factors included a decline in risk premium and expectation of real estate price appreciation.[58] The Japanese practice of assessing corporate worth by looking to a firm's 'hidden assets' also helped the stock prices spiral. The hidden assets include tens of billions of dollars worth of unrealised capital gains on cross-holdings of corporate stocks, with Japanese firms are known to keep, and the real estate holdings.

After Japan was established as a creditor nation, foreign firms increasingly began to flock to the TSE to list their shares. It provided them with a broader base of shareholders among Japanese cash-rich institutional investors and developed new sources of funding. In addition, a TSE listing is taken as an evidence of a company's commitment to Japan and its assessment of the importance of the Japanese market. Thus, for a modest cost the benefits were large. As the depth of the TSE grew, the number of foreign companies listed soared. It grew from 112 in 1988 to 120 in 1990.[59] The depreciating dollar after the Plaza accord also helped the demand for the non-dollar securities and the Japanese securities firms were the direct beneficiaries of the keenness to diversify among the major institutional investors of the world. The total capitalisation of the TSE at the beginning of 1990 grew to ¥ 550 trillion.[60] As we saw, some of the world's most liquid investors like the Japanese life insurance companies and trust banks were at the doorsteps of the TSE and they increasingly took to investing in foreign securities. The statistical dimension of this trend has already been amply demonstrated. While the large securities firms of London and New York struggled to earn modest returns in an industry known for excess capacity, their Tokyo rivals basked in a balmy financial environment and prospered. This propensity was not limited to the Big Four. Even the second-tier securities firms like Sanyo, Wako and Okasan became larger than the Midland Bank or the Bank of Boston in terms of market capitalisation.

The new decade began with Tokyo's return to reality. Sharp falls in stocks, bonds and the yen ended the surrealism. The official discount rate (ODR), as noted, was revised in Japan as well in May 1989 and a string of upward revisions continued in 1990. There was concern regarding the weakness of the yen which had depreciated from a monthly average of 129.1 to the dollar to 143.4 to the dollar between January and December 1989. Its slide continued until the mid-1990s. The rate of inflation inched upwards after the first quarter of 1989 to reach 2.6 per cent in December 1989, high by Japanese standards. Its climb continued in 1990. Uncertainties regarding international trade worsened the situation. The equity price run-up was viewed with concern by both the Ministry of Finance and the Bank of Japan. According to a commentator the fall of the TSE was orchestrated by the two of them acting in concert and fabricating the story that they had fallen out with each other and that their incestuous alliance was over.[61]

The environment around Kabutocho changed out of recognition and buyers' optimism was snuffed out. This was the end of the world's greatest bull market. Helium began to leak out of the balloon and in the first four months of 1990 the Nikkei plunged by 23.3 per cent, taking about a trillion dollars worth of stock market value with it. Over the next three months the market stabilised, responding to the sound domestic macroeconomic policies and *détente* in trade-related tensions. Heavy buying by the securities firms prodded the Nikkei index back up to the 33 100 mark in July but Iraq's invasion of Kuwait again sent the TSE into a tailspin. Sharp decline in the Nikkei continued and it ended the year at 23 740.50. The market firmed up a bit in the first quarter of 1991 when the index hovered around 26 600. Trading volumes retreaded to their 1985 levels and the investors' sentiment in general was muted.[62] The stockmarket fell by 48 per cent from peak to trough, albeit a cataclysmic crash was avoided. The fortunes of the banks and securities firms plunged with the Nikkei index. There were varying speculations regarding the age of the bear market. Investors' attention returned to the low payout ratios and the life insurance companies – which held roughly 12 per cent of the total stock market – called for a change. The mutual funds and *Keidanren*, which is a federation of chambers of commerce, also exerted pressure for average dividend yields on the TSE to rise. Following the fall of the Nikkei index, the New York Stock Exchange (NYSE) reclaimed its title of being the largest stock exchange in the world.

Although the jury is still out on the long-term impact of the collapse in asset values, certain influences are clear. The cost of raising capital – both debt and equity – has increased. Firms are feeling the squeeze more directly because a cheap source of finance has vanished. In the first three quarters of 1990, funds raised by Japanese corporations through equity-linked securities, including convertible bonds and warrant bonds, fell to about 25 per cent of their previous year's level. While the large groups could fall back on their cash balances, the medium and smaller companies were paring back their investment plans. Banks were used to reporting large operating profits and capital gains from securities trading. Their performance on these two counts collapsed with the stock market. All the 22 city, trust and long-term credit banks reported lower pre-tax profits in 1990, the first fall in more than a decade. The aggregate net profits of the 12 city banks dropped by 19.7 per cent in the year ending March 1991. The three long-term credit banks slipped by 3.6 per cent and the seven trust banks were the worst sufferers, with profits crashing by 26.9 per cent.[63] With the stock market in the doldrums, banks are sure to have problems raising fresh capital through stock sales. If the property asset values deflate – which seems a likely possibility – their troubles would aggravate. The two credit rating agencies, namely, the Moody's Investors Service and the Standard and Poor's (S&P) downgraded the ratings of Dai-Ichi Kangyo Bank and Fugi Bank from AAA to AA1 in mid-1990, and in early 1991 they did the same to the following four major trust banks: Mitsubishi Trust, Mitsui Trust, Sumitomo Trust and Yasuda Trust.[64] All four had high real estate exposure. Also, rising interest rates made them vulnerable because they funded themselves largely through long-term floating rate trust products while they held sizeable fixed-rate assets. By mid-1991, all the large Japanese banks were marked down a notch and apart from the Industrial Bank of Japan, none had an AAA rating by Moody's and S&P.

The securities industry bore the full brunt of the Nikkei plunge and firms registered a dramatic plunge in earnings. Pre-tax profits of the Big Four were down by as much as two-thirds in the year ending March 1991. Trading volume sank more than a third in 1990 which compounded the effect of lower stock prices. The pre-tax profits of Nomura – the most closely followed earnings gauge in the financial industry – slid by 52 per cent. Be it noted that despite the drop, Nomura remains among the most profitable securities firms in the world. Daiwa reported a fall of 62 per cent, Nikko 73 per cent and Yamaichi 71 per cent. The second-tier securities firms like Sanyo, Kankaku and Yamatane suffered more than the giants.[65] They reported a pre-tax decline of 90 per cent or more. There was a dramatic fall in their equity brokerage earnings as well as the non-brokerage earnings. This applied to both the Big Four and the second-tier securities firms. The latter's dependence on operating revenues from equity brokerage ranged from 80 per cent to 90 per cent. The foreign operations of the securities firms began to wither away because they were inextricably tied to their domestic equity operations. Their overseas operations did not contribute much to profits; even during the boom years they accounted for less than 10 per cent of the total. In 1990, the overseas operations were expected to slip in the red. Three of the Big Four have reported that their commitment to international expansion will ebb due to their 1990 performance. Daiwas Securities was the only exception in this respect. The domestic economic tribulations have succeeded in lowering the international profile of the Japanese financial markets. Nowhere is it better reflected than in the Eurobond market where the Big Four lead-managed a puny 20 per cent of the $175 million raised in 1990. In 1989, they had a hold over 38 per cent of the Eurobond market.[66] Hegemony of the Big Four in the international book-runner's club broke in 1990. Daiwa slipped to fourth position, Nikko to seventh and Yamaichi to eleventh. Only Nomura succeeded in remaining in the top slot.[67] On pp. 86–8 above, it has been shown that Japan's share of international assets contracted in 1990, that the long-term capital outflows plummeted dramatically, and that the rate of growth of foreign securities holdings by institutional investors flattened.

The new capital adequacy norm of the Basle Committee on Banking Regulations and Supervisory Practices proved to be yet another pernicious turn of the screw for the Japanese banks. According to its last recommendations, published in July 1988, the minimum capital reserves were to be 8 per cent by the end of 1992. These reserves were defined in terms of tier-1 and tier-2: the former consisted of the core element, that is, equity capital and disclosed reserves from post-tax retained earnings, while the latter comprised (1) undisclosed reserves, (2) asset revaluation reserves subject to a discount of 55 per cent, and (3) general provisions and loan loss reserves.[68] This capital adequacy norm has come to be known as the BIS ratio or the Basle ratio and has been universally accepted. In March 1989, most city banks were comfortably above the 8 per cent requirement but a year later, 8 out of 12 city banks were below the mandatory level. In March 1990, then unrealised gains which could be counted in reserves, after applying the 55 per cent discount requirement, constituted almost half of city, trust and long-term capital banks' total qualifying capital. By September, the market value of unrealised gains, after applying the 55 per cent discount, fell by a third. The Nikkei plunge thus savaged the tier-2 capital of the Japanese banks. The tier-1 capital during the same six months dipped from an average ratio of 4.53 per cent to 4.49 per cent.[69] To meet the capital adequacy ratio banks either have to raise fresh capital or reduce assets. Given the environment at Kabutocho and the changes in the economy during 1990, the probability of the latter course far exceed that of the former.

Banks' eagerness of the 1980s to lend in the international markets was supplanted by the reluctance of 1990. Japanese banks were revising their lending plans with a view to cutting back the rate of asset growth, particularly in the international markets. A depreciating yen accelerated this process. As alluded to earlier, a large proportion of these loans were made at wafer-thin margins. Profits on them suffered further because Japanese banks had to sometime borrow at high cost in the interbank market to make these loans. Therefore, it stands to reason that Japanese banks cut loans to non-Japanese borrowers first. In the domestic market there is no generalised asset pruning but adjustment began without delay and credit lines to property developers were the first to be cut off. One of the impacts of the asset pruning was a rise in bankruptcies. The total liabilities of corporate failure in Japan was ¥ 1.2 trillion in 1989. Next year it rose to ¥ 2.0 trillion and the trend for 1991 was upwards. Mikuni & Co., an independent credit rating agency, reckoned bankruptcy liabilities for 1991 to be around ¥ 4.0 trillion.[70] The strategy of the 1980s of high-volume and low-margin was abandoned by the Japanese banks for one of more profitable loans and development of financial services. The priority of the 1990s is to lift overall returns and hold the costs on a tight rein. The margins will rise and borrowers should expect to pay 50 basic points or more on their debts.[71] Many large banks and trusts are cutting investment exposure to the stock market. In a bid to reduce dependence on balance sheet business, banks are accelerating their plans to diversify into fee earning corporate finance services. They are trying to build up the swaps and options sectors which generate income on modest capital outlays. The asset and liability management techniques are being re-examined and so are the domestic and overseas loan portfolios.

The Japanese banks feel a pressing need for higher returns and they will be more selective in their international lendings. On the one hand there is an increased demand for investment in the industrialised, developing and East European countries. The US Federal Government was expected to borrow in excess of $300 billion in 1991 and the developing economies need capital for investment and debt servicing.[72] On the other hand large Japanese banks were retreating from international lending. This will create a resource crunch in the international economy. The long-term real interest rates will rise, undermining the medium-term global economic growth. This scenario looks *a fortiori* plausible because the traditional surplus countries of the Middle East have turned into borrowers and Germany began to run a current account deficit since the beginning of 1991. Japan's current account surpluses were sharply reduced in the late 1980s and 1990. The US is likely to suffer first due to the resource crunch because Japanese banks are downbeat about it and may begin to sell off their US assets. The developing countries will be the next to be affected. In 1991, Japanese banks, like the European and American banks, emerged as important sellers of developing country assets.

Although there is no hint of panic, or even disorderly, selling, exposures to developing countries were being scaled down.[73] Supranational institutions have expressed concern over the probability of Japanese banks declining to roll-over the syndicated credits to developing countries. Asking for higher spreads before the roll-over is seen as a certainty. Also, the Japanese activity in the interbank markets would be much less than that in the past, adversely affecting the international finance and payments system.

Admittedly, the international economy would feel the consequences of the Japanese financial downswing and, as elucidated, it may be manifested in a short-term global credit contraction. However, writing off the long-term potential of the Japanese banking and financial industry merely because it is on a down beat would be imprudent. The Japanese banks will draw in their horns and the securities firms will assume a lower profile in the international financial markets in the near term, yet they have arrived and will continue to have a significant presence there.

SUMMING UP

Sustained economic growth, recurrent current account surpluses, appreciation of the yen and deregulation of the domestic banking and finance sector turned Japan from being a small net creditor in 1981 to the largest creditor and leading banking power of the world by the last quarter of 1986. In the latter half of the 1980s, Japanese banks and securities firms became the largest of their kind and began to sway the international financial markets. By 1989 their dominance over the international capital markets was complete. However, the Japanese banks had low returns on capital and assets. Despite huge assets their profitability was low.

A large number of measures were taken to deregulate and liberalise various sectors of the hitherto stringently controlled financial system. Efforts in this direction were stepped up after 1984. Conscious endeavours were made to transform the bank-oriented Japanese financial system into an open-market-oriented system and to align it with the Anglo-Saxon systemic norms of the international financial markets. Contemporaneous policy measure were taken to liberalise and promote international yen transactions and Euroyen transactions as well as to make financial markets attractive for non-residents. To this end, the Japan Offshore Market was established in 1986. Deregulation enabled the highly liquid institutional investors to become active in the international securities markets, where they soon became a force to reckon with.

The long-term capital account deficit – which implies capital outflows – increased monotonically after 1980, with a dramatic rise after the appreciation of the yen. A dominant proportion of the capital outflows was in the form of investment in foreign securities, large parts of which went to the US and the EC, in that order. The institutional investors played an active role in this game because of their higher propensity to hold foreign securities and lower risk aversion. Capital outflows declined in 1989 and 1990 due to a steep fall in net investment in foreign securities and increased investment by non-residents in Japanese bonds and stocks. Although the standard balance of payments identity tells us that capital outflows equal the current account surplus, after 1984 the long-term outflows were greater than the current account surpluses for the respective years. The ability of the Japanese economy to maintain a high rate of saving and financial intermediation made this feat possible.

Internationalisation of the yen made slow progress despite Japan's status as the largest creditor nation. On the one hand, the yen has remained the currency of low inflation, the deregulation of the financial markets has made a good deal of headway, use of the yen as a reserve currency and its weight in the SDR currency basket has increased and so has the volume of yen traded on the forex markets. Also, the dollar/yen rate is the second busiest exchange rate in the forex market. On the other hand, the yen-denominated current account transactions of Japan and yen-invoicing of international trade has not made much headway. Raising of funds by non-residents increased somewhat after 1980 but all the three bond markets, namely, *Samurai*, *Shibosai* and *Shogun* stagnated despite low coupon rates. Only the Euroyen markets perked up and recorded a relatively higher volume of activity after 1985. The yen was more widely used in capital account transactions. Japan's composition of debt instruments as well as the direction of its long-term capital outflows were not conducive to internationalisation of the yen. In spite of the progress made in this direction, the yen is likely to remain the third international currency in the foreseeable future after the dollar and the Deutsche Mark.

The equity markets were extremely buoyant over the 1980s but began the new decade with a sharp plunge. It changed the domestic and international financial climates out of recognition. Profits and credit ratings of Japanese financial institutions dipped and they had to adopt a lower international profile. Capital outflows and investment abroad were on a downswing and there was a hiatus in the international expansion plans of Japanese banks and securities firms. Since the time limit of adhering to the Basle ratio of capital adequacy was close, banks had to hasten in pruning their asset portfolios, which included international assets. It may lead to a resource scarcity and a credit squeeze in the international financial and capital market.

4 Acceleration in Foreign Direct Investment

COMING ON THE SCENE

Until recently Japan was considered a minor player in the arena of foreign direct investment (FDI). Before the Second World War its FDI was negligible while after the war stringent restraints had to be imposed on capital outflows because of an overwhelming domestic need and a weak balance of payments situation. The rapid economic growth of the 1960s eased the balance of payments situation but the FDI flows remained small. They ranged between $200 million and $300 million a year during this decade, with the largest share (25 per cent) going to North America and 20 per cent to Europe. Less developed countries (LDCs) attracted above half of the FDI with Asia alone accounting for 20 per cent of the total FDI. In the early 1970s, the volume recorded a substantial rise. In 1972 it crossed the $2 billion mark and the Japanese economists call it the *gan-nen*, or the very first year, of the FDI. Apart from the economic growth and export successes of the 1960s, there were three more reasons behind this ripple of FDI in early 1970s. First, between end-1970 and end-1972 the yen had appreciated from 358 to the dollar to 302 to the dollar – a 14 per cent appreciation in nominal terms. This appreciation was brought about by the collapse of the Bretton Woods system and affected the yen's value not only *vis-à-vis* the dollar but also the East and South East Asian currencies which were pegged to the dollar. Second, in the early 1970s wages in Japan were rising with an annual average rate of 15 per cent. Third, the two institutional factors behind the rise were easing of restrictions on FDI by the Ministry of Finance (MOF) and lowering of interest by the Export-Import Bank of Japan on funds for foreign investment.

However, since the 1970s was a decade that was buffeted by supply shocks from OPEC, stagflation in the industrialised economies of the

West and other economic disturbances, economic growth was relatively sluggish in Japan as well as in the world economy. Therefore, the financial authorities delayed further liberalisation of capital outflows. Investment by the private sector, both domestic and foreign, slowed down due to the uncertainty regarding the international demand growth. Therefore the momentum of 1970–72 could not be maintained during the rest of the decade and the FDI flows stagnated, remaining below the peak attained in 1972. North America received about the same (26 per cent) proportion as in the 1960s. The proportion going to Europe declined to 12 per cent. The LDCs again were the recipients of over half of the FDI flows, with the share of Asia increasing to 28 per cent of the total.[1] The four Asian Newly Industrialising Economies (ANIEs) – South Korea, Taiwan, Hong Kong and Singapore – grew particularly attractive from the view point of FDI over the 1970s and their proportion increased from 4.8 per cent of the total in the 1960s to 10.2 per cent. Large amounts of FDI going to LDCs were accounted for by resource development related investment, especially in Asia. Large investments made in oil and natural gas extraction and iron ore and copper mining in North Sumatra, Indonesia, Malaysia, the Philippines and India come under this category. Securing stable supply sources for natural resources were high on the priority list of Japan. The financial authorities, therefore, encouraged resource development related investments. Factors of production also moved in response to the appreciation of the yen and wage increases and the ANIEs attracted many Japanese enterprises in labour-intensive industries such as textiles and electrical machinery during the 1970s. During this period Japan was considered a mere regionally focused investor in resource-based and low-tech light manufacturing industries.

A clarification regarding the definition of FDI would not be out of place. Drawing a clear line between foreign direct and indirect investment is not easy. The latter implies investment in securities with an objective to earn a return on investment, which is generally higher than the return on capital at home. In this case the investor does not expect to be involved in the management of the enterprise. FDI, however, may include purchasing an existing enterprise or production facility, establishing or managing new ones and managing or having an effective say in the management of the enterprise. It is not always obvious which investment is being made with the objective of controlling or participating in the management and which is not. Therefore, often a rule-of-thumb is followed. When 10 per cent or more of corporate stock is acquired in a foreign enterprise, the investment is classified as FDI. The statistics published by the Japanese Ministry of Finance, adhere to this criterion of classification.

Although capital outflows were further liberalised in 1978 and the domestic economy had recovered from the recession, FDI flows did not start growing until 1980. The second oil-price hike had precluded any such possibilities. In 1980, outflows were $2.11 billion but soon grew in volume and the average for the four years 1980–83 was $3.52 billion. With the boom in the world economy, they escalated further in 1984 and 1985 to $5.89 billion.[2] It is in the first quinquennium of the 1980s that Japan stopped being taken as a minor foreign direct investing economy. From this perspective, 1980, not 1972, should be named the *gan-nen*. There was an unprecedented surge in FDI in the international economy in the 1980s and it began to play an increasing role. In the five years between 1985 and 1989 new FDI flows worldwide rose at an annual rate of 29 per cent, three times as fast as international trade, taking the total stock of FDI in the world to $1.5 trillion.[3] Two structural changes are considered responsible: (a) the liberalisation of service industries, specially banking, insurance and telecommunications, for which FDI is the only means of diversification, and (b) the emergence of Japan as a major investor.[4]

The broad sectoral trends between the early 1950s and the mid-1980s were as follows. First, the proportion of FDI in the primary sector recorded a steep decline over this period. It was steeper in LDCs compared to that in industrialised countries because the latter did not attract much of Japanese FDI in their primary sectors in the first place. Second, the proportion of FDI in the manufacturing sector also showed a small decline over this period, with the two country groups showing divergent trends. Its proportion in LDCs increased over the 1970s but declined over the 1980s. Conversely, the share of FDI in manufacturing in the industrialised economies fell until the mid-1970s but this trend has reversed since. Third, FDI in services like finance and insurance, real estate, transport and communications increased, particularly over the 1980s. Fourth, the proportion of FDI going to LDCs had tended to decline since the mid-1970s. This trend analysis is based on the Ministry of Finance (MOF) data, which tried to see them in constant (1985) yen.[5]

POST-APPRECIATION ESCALATION

The net FDI flows recorded a sharp spurt in 1986. The amount of Japan's FDI on the basis of the flow data of balance of payments grew two-and-a-half times between 1985 and 1986 and continued to grow at an extremely brisk rate. This was a watershed point in the FDI flows and the statistics cited understate the vast movement of Japanese capital abroad. Many of the new factories built by Japanese investors were financed by borrowings in the host countries. Therefore, the outflow figures do not reflect the total investment.

For the 1986–90 period they averaged $31.12 billion per annum. This volume of FDI flows was more than seven times the average volume for the 1980–85 period. There was a steady rise in FDI over 1986–89 and the average annual increase was 44.8 per cent (Table 4.1). Thus, the upsurge of the first quinquennium picked up a great deal of momentum in the second. The same trend is reflected by the annual number of FDI cases. Between 1980 and 1985, they varied between 2499 and 2613 per year but in 1986 they soared to 3196 and continued to rise steadily. In 1989, they had doubled to 6589. In 1990, the annual number of FDI cases fell to 5863.[6] According to the MOF approvals/notifications statistics, the volume of FDI dropped 10.2 per cent between April and September 1990.[7] The curtailment was across the board and applied to both the sub-sectors of FDI, namely, manufacturing and services. The principal causal factors behind the decline were the Nikkei plunge-related turmoil in the financial markets, the stringent monetary policy of the late 1980s and depreciation of the yen in 1989.

In terms of total outstanding amount, or the stock data of FDI, Japan's status improved constantly in the latter half of the 1980s. Over the decade of the 1980s, its status changed from an economy investing small, if not trivial, amounts to North America and the ANIEs to a major foreign investing economy having far wider economic interests. While it stood fifth with $44 billion outstanding in 1985, three years later it was third after the US and the UK with $110.8 billion outstanding (Table 4.2). By 1988, Japan's FDI flows had grown to 1.2 per cent of GNP. This level was lower than that for the UK (3.7 per cent), which has remained at the top in terms of the ratio of FDI flows/GNP for the last two decades, but exceeded those for the US (0.4 per cent) and Germany (0.8 per cent). Only 10 years earlier, in 1978, this ratio stood at a paltry 0.24 per cent for Japan. In terms of world-wide international payments statistics, in 1989, Japan

Table 4.1   NET FOREIGN DIRECT INVESTMENT, 1982–89
(IN BILLIONS OF $)

	1982	1983	1984	1985	1986	1987	1988	1989
1. Japan	4.10	3.19	5.98	5.81	14.25	18.35	33.72	43.08
2. US	12.83	5.26	13.80	5.87	15.40	15.85	42.24	40.50
3. UK	1.75	3.00	8.27	6.47	9.39	16.98	20.62	−0.23
4. Netherlands	2.22	2.37	3.37	1.79	0.31	5.63	−0.24	4.22

NB. Minus sign implies net inward flows.
SOURCE   International Monetary Fund, *Balance of Payments Statistics,
1990 Yearbook*, Part I (Washington DC, 1990).

Table 4.2   OUTSTANDING AMOUNTS OF FOREIGN
DIRECT INVESTMENT FOR THE MAJOR INVESTING
COUNTRIES

	1985		1988	
	Amount (Billion of $)	Percentage share	Amount (Billion of $)	Percentage share
1. USA	232.7	36.1	326.9	31.7
2. UK	116.9	18.1	183.7	17.8
3. Japan	44.0	6.8	110.8	10.7
4. Germany	52.4	8.1	97.3	9.4
5. Netherlands	55.5	8.6	70.2	6.8

SOURCE   Japan External Trade Organisation, *White Paper on Foreign
Direct Investment, 1990* (Tokyo, 1990).

made the largest net FDI ($43.08 billion) among the major foreign
direct investing economies and emerged as the most active direct
investor in the world.

As for the form of investment, Japanese investors generally preferred to establish new enterprises with 100 per cent ownership as
opposed to joint ventures. According to the 1988 Ministry of International Trade and Industry statistics, the number of cases where direct
investment involved establishment of new enterprises in manufacturing industry and commerce were 80 per cent of the total. Mergers and
acquisitions (M&A) accounted for only 15 per cent in the manufacturing industry and 9 per cent in commerce. In North America and

Western Europe, preference was greater towards establishing 100 per cent owned subsidiaries while in Asia, because of local equity requirements, many cases of joint ventures came into being. Since 1987, the use of M&A has grown in the US and Europe also. Its use increased particularly in the manufacturing sector.

According to the statistics published by MITI in 1991, the total sales value of Japanese-affiliated companies and subsidiaries abroad reached ¥ 93.2 trillion or $589.7 billion in fiscal 1989/90. Of this, the total sales of manufacturing affiliates reached ¥ 22.3 trillion or $140.9 billion. The ratio of Japanese affiliates' production to the total production of their parent companies in Japan was 5.7 per cent in 1989/90. This proportion was almost half (3.0 per cent) in 1985 and since then it has increased monotonically.[8] It has recorded highest increases in the auto and transport machinery sub-sector and electronics and electrical machinery sub-sector.

A THEORETICAL PERSPECTIVE

From an economic perspective FDI, like international trade, takes place as a market response to opportunities provided by differences in production capabilities between countries. This is the basic Heckscher-Ohlinian explanation of both international trade and foreign investment between countries. Furthermore, the eclectic theory of FDI relates an economy's ability to invest abroad to the level of development as measured by the value of its GNP.[9] In the case of Japan, as we have seen, the GNP had expanded enough by 1980 to make it an important foreign investing economy and subsequently, when the yen appreciated, the resulting wealth effect turned it into a major foreign investing economy. The investing economy may have one or more of the following objectives: (1) development of natural resources in the host economy for eventual use by the investing economy, (2) the export-oriented FDI, and (3) FDI to exploit the domestic markets in the host economy. It has been stated on p. 117 above that more than half of Japan's FDI during the 1960s and the 1970s went to LDCs and that this was essentially aimed at the development of natural resources. The host economy benefited from the capital of the investing firms as well as the technology-intensity of the resource extraction process. Both have high material significance for the host LDC. During the 1980s, however, the second and third motives overwhelmingly dominated Japan's FDI flows.

Comparative advantage is a dynamic phenomenon and changes in it in the investing economy encourage FDI flows. These changes may be brought about by advancement in technology over time, differing rates of accumulation of factors of production and changes in the prices of traded goods. The appreciation of the yen affected the prices of traded goods in a big way and, thereby, changed Japan's comparative advantage. The economy was no longer competitive in a whole range of low- or intermediate-technology products. Its comparative advantage shifted to a high-value-added, high-tech and knowledge-intensive range of products. This change in comparative advantage inflicted both individual and social costs. Firms or industries that lost comparative advantage were forced to contract due to falling profits or rising losses. The contraction, however, can be facilitated by FDI and the affected firms can, to a substantial extent, maintain the value of their capital. Thus, the cost of losing comparative advantage becomes lower than what it would have been in the absence of FDI. Implicit here is the assumption that the value of the capital does not change whether it is invested at home or abroad. There is, however, a negative factor, that is, some of the capital is always industry-specific, not all of it is firm-specific. An additional benefit of this kind of FDI is that the investing firms can produce and market the same line of products utilising its industry-specific and firm-specific intangible capital and some industry-specific physical capital transferred from the home country. An example of the industry-specific intangible capital is marketing know-how. It matters little whether the market for the product is in Japan or a third country, the investing firm will utilise its existing marketing channels and in the process will save on the cost of finding new markets and new marketing channels.

Again, there are individual and social costs of moving capital abroad and doing business in an alien economic setting. The choice of moving into another industry in which there is a comparative advantage is generally open to firms but if they decide to do so, they have to relinquish their industry-specific intangible and physical capital. Therefore, comparing the two costs becomes a vital necessity for the firms making FDI. In case the firms decide on inter-country intra-industry movement, the value of the firms' total capital will not change a great deal. However, an intra-country inter-industry movement will diminish the value of capital by their industry-specific capital. Therefore, *ceteris paribus*, firms would be more inclined to invest abroad than at home.[10] Increased investment by Japanese firms during the decade of the 1980s, in the ANIEs and the ASEAN countries is explained by this rationale. It assisted the host country groups in realising their latent comparative advantage in various industrial sub-sectors.

LONG-TERM FACTORS AT WORK

The revision of the Foreign Exchange and Foreign Trade Control Law in 1980 facilitated the expansion of the FDI over the rest of the decade. The escalation in the early 1980s was to a great extent in response to the resurgence of protectionism in the mid-1970s in the industrial economies, particularly in the US. Several Japanese product lines in these countries had to face import restrictions, anti-dumping duties and several 'grey area' measures like orderly market-ing arrangements (OMA) and voluntary export restraints (VERs). In order to circumvent these as well as to exploit potential market growth, Japanese enterprises established production facilities in North America and Western Europe. Protectionistic barriers also encouraged FDI in the ANIEs because exports from these countries were not subject to trade barriers aimed at Japanese exports. Large investments were made by exporters of finished products in their final markets. Production of colour TVs, VCRs, autos, copiers, machine tools and consumer durables in the US and Western Europe was promoted by trade-barriers-related FDI.

The sharp spurt in 1986 was largely in response to the appreciation of the yen and rising current account surpluses. That is, a confluence of currency valuation effect and wealth effect supported the 1986 spurt.

This was also the year when indirect foreign investment, or invest-ment in foreign securities, peaked at $101 billion and a structural change became evident in Japan's outward capital flows. Between 1986 and 1990, indirect foreign investment declined from $101 billion to $5 billion while direct investment soared from $14 billion to $46 billion. Exploring the driving forces behind this change, one first comes to the demand- and supply-side effects of currency apprecia-tion which combined to move the productive capacity abroad to lower-cost areas and in turn increased the FDI flows. The apprecia-tion transfigured the domestic industrial structure by making several products cheaper to import than to produce. Profitability in the tradable sector was adversely affected while that in the non-tradable sector improved substantially.[11] The yen appreciation also altered the comparative advantage of the economy, domestic production moved upscale towards high-tech and high-value-added products, and imports of low-tech manufactured goods and semi-finished material increased dramatically. It was utilised in domestic industrial production which, in turn, prevented the 'deindustrialisation' or 'hollowing out' of the Japanese industrial sector. In addition, the low-tech and less sophisticated industries became less competitive and moved abroad and became the cause of the extra FDI.

Currency appreciation also reduced the prices of overseas assets and, therefore, the cost of investing abroad. In yen terms it was reduced by half. Likewise, in the countries whose currencies were pegged to the dollar, like the East and the South East Asian LDCs, Japan's cost of investment came down substantially. For manufacturers of semi-finished goods, therefore, there was a clear reason for locating capacity in the Asian region. It also enabled them to maintain their competitiveness against newer rivals in South Korea and Taiwan. The yen had also appreciated *vis-à-vis* the pound and the Deutschemark, although to a lesser extent. Therefore, the cost of investment advantage also existed in the UK and Germany. Second, Europe's movement towards unification was yet another driving force. Apprehensions regarding the possibility of trade diversion due to the market unification of the EC in 1992 were real and they encouraged Japanese firms to actively invest and set a foot-hold in Western Europe before 1992. Third, the motive of circumventing the protectionism and avoiding trade friction had continued to exist in the latter half of the 1980s as well.

In the latter half of the 1980s large investments were made in overseas real estate and fine arts. The former by definition comes under investment in the tertiary or services sector. Some of the high-profile real estate purchases included prime buildings like Arco Plaza in Los Angeles, Rockefeller Centre, Exxon's headquarters in New York and Yosemite National Park. Japanese investors snapped up a long list of paintings by old masters like Van Gogh and Picasso. The real estate investments were motivated by the combination of yen appreciation and escalation of local land prices. In Japanese cities and resort areas real estate prices had increased sharply after 1986, which reduced returns on real estate investment in Japan. The price gap between domestic and foreign prices widened dramatically, which encouraged outward investments. The yields on investments in foreign real estates became much higher than those in the domestic market. There were cases where these yields were as high as the returns on securities investment.[12] This kind of FDI also enabled institutional investors as well as the real estate companies to borrow using real estate as collateral. Therefore, large amounts were invested in big cities in the industrialised countries and resort areas in Hawaii and Australia. Institutional investors treated these investments like their portfolio investments and were motivated by good returns. The cash-rich life insurance companies were very active in the real estate markets abroad. Conversely, individual investors were largely driven by the expectations of capital gains on future price rises. They mainly invested in condominiums which could be liquidated easily.

Another set of motives behind the enhanced FDI flows were acquiring know-how, skills and experience in intricate industries like financial services as well as augmenting market shares. Japanese institutional investors own four of the top 10 California-based banks.[13] In all, Japanese banks hold some 25 per cent of the total banking assets in the State.[14] Associated with this has been the increase in acquisition of equity in the large US securities groups. Two of the significant moves were: Sumitomo Bank buying 12.5 per cent interest in Salomon Brothers and Nippon Life buying 13 per cent state in Shearson Lehman. Fugi Bank acquired Walter E. Heller, the Chicago-based finance company. Several similar moves were made which provided Japanese investors with valuable expertise and experience and boosted their presence in the international financial markets.

A unique feature of Japanese FDI was that, unlike other industrial countries, a significant proportion of it was made by small- and medium-sized industrial enterprises. The reason simply is that in the Japanese economy small- and medium-sized enterprises are more active than in other industrialised economies. Of the total 8567 cases of acquisition of stocks of foreign corporation by Japanese enterprises over 1980–87, 3507 cases related to small- and medium-sized enterprises which put their participation in FDI at 41 per cent in terms of the number of cases.[15] After the appreciation of the yen small- and medium-sized enterprises became more active in FDI. During the first half of the 1980s investments made by them averaged around 300 cases per year. They almost doubled every year between 1986 and 1988, to reach 1625 cases of FDI in 1988. Although their number declined to 1401 in 1989, they stayed at a high level.[16] The following trends were obvious in the overseas investment by small-

and medium-sized firms: (a) the share of investment in manufacturing (38.2 per cent) was higher than the average for Japan's total FDI in manufacturing (24.1 per cent), and (b) these enterprises overwhelmingly concentrated on Asia (64.7 per cent) as opposed to North America (24.3) and Europe (9.0 per cent).[17] The small- and medium-sized firms that began to lose their comparative advantage, were helped by the Government through institutions like the Japan Overseas Development Corporation and the Overseas Mineral Resource Development Corporation in making FDI. Bearing in mind the high social cost, FDI by the small- and medium-sized industries was subsidised. The small- and medium-sized enterprises have been rather active in manufacturing industries, therefore, their involvement in FDI in the future is expected to remain significant.

Manufacturing abroad for domestic consumption by Japanese corporations was relatively lower. This is known as 'boomerang imports' or reverse imports, that is, the output of the firms created with the help of Japanese FDI being exported to Japan. According to a MITI survey, domestic sales of overseas subsidiaries of Japanese manufacturing corporations amounted to 4.9 per cent of total sales for Japan in March 1989.[18] The corresponding proportions for the US and German corporations were much higher; they ranged between 18 and 20 per cent for the US and 17 and 19 per cent for Germany. There were two reasons behind it. First, Japan's FDI flows only accelerated in the latter half of the 1980s and it takes time to establish well co-ordinated subsidiaries and their output. Second, since the majority of these enterprises are new, their first endeavours are to produce and market locally. In fact, certain regional characteristics in this regard were obvious. Japanese affiliates in the US sold an overwhelming proportion of their output locally, suggesting that production in the US took place to replace exports and serve the local markets. The reverse imports from the US were limited to 3.4 per cent of production and concentrated in foodstuffs.[19] A characteristic of investment in the EC was that firms aimed their sales efforts at the EC region as a whole as well as the host country, and together they represent over half of the sales activity. As a rule-of-thumb, the sales destinations of overseas affiliates in the industrialised countries were domestic markets of the host country or region; the affiliates and subsidiaries in the developing countries of Asia aimed their sales efforts at third country markets. Japanese subsidiaries located in the ANIEs exported 16.3 per cent of their output to third countries and 6.6 per cent to Japan as reverse imports. Similarly, from the ASEAN countries 11.1 per cent of the output was exported to third countries and 10.4 per cent to Japan.[20] The total amount of reverse imports was estimated to have reached ¥ 1767 billion or $11.2 billion in March 1990. This represented 5.2 per cent of total Japanese import value and 10.4 per cent of manufactured import value.[21]

The same MITI survey also noted the lower profitability of the Japanese foreign subsidiaries compared to those from the US and other major investing countries. The US subsidiaries were not only noted for higher profits but they also were a rich source of profits for their parent companies. This did not apply to the Japanese subsidiaries largely because they were new in the game and had not fully stabilised and expanded their operations. The profit rates of subsidiaries have been found to be a function of the age of the establishment. Besides, not all the post-1985 FDI expansion and mega-deals made by Japan were spectacular successes. Many of them fell short of expectations and potential. It took Fugi Bank six years and large capital injections to turn around Walter E. Heller. Nippon Mining's acquisition of the mini-conglomerate Gould proved to be an erroneous move, so did Bridgestone's acquisition of Firestone.[22] In the early 1990s, Japanese investors were more cautious and began to recognise that successful acquisition is a matter of careful choice.

The post-appreciation pattern of FDI has influenced Japan's export structure. Exports of durable consumer goods like electronics products and automobiles have suffered while capital goods like telecommunications and data processing equipment, and parts such as semiconductors and auto parts have soared. The reason for increased exports of parts was that Japanese firms that had established production bases in the US and Europe were only beginning to operate and were relying more on domestic supplies of parts and accessories. In case of auto parts 55 per cent or 257 firms established production facilities in the US during the latter half of the 1980s. Once they go on stream and start local production, parts imports from Japan will decline.

An encouraging feature that emerged was that despite (a) high levels of domestic investment during the post-appreciation period, and (b) the marginal depreciation of the yen after the fourth quarter of 1988, FDI flows continued to expand in 1989 both in terms of volume and the number of cases. This implies that although the dramatic expansion of FDI was made feasible by currency appreciation and current account surpluses, it developed into a long-term characteristic of the Japanese economy. To be sure, large-scale involvement of Japanese firms in FDI is relatively recent but it can be expected to continue in the future. It will not continue to grow monotonically. As alluded to earlier, the number of cases as well as the volume of FDI recorded a small decline in the first half of FY 1990. Yet, the overseas business activities of Japanese corporations have developed into a new phase and their endeavours to globalise their activities would keep the FDI at a high level.

REGIONAL DISTRIBUTION

In this section I focus on the post-appreciation dispersal of FDI among various regions. The three regions that have traditionally absorbed four-fifths of Japanese FDI are: North America, Europe and Asia. Together they accounted for 79.5 per cent of cases of FDI over the 1951–90 period. Of this, North America had the largest share (38.3 per cent) followed by Asia (30.2 per cent) and Europe (11.0 per cent).[23] These statistics summarise the long-term regional trends of the FDI flows. The term North America can be taken to mean the US because virtually all of the FDI marked for this region goes to the US. In Asia, two country groups are of special signifi- cance, namely, the ANIEs and the ASEAN. The following mem- bers of the ASEAN group have become increasingly important in recent years: Indonesia, Thailand, Malaysia. The Philippines re- ceived much less attention. The proportion of FDI going to Europe recorded a spurt in the latter half of the 1980s. The approvals/ notifications statistics of the Ministry of Finance (MOF) will be used in the following analysis.

North America

The largest market in the world exercises its centripetal force. In addition, Japan's FDI strategy for the 1980s was low cost production near the consumption centres and positioning for future markets. These two cogent reasons made the US an attractive proposition. Besides, the US has been the closest economic partner of Japan, which is obvious from the trade and capital flows statistics for the last four decades. Over the second half of the 1980s, this relationship continued to be strong in terms of capital flows, although it became less so in the case of trade. According to the MOF statistics, North America's share in total FDI flows rose to 46.8 per cent in 1986, while

Table 4.3 REGIONAL DISTRIBUTION OF FDI, 1981–89
(IN PER CENT)

	North America		Of which US	Asia	Of which ANIEs	Of which ASEAN	Europe	Middle East	Oceania	Other Regions
1981–85	36.4	34.8	20.4		8.7	10.8	13.9	1.5	3.6	24.2
1986	46.8	45.5	10.4		6.9	2.5	15.5	0.2	4.4	22.7
1987	46.0	44.1	14.6		7.7	3.4	19.7	0.2	4.2	15.3
1988	47.5	46.2	11.8		6.9	4.1	19.4	0.6	5.7	15.0
1989	50.2	48.2	12.2		7.2	4.1	21.9	1.0	6.8	7.9

SOURCE Ministry of Finance, *Statistics of Approvals/Notifications of Overseas Direct Investment* (Tokyo, 1990 and earlier issues).

the average for the 1981–85 period was 36.4 per cent (Table 4.3). As stated, almost all of it went to the US. For instance, in 1986 the US received 45.5 per cent of the total and its average for 1981–85 was 34.8 per cent. Subsequently, the proportion of North America grew to 50.2 per cent in 1989, with the US share growing to as large as 48.2 per cent of the Japan FDI. It received $32 billion in 2668 cases of FDI.

Investment in the manufacturing sector has made impressive gains in recent years. From close to $4 billion in 1984, it increased to a gross of $33.5 billion in 1989. Major industries that attracted Japanese investment were autos and transport equipment, electronics, machinery and chemicals. Japanese firms have set up over 1000 manufacturing plants in the US. Their most noticeable presence is in the auto industry where they have captured 21 per cent of the US market. In the electronics industries, 162 US companies were either acquired by or formed joint ventures with Japanese firms.[24] The non-manufacturing or service industries that attracted large FDI were real estate, finance, insurance and retailing. The gross investment in these activities in 1989 was $71.5 billion. The resources development sector, which includes mining, fisheries and agriculture, was traditionally ignored by the Japanese investors, but in 1989, they invested $2.5 billion in purchases of farmland, meatpacking plants and grain-handling facilities and ruffled a few feathers. According to the US Department of Commerce statistics, by 1988 Japan had become the second largest foreign investor in the US after the UK.

Since the mid-1980s, Japanese investors have paid large amounts to acquire hotels, golf courses, office buildings, condominiums and prime land. Beginning with almost nothing in the early 1980s and close to $6 billion in the mid-1980s, real estate investment has swelled like *tsunami* and crossed the $20 billion mark in 1989. These investors were not passively investing their surplus capital but were busy establishing a major presence in the US real estate industry. In the process, Japanese capital shored up a nearly crippled US real estate industry. Japanese institutional investors took up the slack in real estate lending in the wake of the S&L (Savings and Loans) crisis. As stated, following the steep rise in the real estate prices in Japan, returns on property investments abroad became attractive for institutional investors. They were as high as 8 per cent in New York compared to 1 per cent or less in Tokyo.[25]

While Japan's continual purchases of Treasury bonds concerns no one, an acceleration in FDI has had a startling effect on American popular opinion. Opinion polls show that about 70 per cent of Americans think that Japanese corporations have invested too much in the US and that they are colluding with each other and with the government to extract technology and profits from their American acquisitions.[26] The high-profile deals, like Sony purchasing Columbia Pictures or Mitsubishi Real Estate's acquisition of the Rockefeller Center stirred up anti-Japanese sentiments and political anguish. Some did not hesitate to go to an absurd extreme and contended that Japanese FDI is tantamount to the economic colonisation of the US. In fact, both national and state politicians are keen for 'greenfield site' investments in which the investors establish a new enterprise that creates new jobs. This may not always be the optimal *modus operandi* for the investors. In many cases they sensibly prefer to enter it by taking over an American company, thereby acquiring experienced staff and existing production and distribution facilities.[27] However, professional opinion, unlike popular opinion in this regard, was not united. Academia saw virtue in it and the Federal Reserve Board Chairman Alan Greenspan in a Ways and Means Committee hearing[28] called it 'beneficial and positive' for the American economy.

Europe

Compared to the US, Japan's economic ties with the European countries were tenuous, although the UK was an exception in this regard. Accordingly trade, capital flows and FDI remained much lower in volume. Between 1951 and 1990, the total number of FDI cases for Europe was 7425 while the comparable number for the US was 22 944. The gross investment in Europe was $59.27 billion while that in the US was $130.53 billion. That is, over this period Europe received less than half of the US amount.[29] But in the first quinquennium of the 1980s Japanese FDI began to increase but Europe absorbed only about a third of the US share. However, after the appreciation of the yen a dramatic increase was observed. Europe received 13.9 per cent of total Japanese FDI over 1981–85. This proportion increased to 15.5 per cent in 1986, the first post-appreciation year, and increased continually thereafter. It reached 21.9 per cent in 1989 (Table 4.3). To be sure, in absolute and relative terms, the FDI flows to Europe are much smaller than those to the US but they have grown impressively since 1986 when they were a mere $3.5 billion. Even in the latter half of the 1980s, the UK absorbed the largest part – a third – of the total FDI going to Europe. Other important recipients were the Netherlands and Luxembourg, and the latter received banking and finance-related capital. Germany and France stood next, in that order, followed by Switzerland. A rapid rise in FDI stirred political anguish in Europe as well. The antipathy was spearheaded by France. This reaction is out of proportion to its economic significance because in 1989 Japan was responsible for only 6 per cent of the cumulative stock of FDI in the EC. Furthermore, less than $8 billion of FDI was in manufacturing and half of it was in the politically sensitive sectors of autos and electronics.

The attraction of the huge EC market, comparable to that of the US, was one of the strong driving forces. Although various segments of the European market were not homogenous and Japanese entrants had to face severe indigenous local competition, European economies offered the benefits of moderate labour union activity and – notwithstanding the trenchant French criticism – a softening in general attitude towards FDI. Investing allowed Japanese producers proximity to European consumers and the distribution networks and made it easier to do market research in the matured European markets. It was good logic for them to extend and deepen their market presence in activities where they possessed clear comparative advantage and had already built up substantial exports. Secondly, as adumbrated earlier, the EC-1992 phenomenon of an integrated market, coupled with the apprehensions of 'fortress Europe', created a great deal of concern in the Japanese corporate world and several surveys were conducted to work out and analyse the corporate response. The important ones were: (1) A General Survey of Overseas Japanese Affiliates undertaken by Tokyo Kaizai Shinposha in 1990, (2) the Questionnaire Survey Concerning EC Market Unification undertaken by the Federation of Economic Organisations in 1989, (3) the Unification of the EC market in 1992 and Response in Japanese Companies undertaken by the Japanese Committee for Economic Development Association in 1989, (4) the Questionnaire Survey of Trends in Entry into the EC Market by the Japanese Manufacturing Industry undertaken by the Long-Term Credit Bank of Japan Research Institute in 1989, and (5) the Sixth Survey of Management Conditions in Japanese Affiliated Manufacturing Firms in Europe undertaken by Japan External Trade Organisation in 1990. A summary of responses made by Hirata *inter alia* indicated that the perception of Japanese corporations was that the post-1992 period the EC would be more difficult to export to and invest in. Therefore, they believed it would be desirable to secure production bases inside the EC region prior to unification.[30] The two preferred modes of entry were: first, formation of partnership with European firms by providing them with technical expertise, and thereby developing a local production base. Second, setting up a new venture or resorting to M&A. The Japanese corporations have restructured their strategy towards the EC and between 1987 and 1989, their FDI more than doubled. The firms that had made only half-hearted attempts, intensified their activities in various industrial and service areas.[31]

Trade friction was created by rising high-tech exports, which increased with the passage of time and anti-dumping law suits were brought against Japanese companies by the EC countries in the areas of electronic products, machinery and other products. A good deal of FDI was made to ameliorate this situation. FDI in products like VCRs, microwave ovens, CD players and office equipment was made to atone for the European criticism regarding aggressive trade practices. The electronic home appliance manufacturers moved in to cope with consumer needs and reduce transport costs. Textile and clothing and chemical industries were attracted by abundant raw materials and the European sense of design and artwork. Bulk manufacturing plants were established in both chemical and pharmaceutical industries. Some FDI in Europe has been made by large Japanese corporations only because their competitors have done so, instead of for sound economic reasons. For instance, in the auto industry Japanese auto makers had 11 per cent of the European market. Therefore, initially Nissan and Toyota were not interested in producing in Europe but in the early 1990s they reversed their stance and decided to invest in a big way, to march in step with their competitors.

As in the US, non-manufacturing or services sectors have attracted greater amounts of FDI in recent years than the manufacturing sectors, the largest investments going into finance and insurance industries. Other important sectors were commercial services and real estate. The three large life insurance companies, namely, Nippon, Meiji and Sumitomo and real estate firms like Mitsubishi Estate have taken a great deal of interest in the European property market, particularly in the UK and France. Returns on property investments in London and Paris are as high as 5 per cent. In the manufacturing sector, electronics, autos and transport equipment and machinery sub-sectors have been important destinations of FDI. Japanese firms also advanced into Europe through mergers and acquisitions (M&A) and joint ventures. The link between two giants, the Mitsubishi group and Daimler-Benz AG is an important example of the latter. Joint ventures were a popular mode of M&A among the small- and medium-sized companies.

Although the UK has attracted the largest amount of Japanese FDI both in manufacturing and non-manufacturing sectors due to an open-door approach followed by the Tory government towards foreign investment, several other European countries are becoming the new focal countries. For instance, Spain has the lowest labour cost and a record of sustained growth, therefore, it has lately attracted a good deal of investment in manufacturing sectors. Notwithstanding the European ambivalance about Japanese economic expansion, there are strong political factors supporting closer future relations between Europe and Japan (cf. Chapter 2). It was obvious in the early 1990s that economic and geopolitical ties between the US and Japan could no longer be taken for granted.[32] In relative terms, the expansion in FDI in Europe in the latter half of the 1980s was not at the cost of the US but the LDCs. However, there are good prospects of it being at the cost of the US in the short- or medium-term future.

Asia

Compared to the decade of the 1970s the importance of Asia, which essentially implies the four ANIEs and the four ASEAN members (Indonesia, Malaysia, Thailand and the Philippines), declined in relative terms in the early 1980s. As stated above, increase in the proportion of FDI to North America as well as Europe had a lot to do with this decline. However, this does not imply that FDI flows to Asia stagnated in absolute terms. This tendency can be seen in Table 4.3. The proportion of FDI flowing to Asia dipped in the latter half of the 1980s, whereas that to the US and Europe grew. However, in absolute terms FDI flows to Asia grew from $2.3 billion in 1986 to $8.2 billion in 1989, a three-and-a-half times increase.

Japanese FDI in the East and South East Asia has economically transformed the region. In the latter half of the 1980s the four ANIEs were the most important group, of which Hong Kong and Singapore were the largest FDI recipients. The ASEAN-four came next, which was a reversal of the situation from the early 1980s when they received larger investment than the ANIEs, with Indonesia topping the list. Among the ASEAN-four, Indonesia was considered attractive because of its large natural resources, low labour cost and domestic market potential. In Malaysia, Japanese corporations were given near *carte blanche* to invest in and export to, with little concern about bilateral relationships getting seriously out of joint. Malaysia has become a microcosm of precisely the sort of relationship that Japan would like to have with its neighbours. Thailand has benefited the most from Japanese FDI by transforming its economic policy structure and by integrating its economy with the international economy, including that of Japan. It is most aptly suited to became the fifth dragon of Asia in the near-term. The Philippines has lagged behind because of its confused macroeconomic stance, lacklustre economic performance and unwelcoming policies towards FDI.

Countries of South Asia were not considered an attractive proposition and, in turn, in their own scheme of things FDI did not have much significance. If anything, it was something to be shunned. These economies are known for slothful and inefficient bureaucracies which were as powerful as they were over-extended. Any FDI decision had to pass through a labyrinth of procedures and protracted negotiations. Also, their economic performance ranged from tepid to absolutely poor. India, the large regional economy, shackled its centrally-misplanned economy and failed to show any promise. It received a paltry $18 million in 1989 in 9 cases of FDI, which was less than 0.1 per cent of total Japanese FDI for that year. There has been far more interest in China which had received over $2 billion by 1988. It received $438 million in 1989 in 126 cases, which was 0.6 per cent of the total FDI.

During the post-appreciation period, electronics and electrical goods, chemicals and ferrous and non-ferrous metals were among the sub-sectors that attracted large amounts of FDI, with electronics and electrical goods topping the list in the manufacturing sector. Although the ANIEs recorded impressive growth rates and their industrial structures acquired a good deal of sophistication, their currencies began to appreciate and the labour cost rose. On this score, FDI in manufacturing began to shift from the ANIEs to the ASEAN-four. For the first time in fiscal 1988, Japanese FDI in the manufacturing industries recorded a shift from the ANIEs to the ASEAN-four; it reached $1360 million and exceeded those in the ANIEs ($776 million). Large increases in investment in Thailand and Malaysia were recorded in the electronics and electrical goods sectors.

In the non-manufacturing sectors, retailing and other services and finance and insurance accounted for a dominant part of the total FDI during the post-appreciation period. Real estate and commerce were also substantial sectors. A large part of expansion in finance and insurance-related FDI took place in Hong Kong. Deregulation and liberalisation in Japanese financial markets and the demand by Japanese affiliate banks and their subsidiaries in the ANIEs and the ASEAN countries, were responsible for expansion in finance and insurance-related FDI in Asia.

As stated, immediately in the post-yen-appreciation years, investment in Asia was catalysed by a strong yen and rising labour costs and the Japanese firms were relocating themselves for exports. The dispersal process was particularly notable in less sophisticated products. Japanese groups like Uniden boasted that they neither produced anything nor sold anything in Japan. Likewise, many firms had their production facilities in Hong Kong, Taiwan, Malaysia and the Philippines and they marketed their output in the US and Europe. This strategy, in the late 1980s and early 1990s, underwent a change and increasingly Japanese firms began to invest in the East and South East Asia to sell locally. The economic boom of the region justified their positioning to take advantage of expanding Asian markets, an approach so far adopted only for industrialised economies. The new strategy was expected to benefit the whole of the South East Asian region, particularly Indonesia and Thailand. In the world of high-tech electronics and electrical products, this region has acquired the well deserved reputation of being the highest growth potential region. Japanese firms were planning to set up production facilities in products like elevators, refrigerators, washing machines, audio sets, video-cassette recorders, colour TV tubes, cordless telephones and other electrical appliances to meet the growing local demand.[33]

Curtailment of Japanese FDI flows in 1990 has been noted on pp. 86–8 above, and Asia was no exception. However, it is not taken as an indicator of a shift of FDI away from Asia. The slowdown is part of the broader cyclical factors that have constrained Japanese investment world wide. This fall is the first in eight years and investment flows are expected to pick up in the not-too-distant future. The silver lining to this cloud is that some Japanese corporations in the region began to face manufacturing overcapacity and some countries in the region, like Thailand, are feeling their infrastructure being strained. The respite, therefore, may not be utterly frustrating.[34]

SECTORAL DISTRIBUTION

More than a third of the total Japanese FDI went into manufacturing over the 1970s. In the first quinquennium of the 1980s this proportion declined and in 1985 and 1986 it sank to under 20 per cent. But during the next two years it showed a strong recovery (Table 4.4). However, for more than two decades Japan's FDI in manufacturing in all host regions had grown steadily. It grew not only in terms of nominal dollars but also in terms of constant (1985) dollars and constant (1985) yen.[35] These growth rates accelerated after the appreciation of the yen. The rate of acceleration was particularly high for the industrial countries. Although the same accelerating trend was observed for developing countries, the pace was much slower. Industries that received large amounts of Japanese capital were electronics and electrical machinery, autos and transport equipment, ferrous and non-ferrous metal and chemicals and pharmaceuticals, in that order. In 1989, $4.48 billion or 6.6 per cent of the total FDI went into electronics and electrical machinery. It decreased in the US over the late 1980s while it increased in Europe. Its share also increased in the ANIEs and the ASEAN-four. The automakers and transport equipment manufacturers invested $2.05 billion or 3.0 per cent of the total. Again the US share decreased in the late 1980s because big Japanese

Table 4.4   SECTORAL DISTRIBUTION OF FDI, 1986–89
(IN PER CENT)

	Manufacturing	Resource Development	Commerce	Finance and Insurance	Transport Service	Real Estate	Others
1986	17.1	3.3	8.3	32.4	8.6	17.9	12.4
1987	23.5	1.9	6.8	32.0	6.4	16.3	13.1
1988	29.4	2.7	6.8	27.9	5.0	18.4	9.8
1989	24.1	2.2	7.6	22.8	4.3	20.9	18.1

SOURCE   The Ministry of Finance, *Statistics of Approvals/Notifications of Overseas Direct Investment* (Tokyo, 1990 and earlier issues).

assembly plants of the principal Japanese automakers were already completed. Europe recorded an expansion because most of the large Japanese automakers were building up their production facilities. Auto-parts makers were following the automakers in a natural sequence. They also set up facilities in South East Asia to export parts to Japan. Ferrous and non-ferrous industries in the US, Europe and South East Asia attracted investment in aluminium and copper projects and manufacturing of steel plates for automobiles. In the US and Europe there were several large M&A cases in this sub-sector. Another major sector was chemicals and pharmaceuticals where the M&A strategy was found to be suitable and active.

Unlike the 1970s, investment in resources development in the 1980s diminished in volume and significance. In the latter half of the 1980s it grew in a minor proportion. As noted in another context, some investments were made in the purchases of orchards in California and farmlands and meat-packing plants in other places in the US. However, mining and oil extraction related investment were substantial in Indonesia, Australia and Mexico.

In the services sector finance and insurance and real estate were the two largest sub-sectors; FDI in them has increased rapidly since the yen appreciation. In 1989, the former received $15.39 billion, which was 22.8 per cent of the total. Investment in finance and insurance was in the form of investment to expand juridical entities of banks and securities firms abroad as well as for establishing subsidiaries of financial companies for investing in financial operations. At the end of March 1990, the number of Japanese banks' overseas subsidiaries totalled 276.[36] Globalisation of Japanese corporate activities also contributed to the establishment of overseas financial subsidiaries in non-banking sectors. While internationalising their finances, firms had to find ways to control the supply of funds and foreign exchange fluctuations and manage surplus liquidity. Trading and manufacturing firms loaned surplus liquidity to their overseas financial subsidiary at low interest rates, which in turn they invested profitably in the Eurobond markets. Establishment of such subsidiaries contributed to an increase in finance-related investment. These investments were essentially made in the US, Europe and Hong Kong. Purchases of banks in California comes under this category. As alluded to earlier, the real estate investments became huge in the late 1980s. In absolute terms, they grew from $3.9 billion in 1986 to $14.14 billion in 1989. Other than the large and attention-catching acquisitions noted earlier, there was a boom in the development of overseas resorts by Japanese companies. The largest share of this investment went to the US, followed by the Pacific region. Europe was discovered late by real estate investors but they were very active in the latter part of the decade.

It has been set forth that Japan's FDI in the manufacturing sector in LDCs grew at a much slower pace than that in the industrialised economies, but the proportion of FDI going to the manufacturing sector in Asia kept growing steadily. Therefore, Asia's share rose from 50 per cent of the total manufacturing FDI in LDCs in the mid-1970s to 61 per cent in early 1980s and further to 81 per cent in the late 1980s. Japan's FDI affiliates in Asia were more export-oriented than those in other LDCs. FDI in general tends to promote manufactured exports from LDCs and this tendency is not limited to Japanese FDI.[37] A case study for Thailand corroborated this observation and concluded that FDI by transnational corporations played a significant role in creating and promoting manufactured exports from Thailand.[38] In several sub-sectors, Japan's FDI in Asia has resulted in 'boomerang imports'. In the electrical machinery sector these exports were the highest. They were also significant in transport machinery and auto-parts, and were also increasing in the precision machinery and general machinery sub-sectors. In other sub-sectors such exports were small, that is, a quarter or less of the total output.[39] In FY 1989–90, reserve imports reached $11.2 billion, a 40.8 per cent increase on yen basis or 18.7 per cent increase on dollar basis over the previous fiscal year. This represented 10.4 per cent of manufactured import value.[40]

FDI IN JAPAN

According to the MOF notifications statistics, FDI in Japan in 1985 was a mere $930 million, of which $650 million, or 69.9 per cent, was in the manufacturing sector. The US was traditionally the largest foreign direct investor in Japan, accounting for as much as 60 per cent of the total, while the EC came next with about a quarter of the total. The volume of inward FDI in Japan is very small compared to its own expansion abroad on this count. In 1989, the ratio of out-standing balance of Japan's FDI to the outstanding balance of inward FDI in Japan was 16.8. The comparable figure for the US was 0.9. In case of the UK and Germany this ratio was 1:5. One of the reasons why inward FDI has remained low is the general perception outside that the Japanese economy is virtually closed to inward investment. Second, during the 1980s, there was a good deal of withdrawal of FDI. Some foreign firms pulled out of Japan because they lost their technological advantage and with it their competitive edge. Third, after 1985, high costs due to an appreciated yen became an effective deterrent. The high cost of land and the labour shortage had the same daunting impact on foreign investors in Japan. The appreciation of the yen also encouraged some foreign firms to liquidate their assets to make capital gains. Several large firms like Chrysler, Merk, Honeywell and General Motors decided to make capital gains and withdrew. Another associated trend was the purchase of parent companies by their Japanese subsidiaries; the buying-out of CBS records and Shaklee can be taken for two high-profile examples.[41] Fourth, although institutional and regulatory impediments were re-moved to a great extent and inward investments were completely liberalised in 1980, traditional Japanese business practices and structural impediments stood in the way. They originated from the *keiretsu* tradition of Japanese business. A *keiretsu* is a developmental conglomerate of mutually co-operating firms. There are six *keiretsu*, namely, Mitsui, Mitsubishi, Sumitomo, Fugi, Sanwa and Dai-Ichi Kangyo. There is an intense mutual competition among them. The *keiretsu* arrangement goes part of the way in explaining the shallow penetration of FDI in Japan. The low level of inward FDI has become responsible for 'investment imbalance' which in turn became an additional source of friction between Japan and other industrial-ised countries. In order to allay international resentment on the investment imbalance count an advisory panel was set up by the Ministry of International Trade and Industry which suggested in

1991, that new incentives should be given to encourage FDI in Japan. Foreign companies have complained of the high starting-up costs in Japan and of complex import regulations. Therefore, based on the recommendations of the advisory panel, the Japanese Government is considering establishing ten free trade zones where foreign investors would be eligible for preferential tax treatment. They will also have access to concessional finance and be entitled to make duty free imports.[42] Subsidised loans are to be made from Japan Development Bank and the Hokkaido-Tohoku Development Corporation, a regional agency. The proposed zones are to be set up near airports and ports. Chitose airport in Hokkaido is a prime candidate for such a zone.

We shall see below that the manufacturing sector accounted for the lion's share of inward FDI in Japan, with large proportions going to machinery and chemicals sub-sectors. Between 1982 and 1986, according to the MOF notifications statistics, there was no noticeable increase in the inward FDI. It increased from $749 million to $940 million over this period, which is a 25.5 per cent increase in four years. On a cumulative basis, 64.4 per cent of this went into manufacturing. During 1987 and 1988, a sudden spurt was observed and the inward flows reached $2.21 billion and $3.24 billion, respectively. A large part again went to the manufacturing sector during both the years. Its proportion stood at 64.5 per cent and 74.7 per cent, respectively. Growth in manufacturing, particularly in semiconductors and transport machinery, was specially high. In 1989, foreign business invested $2.86 billion in Japan, which was an 11.8 per cent decline over the preceding year. This fall was despite a 33.3 per cent increase in the number of investment cases. The decline was attributed to a sharp drop in investment in the manufacturing sector. As opposed to this, the non-manufacturing sector recorded a 106 per cent increase. Noteworthy was the investment in real estate in 1989; it increased eight-fold over the previous year, soaring from 2.2 per cent of the total inward FDI in 1988 to 22.6 per cent in 1989. Other than real estate, research and development (R&D) and distribution channels attracted the attention of foreign investors in the late 1980s. More recently, Japanese firms became technological leaders in several high-tech areas. Their growing prowess in technology development was noticed by firms in the other industrialised countries, which encouraged them to establish R&D centres in Japan. Increased investment in distribution channels stemmed from the need to establish marketing networks for entering the massive Japanese market.

SUMMING UP

Japan's FDI in the industrialised and developing economies did not come into reckoning until the beginning of the 1980s. Before this point in time, Japan invested trifling amounts in the US and the developing countries of the East and South East Asia. FDI in the latter country group was made for the development of natural resources and ensuring their supply for the Japanese industries. After the appreciation of the yen, FDI flows recorded a dramatic spurt and by the end of the decade, in terms of net flows, Japan became the largest investing economy in the world. Other than the rising current account surpluses, the wealth effect of the yen appreciation and the changes brought about by it in the comparative advantage of the Japanese industry were responsible for the spurt. Generally Japan preferred to invest in new enterprises with 100 per cent ownership but after 1987, the use of M&A increased.

There were several driving forces behind the expansion of FDI. Neo-protectionism in the industrialised countries gave an impetus to Japan's FDI in these countries. It was seen as a means to circumvent the ingeneous array of barriers created for Japan's exports. The demand and supply-side effects of currency appreciation combined to force the Japanese economy to move its productive capacity abroad to lower-cost areas. The currency appreciation had reduced the cost of investing abroad by reducing the cost of foreign assets. Acquiring know-how and skills in intricate industries like financial services was another motivating factor. Rise in domestic real estate prices and expectations of high returns abroad increased FDI in real estate. Other than the large real estate companies, the cash-rich insurance companies were active in the real estate markets abroad. The confluence of all these factors turned the Japanese economy into a high foreign investing economy and when the yen began to depreciate, it did not affect the FDI flows. FDI flows came to be established as a long-term feature of the Japanese economy.

A significant proportion of FDI was made by small- and medium-sized enterprises. They were rather active in the manufacturing sector. Manufacturing abroad for domestic consumption was lower for Japanese corporations than their US and German counterparts. Japanese affiliates in the US sold an overwhelming proportion of their output locally, suggesting that FDI in the US took place to replace exports and serve the local markets. The reverse imports were tiny. FDI in EC firms led to sales efforts in the EC region as well as the host country. Japanese firms located in the ANIEs exported substantially to third countries and to Japan. The profitability of Japanese firms' FDI was found to be lower than that of US and German firms.

There were three regional foci of FDI: North America, Asia and Europe, in that order. The traditional focus of Japanese FDI was the US which maintained its status during the post-appreciation period. Europe's importance was enhanced at the expense of the developing countries. In the US the manufacturing sector recorded impressive gains in the recent past and so did investment in real estate. Increases in Europe were driven by the lure of the large EC market and the EC 1992 phenomenon. Both manufacturing and non-manufacturing sectors attracted FDI. Investment flows to Asia did not stagnate in absolute terms. During the latter half of the 1980s, the four ANIEs were the most important group, the ASEAN-four came next. The South Asian LDCs were not considered an attractive proposition, while China attracted a substantial amount of FDI in the late 1980s.

The manufacturing sector was singularly the most important sector. During the post-appreciation period investment in this sector accelerated, the rate of acceleration was particularly high in the industrialised countries. Although the same trend was observed in the LDCs, the rate of acceleration was much lower. The most prominent sub-sectors were: electronics and electrical machinery, autos and transport equipment, ferrous and non-ferrous metals and chemicals and pharmaceuticals. FDI in resources development diminished in volume and significance. In the services sector, finance and insurance and real estate grew enormously in significance. The manufacturing sector attracted a great deal of FDI in Asia as well. Most of it went into export-oriented sectors and influenced the export performance of the host countries favourably.

The general perception is that the Japanese economy is virtually closed to inward investment. FDI in Japan was skimpy as compared to Japan's own FDI all over the world. There was international resentment due to this investment imbalance which Japan is trying to redress. After 1985, the high cost of investing in Japan due to the yen appreciation became an effective deterrent. The US was the largest investor in Japan and accounted for more than half of the inward FDI. The manufacturing sector made up for the lion's share of the inward-investment, with machinery and chemicals having high weights. Due to Japan's growing prowess in R&D and technology development, FDI in R&D increased rapidly in the late 1980s.

5 Economic Assistance to the Developing Countries

GENESIS

Although at present Japan is the largest bilateral donor to less developed countries (LDCs), only about a quarter of a century ago it was one of the largest recipients of bilateral (from the US) and multilateral (from the World Bank) economic assistance. Since Japan devised a perspicacious macroeconomic policy package and implemented it with admirable dexterity, and since there were measurable results to show for the external assistance, donor countries and organisations were eager to assist the Japanese economy. During the first half of the 1960s it was the second largest recipient of the World Bank fund after India. It borrowed large sums to build highways, electric power stations and the famous bullet train. The final repayment instalment to the World Bank was made in July 1990. Thus, in a short span of time Japan metamorphosed itself from a reconstructing, aid-recipient economy to the largest donor to LDCs.

The origin of Japan's interest in developing economies goes back to its entry into the Colombo Plan in 1954 and to the extensions of reparations to Myanmar.[1] In 1954, Japan entered into its first agreement on war reparations with Myanmar. In 1958, it granted a loan to India under a technical assistance programme which was Japan's first Official Development Assistance (ODA) loan. These were the inceptive moves. A spectacular economic resurgence enabled Japan to expand its involvement in the developing economies. When it participated in the Colombo Plan, its operational economic assistance budget was ¥ 18 million or $50 000. As we shall see, by the end of the 1980s it began to hover around $10 billion.[2] The early documents of the Economic Planning Agency (EPA), the Ministry of International Trade and Industry (MITI) and the Ministry of Foreign Affairs (MFA), while talking about economic assistance to LDCs, always used the words *keizai kyoryok* or economic co-operation. There was no reference to the word *enjo* or aid. This was not a mere accident of choice of words but a matter of attitude and disposition. The economic co-operation mentality of the Japanese aid efforts to LDCs not only persisted but dominated.

Three characteristics of Japan's economic assistance during the earlier years are indisputable. First, when the Japanese economy entered its high growth period in the late 1950s, one of the fundamental planks of its outward-oriented economic policy was to promote exports. Second, given its economic structure, it was obliged to import natural resources, and its dependence on such imports was high. This was what the Japanese called *kako-boeki* or exports based on imported raw materials. Japan used its ODA to both these ends, that is, promoting exports and procuring natural resources and industrial raw materials. From the Japanese perspective, it was in order because it was in keeping with the principle of *keizai kyoryok*. Third, the overwhelming focus of Japan's ODA efforts was Asia. Until the 1970s, more than 90 per cent of ODA flows were directed towards the Asian LDCs because of Japan's close historical, geopolitical and economic links with them. These flows were mostly in the form of tied aid.

In the background of the above characteristics, the rising Japanese exports to LDCs created an impression that Japan's private sector, in collaboration with the Government, is endeavouring to penetrate the markets of the recipient LDCs. Japan's linking of trade and aid was resoundingly criticised all over the world. A callous disregard of such widespread disapproval was not possible for long. In addition, the 1960s were declared the 'Development Decade' by the United Nations, which intensified the international debate on the developing economies as well as economic growth *per se*. The industrialised economies realised that international economic problems could not be resolved without the economic development of LDCs and accepted the notion of international interdependence. When the Pearson Commission Report (1969) and the Tinbergen Report (1970) promoted the view that economic problems of LDCs should be addressed by the international community as a whole, it was well received. The 1971 Report of the Overseas Economic Co-operation Council of Japan called economic development in the developing world a pressing issue and exhorted Japan for 'more co-operation' with the LDCs. International opinion called for an attitudinal change in Japan's external economic assistance.

Ozawa (1989) divides Japanese assistance to LDCs into three components, namely, budget-determined official flows, market-co-ordinated private flows and the hybrid kind which combines the first two. All three have specific functions and objectives. As seen in Table 5.1, they take different names. For instance, official development assistance (ODA) and other official flows (OOF) are the first kind and are budget or Government determined. The second category, that is, market-co-ordinated flows are generated by market forces and take the form of foreign direct investment and bank loans and are beyond the theme of this exposition. The hybrid flows are of relevance to our theme because they represent collaborative financial flows of the Japanese Government and the private sector. This is considered a unique feature of Japan's economic assistance to LDCs. The hybrid flows are essentially organised by Japan's Overseas Economic Co-operation Fund (OECF), the main dispenser of official economic assistance, and the Export-Import Bank of Japan. These institutions take the initiative in arranging joint loans and syndicated equity investments in LDCs with private corporations and commercial banks. In such financial arrangements these institutions serve as risk-sharers. Such flows are classified under the OOF category. Also, the OECF grants and loans with a grant element of 25 per cent or more are classified under the ODA whereas the remaining flows go under the category of the OOF. It also includes financial resources provided by the Export-Import Bank of Japan and other government agencies as export credits.

An analysis of the expansionary process reveals that during the 1960s Japan's ODA expanded due to the sustained high growth rates of the economy, and the disbursement level reached $458 million in 1970. This level soared at a brisker pace during the early 1970s to reach $1148 million in 1975.[3] In 1970 Japan edged past the UK and became the fourth largest donor after the US, France and Germany – a position Japan was to maintain for the remaining years of the decade. However, the first cataclysmic phase in Japan's endeavours as a major donor did not begin until 1977, when the Government adopted its first medium-term ODA target and followed it through by a succession of three more medium-term ODA targets. The objective was to double the amount of annual ODA under each medium-term plan from the base line of the previous plan. The financial allocations and the time-spans of the four medium-term targets were as follows: (1) When the first target was announced in 1977, Japan's ODA disbursement level was $1424 million. The first medium-term target

Table 5.1 FLOW OF FINANCIAL RESOURCES TO DEVELOPING COUNTRIES: NET DISBURSEMENTS, 1980–89 (IN MILLIONS OF $)

	1980	1981	1982	1983	1984	1985	1986	1987	1988	1989
I. Official Development Assistance (ODA)	3.304	3.171	3.023	3.761	4.319	3.797	5.634	7.454	9.134	8.965
1. Bilateral Assistance	1.961	2.260	2.367	2.425	2.427	2.557	3.846	5.248	6.422	6.779
(1) Grants:	653	810	805	993	1.064	1.185	1.703	2.221	2.908	3.037
Grant Assistance	375	472	452	608	626	763	1.104	1.481	1.815	1.556
Technical Assistance	278	338	353	385	438	422	599	740	1.093	1.481
(2) Loans	1.308	1.450	1.562	1.432	1.363	1.372	2.143	3.027	3.514	3.741
2. Contributions to Multilateral Institutions	1.343	910	656	1.336	1.891	1.240	1.788	2.207	2.712	2.186
As percentage of GNP	0.32	0.28	0.28	0.32	0.34	0.29	0.29	0.31	0.32	0.32
(Average of DAC Countries)	(0.38)	(0.35)	(0.38)	(0.36)	(0.36)	(0.35)	(0.35)	(0.35)		
II. Other Official Flows (OOF)	1.478	3.023	2.914	1.954	743	-302	-724	-1.808	-639	1.544
1. Export Credits (Over 1 year)	823	1.410	849	472	493	-152	-858	-2.047	-1.834	-1.245
2. Direct Investment and Other	767	1.490	2.095	1.442	380	-1	332	287	1.410	1.892

3. Finances of Multilateral Institutions	−112	123	−31	41	−130	−148	−198	−47	−211	897
III. Private Flows (PF)	1.958	6.011	2.928	2.151	6.644	8.022	9.586	14.723	12.882	13.502
1. Export Credits (Over 1 year)	74	712	−1.762	−2.069	−655	−994	199	1.081	219	687
2. Direct Investment and Other	1.566	3.699	3.162	2.645	5.090	6.183	8.073	11.777	11.020	12.579
3. Finances to Multilateral Institutions	318	1.599	1.528	1.574	2.209	2.832	1.314	1.865	1.583	236
IV. Grants by Private Voluntary Agencies	26	27	23	30	41	101	82	92	107	112
Total Official and Private Flows (I + II + III + IV)	6.766	12.231	8.889	7.896	11.746	11.619	14.578	20.462	21.423	24.133
As Percentage of GNP	0.66	1.08	0.82	0.67	0.93	0.87	0.74	0.86	0.75	0.85
(Average of DAC Countries)	(1.04)	(1.25)	(1.15)	(0.91)	(1.00)	(0.54)	(0.63)	(n.a.)		

NOTE The figures are rounded off and may not necessarily add up to the totals.
SOURCE Ministry of Foreign Affairs. *Japan's Official Development Assistance* (Tokyo, various issues).

was kept at approximately $9.0 billion spread over a four-year (1977–1980) period, with an annual target of $2848 million. The achievement at the end of the period was $9.6 billion and exceeded the target. The disbursement level in 1980 was $3304 million. (2) The second medium-term target set a goal of achieving an ODA disbursement level of $21.36 billion over the 1981–85 period and an annual level of $4272 million by 1985. The achievement level was $18.07 billion, or 84.6 per cent of the target. The ODA disbursement in 1985 was $3797 million, falling 11.2 per cent short of the targeted level. (3) The following third medium-term target kept the ODA disbursement level at $40 billion for the six years between 1986–92, and an annual target of $6666 million by 1992. The ODA disbursement over 1986–88 reached $22.22 billion, with $9134 million disbursed in 1988. (4) The third target had to be revised in view of the yen appreciation and the fourth medium-term target was kept at $50 billion for the five years between 1988–92. The revised annual target was $10 billion.[4] The second noteworthy phase began with the announcement of the International Co-operative Initiative in May 1988. Unlike the first phase, which focused on quantitative expansion, the second phase was a qualitative one and reflected Japan's acceptance of its international responsibility as a prosperous industrialised democracy. Several significant moves were made to assist the developing economies and thereby contribute to international prosperity.

With an ODA disbursement of $8965 million in 1989, Japan became the world's largest donor of concessional finance to LDCs (see Graph 5.1). The US and France stood at second and third positions with disbursements of $7659 million and $7450 million, respectively. The number one ranking among the 18 members of the Development Assistance Committee (DAC) of the Organisation for Economic Co-operation and Development (OECD) was attained after a strong second-place showing in the preceding three years. The dollar value of 1989 ODA disbursement represented a fall of 1.8 per cent over the 1988 figures. The reason for the decline was the depreciation of the yen in 1989; the value of the yen in 1989 was 7.6 per cent below its 1988 level. In yen terms, Japan's ODA in 1989 amounted to ¥ 1.2368 trillion, an increase of 5.7 per cent over the 1988 total of ¥ 1.1705 trillion.

FIGURE 5.1   *The Volume of ODA Disbursements of Major DAC Donors (1978–89)*

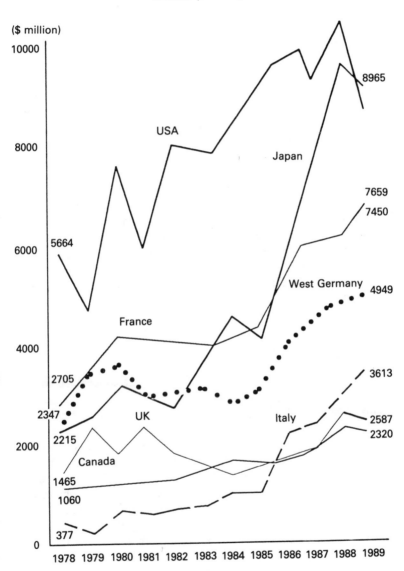

POST-APPRECIATION SPIRALLING

It is apparent from the foregoing exposition that economic assistance to LDCs received a great deal of official attention and, therefore, priority in the general account budget throughout the 1980s. Although only a part of the ODA was funded by the general account budget of the Government, the rest came from *Zaisei Toyushi* or the Fiscal Investment and Loan Programme budget, the general account budget perspective showed an upward trend for ODA allocations throughout the decade. The operational ODA budget is, thus, much larger than the general account ODA budget. For instance, during the fiscal 1990, the ODA general account budget was ¥ 817.5 billion while the operational budget for ODA was ¥ 1.5995 trillion, which was close to double the ODA general account budget of the Government.

The statistics for the decade of 1980s (Table 5.1) indicate that ODA disbursements increased at an average annual rate of 4.9 per cent during 1981–85 but they recorded a marked spurt after 1985. They soared from $3797 million to $5634 million during 1985–86, a 48.4 per cent rise. They further rose to $7454 million in 1987, a further 32.3 per cent increase. Steady spiralling continued even thereafter. To be sure, a great deal of this billowing largesse can be attributed to the post-Plaza accord appreciation of the yen. Be it noted that economic aid figures are conventionally reported on the basis of net disbursement in dollars. The ODA disbursement statistics, when seen in yen, clearly brings out the impact of the yen appreciation. In terms of the dollar, Japan's ODA increased with an annual average rate of 4.9 per cent during 1981–85 and 36.1 per cent during 1985–89. But when denoted in yen, the corresponding growth rates for the two periods becomes 7.4 per cent and 9.1 per cent, respectively. Thus, in yen terms Japan's munificence is much less noteworthy. Assisted by currency appreciation, Japan's share in the total volume of ODA contributed by the DAC countries increased sharply from 12.9 per cent in 1985 to 15.4 per cent in 1986 and further to 18.1 per cent in 1987. As opposed to this, there was a sharp decline in the share of the US after 1985.[5] It can, therefore, be inferred that currency appreciation and increases in ODA in yen terms made Japan the second largest donor after the US in 1986, which accounted for 26.1 per cent of the total ODA against Japan's 15.4 per cent. In yen terms, Japan's ODA increased by 4.8 per cent in 1986. At this point, France and Germany held third and fourth positions, respectively. Subsequently, both of them not only held their positions but also raised their shares of total ODA moderately.

Likewise, Japan's contributions to multilateral organisations were not conspicuous until the mid-1980s, except in 1984 when they were substantial. But since 1985, they recorded a steady rise and Japan emerged as a major source of funds for the multilateral development organisations. As seen in Table 5.1, between 1985 and 1988, disbursements to the multilateral institutions increased by 118.7 per cent, although in 1989 a small decline was recorded. The reason for this decline essentially was a depreciating yen. After 1987, the contributions to multilateral organisations have remained above \$2 billion. There are several advantages of channelling the ODA through multilateral organisations. It provides access to their sophisticated and specialised knowledge and experience as well as to their global networks. In addition, economic assistance is disbursed in a politically neutral manner. Recognition of this is reflected in increasing expansion of Japan's share of total DAC assistance through multilateral organisations. It has risen from an average of 9.0 per cent in 1975/76 to 29.9 per cent in 1987/88. In 1988/89, the ratio dropped to 27.1 per cent. The contributions of the DAC members to multilateral organisations have increased – although somewhat unsteadily – over the 1980s. They added up to \$12 483 million in 1989. A notable feature regarding these contributions is that the US is no longer the largest single source of multilateral funding. In 1987, it was replaced by Japan which accounted for 21.6 per cent of the total contributions, as against 21.1 per cent for the US. The third and fourth positions were held by France and Germany, respectively. Japan has stepped up its co-operation with the World Bank and the International Monetary Fund in a significant manner. It was the second largest contributor to the International Development Association's (IDA) seventh and eighth replenishments, accounting for 18.7 per cent of the total. Its share in the ninth (1990–93) IDA replenishment is likely to rise to 20.8 per cent.[6]

The second oil-price hike had taken the wind out of the sails of ODA flows. They had peaked in 1981 at \$137.4 billion and reached their low point in 1986 when they were \$83.7 billion. There was a recovery in nominal terms since but in real terms, that is, if the effects of inflation and exchange rate changes are taken care of, total resource flows to LDCs fell. After 1985, the net resource flows to LDCs were close to half of the 1981 level. Several donor economies have been showing the signs of 'aid fatigue' due to budget constraints. Particularly, the US which was the largest donor and had played the lead role in tackling development problems by deploying a great deal of financial and human resources, was compelled to cut back on its budget and personnel. At the same time, there was a marked fall in the non-OECD economic assistance. The problem of the developing countries has been exacerbated due to recent 'reverse flows' which entail repayments of principal and interest to the donor countries by the recipient developing countries. Of late, the repayments from the LDCs have exceeded the financial flows from the industrial economies.

Although we have seen the trend in ODA disbursement by Japan and how it became the second largest and then the largest donor, the total flows from the developed to developing countries comprise ODA, other official flows (OOF) and private flows (PF). Therefore, after the ODA it is a worthwhile idea to see the trends in the total financial flows from Japan. Along with the ODA funds from the DAC countries, the private flows, or the ones categorised under the PF, had also recorded a decline in the 1980s. Their rate of decline was greater than that of the ODA. Consequently, their share fell from 54.1 per cent to the total resource flows in 1981 to 32.0 per cent in 1988. As the data in Table 5.1 show, total financial flows to LDCs from Japan over the same period nearly doubled. Thus, Japan can be credited with picking up the slack. The value and significance of its economic assistance was, therefore, high for the recipient LDCs. In 1988, its total contributions added up to $21 423 million which was 20.9 per cent of the total contribution from the whole of the developed world and the multilateral financial institutions ($102.9 billion). This implies that while Japan became the largest donor of ODA in 1989, it became the world's largest supplier of financial resources to LDCs a year earlier. The combined flows increased to $24 133 million in 1989 (Table 5.1), an increase of 12.6 per cent over the preceding year's figures (Graph 5.2). This is equivalent to 22.1 per cent of the overall flows of funds from the developed countries and multilateral financial institutions into the LDCs.

Such a large expansion in the volume of financial assistance during the latter half of the 1980s has increased the significance of Japan's financial resources for several LDCs individually. For many of them, they account for 15 to 20 per cent of the annual national expenditure. The number of LDCs for which Japan is the largest bilateral donor has steadily increased: from 6 LDCs in 1970, 15 in 1980, 19 in 1985 and 29 in 1987. To be sure, the largest number of such LDCs was in Asia. In 1987, for 17 Asian LDCs Japan was the largest bilateral donor. But the other 12 were in the Middle East, Africa and Latin

FIGURE 5.2   *ODA Flows and Total Financial Flows from Japan to LDC's: Net Disbursements (1980–89)*

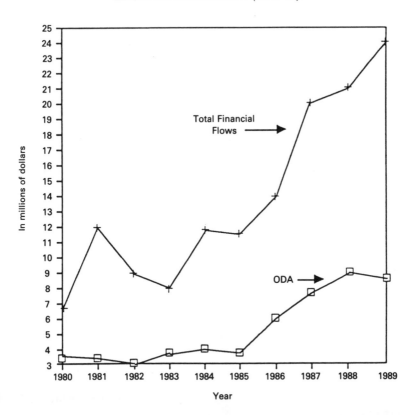

Source: Table 5.1

America. Thus, Japan's economic assistance has begun to exert a great deal of influence on an increasing number of LDCs.

THE RECYCLING STRATAGEMS

Since the mid-1980s Japan acquired the status of the largest creditor nation in the world; it grew to be the second largest economy after the US, accounting for 12 per cent of World GNP and currently it is the third largest trader in the world accounting for 9 per cent of total exports. Added to this is the wealth effect of the yen appreciation. The rising status of the Japanese economy *pari passu* raised the expectations of the LDCs and created mounting international pressure on Japan to play a global economic role commensurate with its newly acquired status. Recycling part of its economic resources and large surpluses to capital strapped LDCs is an important part of such a role. Although it is far from rational, a long-sustained trade surplus is generally seen as an economic evil and a surplus country is seen as one having extra obligations to the international community. However, it is relatively easier for a surplus economy to help put the international economy on a path to sustained growth. Japan responded to international expectations by announcing that it would recycle part of its surplus to LDCs at the 1986 IMF-World Bank annual meeting. A pledge of $10 billion was made at this point but during the Venice Economic Summit in 1987 Japan announced a Capital Recycling Programme totalling $30 billion for the following three-year period. The objective of this programme was (a) to expand the total resource flows, primarily through other official flows (OOF), to LDCs and (b) to contribute to the solution of serious accumulated debt problems of the highly indebted countries (HICs). The World Bank has classified 17 middle-income indebted countries as the HICs. The implementation was prompt and by July 1987, a year before the schedule, over 90 per cent of the target was achieved. While recycling resources through OOF, especial attention was paid to the middle-income LDCs and those of Latin America.

Again, in view of the continuing stagnation of ODA flows, at the time of the 1989 Paris Economic Summit another recycling programme was announced. The basic objective of this programme was to support sustainable development and reform of the economic structures of LDCs through the expansion and reinforcement of the former $30 billion three-year recycling plan to a $65 billion five-year plan, including the original three-year period.[7] The disbursement channel was to remain the same, that is, the OOF. For the HICs, an additional support plan of $35 billion was put into operation. These resources were intended to go to HICs in accordance with the strategy planned under the Strengthened Debt Strategy or the Brady Plan which was announced in March 1989.

Resolving the LDC Debt Riddle

As seen above, the debt problem of LDCs had attracted the attention of Japan so much that in mid-1988 it put forth the Miyazawa Plan for the consideration of the international community. Several low and middle-income LDCs had suffered from debt-related macroeconomic strains since the early 1980s. This included several sub-Saharan and Asian nations with per capita GNP below $425, who have been groaning under high debt pressure. For these LDCs, accumulated external debt became a veritable economic and financial crisis. Since this has serious implications for the world economy as well as for the international financial community, several concerted attempts were made both bilaterally and multilaterally to resolve it.

Under its recycling programme Japan took several initiatives to ameliorate the situation for the indebted LDCs. For instance, when the International Monetary Fund (IMF) proposed tripling of funds under the Structural Adjustment Facility (SAF) to support macro-economic and structural change in policies in sub-Saharan Africa, Japan promised SDR 2.2 billion through its Export-Import Bank. In addition, SDR 300 million were given to the Expanded Structural Adjustment Facility (ESAF) as interest rate support. The Brady Plan incorporated some of the recommendations contained in the Miyazawa Plan and was supported by Japan and other members of the Group of Seven (G-7) nations. Japan announced its enhanced capital recycling programme in support of the Brady Plan. Approximately $10 billion were earmarked for the implementation of the plan which was to be done on a case-by-case basis, according to the needs of the individual indebted LDC in collaboration with the International Monetary Fund and the World Bank.

Global Infrastructure Fund

The proposal of establishing a global infrastructure fund (GIF) to recycle the surplus resources of the industrialised and oil-producing countries to the capital scarce LDC is an old one and has resurfaced in the background of the Japanese surpluses. When it was originally made in 1977 by Masaki Nakajima of the Mitsubishi Research Institute, the volume of resources to be recycled by the GIF was set at $25 billion a year, for five years.[8] At that time critics considered it a preposterously high amount. In its present incarnation, a restructured Japan Development Bank is to work as the GIF and put its rich domestic experience to good international use. The bank will be allowed to float bonds, with a tax exemption offered to the buyers of such bonds. It will be assisted in its operations with an interest subsidy from the government.

An outstanding feature of this proposal is that it does not promote passive financial recycling but emphasises transfer of industrial know-how from Japan to the recipient developing countries. The transfer to the recipient LDCs would include technological and managerial know-how and the necessary project-related skills. Thus, the proposal comes close to having another small World Bank. It has been internationally discussed in two conferences held in 1986 and 1987. In the second conference ten countries participated. As a follow up, the GIF's temporary secretariat was set up in Tokyo to conceive and promote programmes and a study group was appointed to select possible infrastructure projects in LDCs. Needless to say, Japan will contribute a major part of the financial resources while the other participating countries will play a supportive role.

The WIDER Proposal

The World Institute for Development Economics Research (WIDER), at Helsinki, which is a part of the United Nations University head-quartered in Tokyo, has taken a great deal of interest in the idea of recycling Japanese surpluses to LDCs. It has brought out three studies on this theme and kept the idea of recycling alive.[9] The WIDER plan is innovatively contrived. It supports sustained growth of the Japanese economy so that the decline in the growth momentum in the US is offset. It is not averse to Japan's surpluses or their sizes. The variable of capital importance is how these surpluses are utilised. It proposes that at least $25 billion a year should be earmarked for recycling to LDCs. It would entail a certain diversification of Japanese capital away from the US which would be a healthy economic move for the international economy because it would force Americans to tighten their belts and live within their means. The WIDER proposal emphasises a market-based mechanism of transfer of capital to LDCs rather than the conventional official channels. This mechanism is to be supplemented by an enlargement in the lending capacity of the multilateral financial institutions, notably the International Monetary Fund and the World Bank. Additionally, for the low-income LDCs Japan is expected to encourage 'soft' loan operations of the multilateral institutions and the Export-Import Bank of Japan is to step up its 'soft' loan disbursements.

An issue that drew little professional attention in the past was: where precisely should the funds to be recycled come from? Japan's surpluses are not Government's budget surpluses, if anything, there have been years of budget deficit in the Government budget. The surpluses are owned by business firms and, insofar as they are a result of excess savings, by the Japanese household sector. That is, the surpluses are thinly scattered in the economy. The WIDER proposal has hit upon an imaginative scheme to accumulate resources to be recycled using the Japanese capital market. It proposes the floating of government-backed bonds, including zero-coupon bonds, for loan to LDCs. An interest rate subsidy is to be a part of this scheme. Resources are also to be tapped from *Yubin Chokin*, the cash rich postal saving scheme and the government pension funds. Thus, this proposal makes use of Japan's domestic capital market to promote recycling of capital to developing countries. By so doing, keeping surveillance over capital flows to the US will be easier. In addition, market mechanism will not be relegated to the background and the Japanese investors will have an opportunity to diversify their assets. Two noteworthy features emerge. First, the common thread in the above two proposals is that they utilise Japanese capital markets and capitalise on Japan's current status as the leading creditor nation. Second, institutions like the Export-Import Bank, which has played a role in purveying the financial resources through OOF, will come to acquire greater importance. The Export-Import Bank has been an active recycling channel and of the $42.2 billion recycled until the end of 1990, $15.6 billion or 36.7 per cent were recycled through this institution.[10] It has been gearing itself for this role by lowering its interest rate. The interest rate for transfers under the recycling pro-gramme was fixed slightly lower than the long-term prime rate of Japan and maturity was extended up to 20 years. The Export-Import Bank has also begun to align its maturities with those of the multi-lateral development banks – ranging from 15 to 20 years – when cofinancing to reduce annual repayments by the borrowing LDC.

PHILOSOPHY OR THE LACK OF IT

Japan was a late entrant to the economic assistance stage and did not have a well-conceptualised philosophy underpinning its economic assistance efforts. As late as 1980, one could not find a clear-cut, well-articulated statement of principle behind its economic assistance to LDCs. If anything, Japanese assistance efforts were characterised by pragmatism, laced by opportunism.[11] Most earlier economic assistance was diplomatically directed towards resource-rich Asian countries and *vide ut supra* was also aimed at promoting Japanese exports. A 1980 Ministry of Foreign Affairs report called economic assistance the 'necessary cost' of remaining a peaceful nation, being an economic power, maintaining friendship with nations of strategic importance and serving as a non-Western development model.[12] Ozawa (1989) wryly dismissed it as an 'egocentric rationalisation'. Consequently, even the subsequent assistance efforts were at times received with more suspicious criticism than laudable recognition. Even after becoming the largest donor critics charge – not wholly justifiably – that Japan's economic assistance benefits Japan.[13]

The notions of development of the developing countries benefiting the world economic community and that of economic altruism have come to be recognised and accepted as the contemporary philosophy underlying economic assistance. This concept was promoted by the Brandt Commission (1980) and has come to be accepted by the donor nations as a common international rationale of economic assistance to LDCs. Moral and humanitarian considerations are in the forefront while commercial calculations have been relegated to the background. The philosophy of economic altruism has been institutionalised and *noblesse oblige* is considered its justification. The Japanese thinking in the latter half of the 1980s was in consonance with this philosophy of external assistance and the 1987 Report of Overseas Economic Co-operation Council emphasised the imperative need for Japan 'to take the lead in strengthening and supporting the economic development of developing countries'. Soon Japan did take the lead. However, in terms of an aid philosophy it is difficult to ignore Japan's admiration for the better performing LDC economies and its support of their self-help efforts. For instance, even in Asia Japan virtually ignores the stuck-in-the-morass economies of the south Asian LDCs while it lavishes resources on the East and South-East Asian LDCs. Also, it was slow to react to the needs of the sub-Saharan LDCs because there was no semblance of self-help endeavours.

When viewed against the background of lofty altruistic and humanitarian objectives, Japan's efforts seem relatively less generous. There are several indicators to prove this. First, in terms of the volume of ODA Japan has taken the lead but it has consistently fallen far short of the UN target of 0.7 per cent of GNP. This target was adopted in the UN General Assembly in 1970 and was also included in the International Development Strategy (IDS) for the 1980s. It was

Table 5.2   THE ODA/GNP RATIO OF DAC COUNTRIES
(IN PER CENT)

COUNTRY	Rank	1989	Rank	1988	Rank	1986
Norway	1	1.04	1	1.13	1	1.17
Sweden	2	0.97	4	0.86	2	1.01
Denmark	3	0.94	3	0.89	3	0.89
Netherlands	3	0.94	2	0.98	4	0.85
France	5	0.78	5	0.72	5	0.70
(excl. DOM/TOM)		(0.54)		(0.50)		(0.48)
Finland	6	0.63	6	0.59	9	0.45
Belgium	7	0.46	9	0.39	6	0.48
Canada	8	0.44	7	0.50	6	0.48
Italy	9	0.42	10	0.39	10	0.43
West Germany	10	0.41	10	0.39	11	0.40
Australia	11	0.38	8	0.46	8	0.47
Japan	12	0.32	12	0.32	15	0.29
UK	13	0.31	12	0.32	12	0.31
Switzerland	14	0.30	12	0.32	13	0.30
Austria	15	0.23	16	0.24	18	0.21
New Zealand	16	0.22	15	0.27	13	0.30
Ireland	17	0.17	18	0.20	16	0.28
USA	18	0.15	16	0.21	17	0.23
TOTAL DAC		0.33		0.36		0.35

SOURCE   Organisation for Economic Co-operation and Development.
Development Co-operation: 1990 Report (Paris, December
1990).

agreed that the developed countries which have not attained the
ODA/GNP ratios of 0.7 per cent should try their best to achieve it by
1985, or at the latest by the late 1980s, and then proceed to achieve
the goal of 1.0 per cent as soon as feasible. The highest ODA/GNP
ratio that Japan ever reached was 0.34 in 1984 which is less than half
the UN target. Both in 1988 and 1989 this ratio was even lower at 0.32
and as seen in Table 5.2 Japan was ranked 12th in the 18-member
Development Assistance Committee (DAC) of the Organisation for
Economic Co-operation and Development (OECD). There was a
minor improvement between 1986 and 1988 but still Japan is below
the DAC average of 0.33. The best performers in this regard are the
four Nordic members of the DAC which have achieved the UN target,
Norway being the top performer which has achieved the advance
target of 1.0 per cent. The ODA/GNP ratio is an internationally

recognised criterion for economic assistance. Expansion in ODA volume without improvement in the ODA/GNP ratio will not cut much ice in international fora. Looking at Japan's GNP and current achievement, attaining the target will not be an easy task, albeit improvement is a feasible short-term target. Second, in 1989 Japan's GNP was $2836.3 billion, which was 20.3 per cent of the total GNP of the DAC member countries. Japan's ODA disbursement for that year was $8965 million, which was 19.2 per cent of the total ODA disbursement.

Next come the quality considerations of economic assistance in the sense of how much burden it imposes on the recipient. The standard measures of the quality are (a) the grant share and (b) the grant element. They are the indicators of the 'softness' of the financial terms under which resources flow to the LDCs. Japan's performance on these two counts has been dismally poor. As seen in Table 5.3, in 1988/89 Japan gave only 42.4 per cent of its ODA as grant while the DAC average was 75.6 per cent. Five DAC members give all their ODA as grant and six more give more than 90 per cent of it as grant. Compared to them Japan's proportion of grant in ODA appears unimpressive. Little wonder that Japan has always ranked at the bottom of this scale. Except for 1986/87 when this proportion increased to 60.7 for Japan and the DAC average was 84.3, for all the years in the recent past Japan has hardly attempted to increase this proportion beyond 47 per cent. Similarly, in the case of the grant element Japan's performance is not the poorest, but not very much better. As seen in Table 5.4, it was consistently ranked among the bottom two for the last four years. In 1988/89 its grant element was 83.3 per cent when the DAC average was 91.6 per cent and five DAC members reported 100 per cent grant element and nine more had their proportion over 90 per cent. Little efforts have been made by Japan to improve its image as a donor that is only interested in meeting the quantitative targets without paying attention to the qualitative aspects of economic assistance.

Unlike the other major donors, Japan adopts a passive stance regarding the selection of bilateral assistance projects in LDCs. It waits for a project to be brought to it by the potential recipient LDC while the other large donors take considerable initiative in this regard. Some of the smaller donor countries like Sweden, Denmark and Canada are also known to take a great deal of initiative. This 'request basis' approach has prompted a good deal of criticism from the developing and developed countries. They expect activism in this

Table 5.3 SHARE OF GRANT IN ODA (IN PER CENT)

Country	Rank	1988/89	Rank	1987/88	Rank	1986/87
Australia	1	100.0	1	100.0	1	100.0
New Zealand	1	100.0	1	100.0	1	100.0
Ireland	1	100.0	1	100.0	1	100.0
Sweden	1	100.0	1	100.0	6	98.7
Switzerland	1	100.0	5	99.5	5	
Norway	6	99.7	6	99.4	5	99.2
Denmark	7	98.7	7	98.1	15	77.1
UK	8	98.1	8	97.8	1	100.0
Canada	9	97.8	9	97.4	7	98.6
Finland	10	94.4	10	91.9	9	94.7
USA	11	92.6	11	91.2	11	91.1
Netherlands	12	87.6	13	86.4	10	93.7
Belgium	13	(87.0)	12	90.6	13	87.1
Italy	14	76.9	15	76.9	12	90.2
France	15	(73.1)	14	78.2*	14	78.1
West Germany	16	(68.5)	16	69.0	16	75.6
Austria	17	(48.8)	17	64.6*	17	65.1
Japan	18	(42.4)	18	46.6*	18	60.7
TOTAL DAC		75.6		78.4		84.3

SOURCE Organisation for Economic Co-operation and Development, *Development Co-operation: 1990 Report* (Paris, December 1990).

regard. Japan assumes that economic development of an LDC is a multifaceted reform process involving economic, socio-cultural and potential aspects of life of the recipient LDC. Therefore, it must take the responsibility of initiating and directing this process. The external agency or the donor country should only play a supportive role in the self-help endeavours of the recipient LDC. This assumption is in unison with the Japanese maxim of *keizai kyoryok*. Economic assistance is provided with the belief that the recipient LDC recognises its positive value, is committed to the project and, therefore, will make endeavours to initiate and implement it in an efficacious manner, ensuring the most profitable results.

Lastly, in the area of the untying of ODA Japan has done better than in the areas of grant-share and grant-element. As Table 5 shows, in 1988 its untying ratio was 75.6 per cent while the DAC average was 56.7 per cent. This level is much higher than that of any major donor, namely, the US, France and Germany. However, suspicion that

Table 5.4   GRANT ELEMENT (IN PER CENT)

Country	Rank	1988/89	Rank	1987/88	Rank	1986/87
Australia	1	100.0	1	100.0	1	100.0
New Zealand	1	100.0	1	100.0	1	100.0
Ireland	1	100.0	1	100.0	1	100.0
Sweden	1	(100.0)	1	100.0	6	99.5
Switzerland	1	(100.0)	5	99.9	8	99.2
Canada	6	99.7	6	99.6	5	99.9
Norway	6	(99.7)	6	99.6	7	99.4
Denmark	6	99.7	8	99.5	12	97.4
UK	9	99.1	9	99.0	1	100.0
Finland	10	98.2	10	97.7	9	98.4
USA	11	97.5	11	96.9	13	96.8
Belgium	12	(96.7)	13	94.0	10	97.6
Netherlands	13	94.2	12	94.2	10	97.6
Italy	14	(92.8)	14	92.2	14	96.0
France	15	(89.7)	15	89.3	15	89.1
West Germany	16	(86.4)	16	86.1	16	88.9
Japan	17	(83.3)	18	75.4	17	81.7
Austria	18	(68.1)	17	76.2	18	79.6
TOTAL DAC		91.6		90.4		93.2

SOURCE   Organisation for Economic Co-operation and Development, *Development Co-operation: 1990 Report* (Paris, December 1990).

Japan's ODA loans are abused to promote exports has lingered. Further untying of the consultant services portion was also done to increase opportunities for Western consulting firms to participate in implementing Japan's ODA programmes. Similarly, 11.5 per cent of Japan's ODA was tied against the DAC average of 35.6 per cent (see Table 5.5). The other three major donors not only have a substantially higher proportion of tied assistance but this proportion has also increased menacingly in the recent past. However, Japan's adoption of altruistic and humanitarian objectives of the contemporary philosophy would be incomplete unless it improves its performance on the grant-element and grant-share fronts. Japan also needs to learn to take the initiative in development-related issues like the other major donors and atone for its 'request basis' principle.

Table 5.5 SHARE OF TIED AND UNTIED ODA
(IN PER CENT)

Country	Untied 1987	Untied 1988	Partially untied 1987	Partially untied 1988	Tied 1987	Tied 1988
Australia	55.9	67.3	–	–	44.0	32.7
Austria	25.7	31.2	–	–	74.3	68.8
Belgium	50.6	(46.1)	–	–	49.4	(53.8)
Canada	61.0	62.0	3.9	3.5	35.1	34.5
Denmark	70.0	76.1	–	0.9	30.0	23.0
Finland	44.2	52.8	–	–	55.8	47.1
France	55.6	51.0	3.5	3.2	40.9	45.8
West Germany	57.4	52.8	–	–	42.6	47.2
Ireland	66.2	(62.3)	–	–	33.8	(37.7)
Italy	28.2	34.2	–	–	71.7	65.8
Japan	72.1	75.6	16.6	12.9	11.3	11.5
Netherlands	52.3	48.0	33.7	33.1	14.0	18.9
New Zealand	65.8	53.4	–	10.2	34.2	36.4
Norway	74.4	79.2	1.4	–	24.2	20.8
Sweden	75.4	76.0	–	2.8	24.6	21.2
Switzerland	64.1	85.0	–	–	35.9	15.0
UK	38.0	33.4	0.1	–	61.8	66.6
USA	45.4	48.5	36.6	13.7	18.0	37.7
DAC average	54.8	56.7	13.0	7.6	32.3	35.6

SOURCE Organisation for Economic Co-operation and Development,
Development Co-operation: 1990 Report (Paris, December
1990).

THE NEW ETHOS

During the late 1980s, particularly after 1987, Japan recognised its
expanding role and became self-conscious as a leading donor economy. Accordingly it began to prepare for its new role as a positive
and creative donor out to play a substantive and meaningful role in
the developing world. It was done more coherently and in a firm-
footed manner after the announcement of the International Co-
operative Initiative in 1988 and Japan began to break ground in
several new areas. The first such move was in the direction of globalisation of its economic assistance. Traditional concentration of
Japanese assistance in the East and South East Asian countries has

been alluded to earlier. It was *inter alia* because of the growth potential and tenacious self-help efforts of these economies. Their accomplishments and take-off merited the extra attention and resources that Japan lavished upon them. Therefore, as much as 65 per cent of bilateral assistance in 1987 went to Asia. But Japan is now aiming at promoting global development through economic assistance and its regional focus is changing. By 1989, it had extended ODA to 135 countries which indicates the growing geographical diversification of Japan's efforts. All the 128 UN affiliated LDCs with one exception, Albania, were covered by Japanese efforts. The ODA to Africa has expanded. The South Pacific and Central America were traditionally ignored. Japan is increasing its ODA contribution to these regions.

Another such step is Japan's interest in the Least Developed Countries (LLDCs). The UN has classified 41 LDCs as the LLDCs. Their economies are tiny and in terms of the size of the GDP add up to only 2 per cent of the GDP of developed economies. About half of the LLDCs have recorded declines in their per capita incomes over the 1980s. The LLDCs located in the sub-Saharan region are in dire straits because of declining agricultural production due to natural calamities, decreased export revenues caused by falling primary product prices, followed by balance of payments problems and inability to service outstanding external debt. Economic problems of this country group have attracted international attention and a special programme to assist them was designed by the United Nations Conference on Trade and Development (UNCTAD). Although their external debt is only a small part of total outstanding LDC debt, it has become a serious problem for many of them, essentially due to the small sizes of their economies. In various international fora, including the DAC, appeals to increase economic assistance in the form of grants to LLDCs were made. Japan has responded by expanding this kind of assistance from $325 million in 1985 to $988 million in 1987 and making LLDCs a point of especial attention in its economic assistance programmes.

Japan's economic assistance programmes have begun to recognise that LDCs cannot be treated as a monolithic group, that economic conditions and needs are varied and that they have been undergoing considerable change. The East and South East Asian LDCs have maintained strong economic growth due to pragmatic economic policies and expanding capital investments. As opposed to them, many LDCs are suffering from grave economic strains. For instance, those in South Asia, Latin America and sub-Saharan Africa have been suffering from their own brands of economic malaise. These could be poor macroeconomic management, excessive budget deficits, large debt overhangs, deteriorating terms-of-trade and the like. Such diversified economic circumstances generate divergent development needs. Recognising this fact, Japan now selects specific sectors or projects depending upon the need of the recipient LDC. Assistance and its administration have been consciously made more flexible. The traditional stress on project-based assistance has been considerably reduced and disbursement of non-project assistance has been expanded as a relief measure to LDCs experiencing economic difficulties due to the deterioration in their balance of payments. This form of assistance enables the recipient LDCs to make structural adjustments, facilitate efficient economic management and acquire capital or intermediate goods needed in the short-term. The International Monetary Fund and the World Bank have expanded the provision of non-project multilateral assistance on condition that the recipient LDCs implement a concrete and well-defined economic structural adjustment policy package. The most recent example is, when India took several major strides to restructure its economy in mid-1991, the International Monetary Fund provided liquidity from the Compensatory and Contingency Financial Facility (CCFF). The World Bank readily joined the operations and Japan provided $100 million to facilitate the adoption of the structural transformation policy package. The recipient LDCs appreciate this kind of non-project assistance because of its quick disbursement feature which produces immediate benefit in alleviating their short-term budgetary and balance of payments difficulties. A special non-project grant assistance package was announced in mid-1987 for the LLDCs by Japan. It amounted to $500 million and was to be implemented over the following three-year period. This programme got off to a good start and, in the light of the success attained, Japan announced a second programme of providing $600 million of non-project grant assistance in April 1990 for a period of three more years between 1990 and 1993.

Due to international expectation, Japan has stepped up its interest in Africa, especially sub-Saharan Africa. This fact was earlier alluded to in another context. Disbursements to Africa have gone up from 1.3 per cent of the total in 1985 to 9.8 per cent in 1988; they recorded a decline to 8.0 per cent in 1989. A good part of the allocations noted in the preceding paragraph for LLDCs went to LLDCs in the sub-Saharan region as non-project loans for the implementation of macroeconomic policies and restructuring programmes with the help of the World Bank. Changes in the type of countries and objectives of economic assistance is likely to bring about changes in the nature of Japanese economic assistance. An increasing emphasis on poorer LDCs is certain to improve the quality of Japan's economic assistance efforts.[14]

Although designing a well-defined economic structural adjustment policy package – 'conditionality' if you will – is a prerogative of the International Monetary Fund and the World Bank, when Japan extends non-project type economic assistance it has begun to take into account the macroeconomic policy package prescribed by the multilateral financial institutions. A demand of this nature from a bilateral donor is a sensitive issue and the recipient LDC may revolt, but so far the issue has not created any unseemly rows for Japan.

Provision of local cost financing is another example of a more flexible approach that is currently being adopted. Many LDCs, due to economic pressures, have been forced to apply austerity measures to their economies. Consequently, they are unable to allocate sufficient funds to the local currency part of the project budget. The end result is either shelving or abandoning of projects. In the past, Japan expected the recipient LDCs to finance the local cost of the project; only in special cases 30 per cent of it could be granted. It is difficult for the donor to fully accommodate the local currency part of the project budget in projects like agricultural irrigation or regional development. However, in 1989 Japan replaced the 30 per cent ceiling with a new system that makes it possible to finance a specific – albeit predetermined – proportion of the total project expenditure including the local currency expenditure.

Since Japan's involvement and experience in economic development is limited compared to countries like the US, the UK and France, co-operation with them and other organisations like the World Bank will enhance the benefits of its efforts to a level that Japan could not reach alone. It is well understood that in fields and regions in which Japan's knowledge and human resources are limited the above logic will apply *a fortiori*. The impact of economic assistance can also be enhanced by co-ordinating efforts with the major multilateral donors. In view of this, several joint programmes have been undertaken in the recent past. The larger ones among them are: (1) Japan–US agricultural development project in Bangladesh, (2) Japan–UK project of developing the veterinary medicine faculty of Zambia University, (3) co-operation with Australia and New Zealand in constructing an international airport in Vanautu, (4) joining the multilateral aid initiative for the Philippines. Such co-operation efforts are not only limited to single projects but are also directed towards issues that require a long-term, multifaceted approach like restructuring an LDC's complete economic development policy. Japan has collaborated with the multilateral organisations like the International Monetary Fund and the World Bank in such projects. Co-financing for projects with international financial institutions is also being further expanded. Since Japan had scanty knowledge of African economies, it sought the assistance of the United Nations Development Programme (UNDP) and Britain's Crown Agent; both the organisations were experts of long standing in African economies.

PRIVATE SECTOR SLANT

Since the birth of the Japanese economic assistance programme took place essentially in an environment of *keizai kyoryok*, the private sector has had a greater role to play in economic assistance than in other donor countries. One advantage of private sector involvement is that a link is established between the external economic activities of the donor and the recipient economies. If one of the implicit objectives of economic assistance is to help the recipient LDC develop as an open market economy and a full-blooded partner in international trade and investment, elements of commercialism in the assistance package need not be abhorred. If anything, they need to be encouraged, so long as gains are shared by the two sides. If the economic assistance takes place in a private sector framework, exchange of vital commercial inputs like technology, managerial skills and access to markets can be done in an optimal manner. Ozawa (1989) insists that a commercially-motivated and market-mediated economic assistance package has greater chances of turning into a dynamic positive-sum game than one in which economic assistance is based on mere altruistic considerations. Besides, the economies of recipient LDCs will not become vigorous without developing the potential of their private sectors. A dynamic private sector is a necessary condition of economic growth. The thinking of economic planners has changed its course with a bang from Marx to markets. Additionally, in the ultimate analysis, ODA alone cannot sufficiently meet the development needs of LDCs. When it joins hands with the private sector's efforts, the economic co-operation programme is rendered more comprehensive.

The private sector slant of Japanese assistance efforts has persisted over the years. The policy objective of the plan made public in 1987 was to tie together economic assistance, private capital and trade. Its slogan was *sanmi-ittai* or 'three sides, one body'. Sometimes this private sector involvement creates confusion regarding Japan's definition of economic assistance and opens it to the charge that it is trying to promote its exports under the guise of economic assistance and that Japan's motives are more commercial than altruistic. The fact that it did so in the early period of its economic assistance programme enhances such a suspicion.[15] But it strains credulity to believe that an extremely successful exporter like Japan would need a $10 billion economic assistance programme to promote its exports.

In Japan's economic assistance programme, measures to promote comprehensive economic co-operation with the recipient LDCs have been increasing. Under the plan announced in mid-1987, Japan decided to recycle $20 billion in three years in a comprehensive manner, in which the private and official flows both were disbursed to the recipient LDCs on a completely untied basis. The implementation of this programme has made steady progress. It laid extra emphasis on the middle-income LDCs, particularly those that were highly indebted. As stated above, there is a limit to which ODA can help them, therefore ODA flows must be supplemented by non-ODA funds. Another such programme was the ASEAN-Japan Fund, to which Japan pledged $2 billion, to be disbursed over three years. The objectives of this fund were: (1) to promote the private sector of the ASEAN economies, and (2) encourage inter-regional economic co-operation between the ASEAN countries. A similar comprehensive economic plan is on the anvil for China.

In the Asian Development Bank (ADB), where Japan, along with the US, is the largest (14.98 per cent) subscriber of capital and, therefore, has the largest (12.41 per cent) voting rights, Japan has constantly pushed for expansion of private sector activities. In the past, ADB assistance to the private sector was provided exclusively under government guarantee through credit lines to development finance institutions (DFIs) in the borrowing countries. This stipulation has been changed and ADB devised a programme of direct assistance to the private sector. This programme has gained a great deal of momentum since 1987. In 1989, ADB's total lending to the private sector rose by 80 per cent to $705 million.[16] Another noteworthy success of Japan in the ADB was the creation of the Asian Finance and Investment Corporation (AFIC) in 1989 with $35 million in equity investment from the ADB.[17] Japanese officials at the ADB pushed for the creation of a financial corporation identical to the International Finance Corporation, the private sector arm of the World Bank. The total paid-up capital of AFIC is $135 million. The new institution has been designed to provide a wide range of investment finance and merchant banking services to private sector enterprises in the developing countries of Asia and the South Pacific region without any stipulations of government guarantee.

A similar plan has been devised by *Keidanren*, Japan's federation of business associations. It has created the Japan International Development Organisation (JAIDO) which is so ambitious as to seek capitalisation larger than the government's own economic assistance programme. It plans to put capital into joint ventures with businesses or governments in LDCs. Corporations would present proposals which would be vetted by a *Keidanren* committee and then implemented jointly with the recipient country government or private sector. The JAIDO took off in 1989, although it had only ¥ 7 billion or $42 million, largely raised from approximately 100 Japanese corporations.[18] JAIDO's activities are to take the form of financing, technology transfer and taking the initiative in the identification of potential development projects. LDCs' admiration of Japan's export successes is well known. In view of this, the JAIDO is studying ways to contribute to the development of export industries in LDCs. It will take an integrated infusion of Japan's managerial and technological expertise and financial resources. The JAIDO's mission is to promote foreign-currency generating projects in LDCs in which private Japanese and local enterprises jointly make investments. It has plans to undertake 10 to 15 projects each year. The total foreign currency earnings by LDCs through the JAIDO projects is expected to be ¥ 550 000 million annually.[19] The output of the joint enterprises is primarily intended for export to Japan and thereby it is expected to contribute to the accumulation of foreign currency reserves of the LDCs. The other major objective of the JAIDO is to establish links with the multilateral development organisations like the International Finance Corporation (IFC), the United Nations Development Programme (UNDP) and the United Nations Industrial Development Organisation (UNIDO). These organisations are eager to utilise the human and technological resources of the Japanese private sector but Japan's link with such bodies has hitherto been tenuous. It was limited to the government agencies. The JAIDO is endeavouring to establish direct and strong links with the multilateral bodies.[20]

SUMMING UP

Japan entered the LDC economic assistance stage later than the other industrialised economies, its early assistance efforts were more in keeping with its principle of *keizei kyoryok* or economic co-operation. It became a donor country of any significance only in the late 1970s when it adopted its first medium-term economic assistance plan. An increasing volume of ODA and an appreciating yen turned Japan into the second largest donor nation, after the US, in 1986. Soon, in 1989, it replaced the US as the largest donor. Likewise, Japan's contribution to the multilateral financial institutions soared and it became the largest donor to these organisations in 1987. The increase in Japan's assistance occurred while other major donors were showing signs of 'aid fatigue' due to budget constraints. By the end of the last decade, the significance of Japanese resources had increased substantially for a large number of recipient LDCs. For as many as 26 of them Japan was the largest bilateral donor.

In view of its mounting current surpluses and its status as the largest creditor economy, several strategies were chalked out for recycling of its surplus resources. To this end, several initiatives were taken. Japan is trying to extend a helping hand to the highly indebted countries and the least developed countries under various financial recycling programmes. The most notable recycling plan was drawn up by the WIDER. Recycling is done in a co-ordinated manner, ODA funds are added to the OOF and PF resources.

For a long while Japan lacked the philosophical underpinning of its economic assistance efforts. Despite becoming the largest donor, it has fallen far short of the UN target regarding the ODA. As a ratio of GNP, its ODA has not even reached the DAC average. Several indicators show that the quality of Japan's ODA is poor. In terms of the grant-element and the share of grant in total ODA, Japan ranks near or at the bottom of the list of 18-DAC countries. Like other donors Japan does not take initiative in assisting the LDCs and its 'request basis' approach has earned it the criticism of the developing and developed countries. It has done somewhat better in the area of untying of ODA than in the areas of grant-share and grant-element.

The rapid expansion in the volume of ODA made Japan self-conscious as the leading donor economy and in the late 1980s it began to reassess its new role as a positive and creative donor economy. It began to dilute the concentration of its assistance efforts in Asia and adopt a global posture. The African LDCs and the least developed countries became special foci. Japan began to jointly operate with other major bilateral donors and multilateral organisations to increase the effectiveness of its economic assistance. It readily enters into co-financing deals with the latter. The administration and planning of assistance programmes was made more flexible and adapted to the needs of the recipient LDCs. The traditional emphasis on project assistance was abandoned and non-project assistance was expanded. It also became an active supporter of the multilateral financial institutions in implementing the structural adjustment policy packages. There was an imperious need for macroeconomic restructuring in several LDCs. Japan also altered its former approach of insisting on not providing the local currency cost of the projects.

The private sector slant of the Japanese economic assistance has persisted and its private sector is gradually emerging as a partner in the official endeavours. Japan's efforts have resulted in the creation of Asian Finance and Development Corporation (AFDC), which is the private sector arm of the ADB. Also, *Kaidanren* has established the Japan International Development Organisation for assisting the private sector industries in LDCs and participating in joint ventures with the LDC governments. The objective is to try to develop the export sectors of the recipient LDCs' economies and augment their foreign exchange earnings.

6 The Yen Bloc

THE NASCENCE OF A CONCEPT

Despite Jacob Viner's theory of economic integration and the distinction he made between trade creation and trade diversion, the advocates of economic co-operation have stressed the dynamic gains that could be achieved through greater mutual economic co-operation among countries of the same region. The potential members of a trading bloc or any other form of economic union apparently ignore the trade diversion losses and perceive welfare gains in pooled efforts. The other motivation for the formation of a bloc is perception of an external threat which, for the countries of the Asia-Pacific region, comes from the prospect of trade diversion from market unification of the European Community (EC) in 1992 as well as from the proposed trade linkages between the US and both Canada and Mexico. The threat of retaliatory action by the US under section 301 of the Omnibus Trade and Competitiveness Act of 1988 against the Asia-Pacific countries was also a serious one and created a nagging unease among the countries of the region.[1] The possibilities of a dynamic co-operation – trade diversion notwithstanding – are greater for the economies that have followed market-based growth strategies and have dominant participation of the private sector. An adoption of outward-oriented industrialisation strategy in the framework of an open economy further enhances the feasibility of such a dynamic co-operation. Several economies of the Pacific region manifest these characteristics and, therefore, are considered ripe for forming a functional economic bloc of one kind or the other with Japan acting as a catalytic agent and a leading partner.

On a conceptual plane the notion of a Pacific economic community which would enable the countries of the Pacific rim to benefit from such mutual co-operation has been around for three decades. Its possibility was first discussed by Kyoshi Kojima and Peter Drysdale in 1961. Thereafter, on numerous occasions obeisance has been made

172

to this concept. However, in reality there is a polarisation in views regarding the status of the yen bloc. While some are debating whether it will come into being or not, there are others who believe that, spurred by the appreciating yen, market forces have pulled the Asia-Pacific region closer together and that the yen bloc – although uninstitutionalised – exists and is in operation. Whether its creation is under way or it is actively and purposefully functioning, depends upon how it is defined.

If one chooses the broad definition according to which Japan acts as the epicentre of business and economic activities of the Asia-Pacific economies by virtue of the size of its economy and its financial prowess and technological lead, the yen bloc exists. The Japanese economy produces two-thirds of the region's annual output and its corporations attract far more business activity of the region than they ever did in the past. Trade and investment are growing faster within the region than in the rest of the world. While pegging their currencies, countries of the region have begun to give far more importance to the yen in their currency baskets. Do these trends not presage the presence of an uninstitutionalised economic bloc untied by any formal treaty? However, if a narrow definition is chosen whose scope includes a Pacific OECD, or a properly institutionalised customs union, or a monetary union or a free-trade pact, the yen bloc seems many years off.

The swirl of economic forces bringing the Asia-Pacific region together did not emanate from Japan alone. The Asian newly industrialising economies (ANIEs) and the Association of South East Asian Nations (ASEAN) have sustained impressive economic and industrial growth. As expounded, they adopted an export-oriented development strategy, based on light industries at an early stage of economic growth and then turned to diversify towards heavy and high-tech industries. These economies were young when they launched their take-offs, and had few structural rigidities that characterised economies elsewhere. They also adapted flexibly to changes in the external and internal economic environment through rapid and pragmatic shifts in strategy and economic structure. By adopting macroeconomic policy packages based on neoclassical lines these economies dispelled their structural imbalances and turned their domestic economies into diversified and increasingly integrated ones.

To a substantial extent these economies relied on external capital, markets and technology. Their dynamic growth was propped up by expanding world markets in the 1960s, ready access to loan and equity capital, a historical legacy of substantial investment in human capital and physical infrastructure. In case of the ANIEs there was an entrepreneurial and manufacturing base which was constructed during earlier periods of industrialisation. It is difficult to over-emphasise the importance of a sound macroeconomic policy structure on the one hand and flexibility and responsiveness in reorienting it in accordance with the dictates of the economic reality on the other. The ANIEs and the ASEAN economies became a convincing proof of the dictum of the *World Development Report 1991*, that is, the rewards for sound macroeconomic policies, and the cost of the poor ones, have been larger than what one might have visualised. Since these economies were small and relatively open, and relied on foreign markets, capital and technology, this kind of responsiveness and flexibility became a source of brisk and sustained growth. In addition, to varying extents these economies had a strong, developmentalist state whose commitment to economic growth and industrial expansion was high, making their capacity to implement well-chosen development strategies equally high. This trait differentiated these economies from other less developed countries (LDCs) that were better endowed with vital economic assets like natural resources and size of domestic markets. A confluence of these characteristics made the LDCs of the Asia-Pacific region a natural candidate for being grouped with the Japanese economy to form an economic bloc.

The list of potential members of a yen bloc does not end at the ANIEs and ASEAN-4, namely, Indonesia, Malaysia, the Philippines and Thailand. China, a long slumbering giant until 1980, has begun to stir. Despite high growth rates in the first half of 1980s, it was initially not taken as a serious contender for a place in the yen bloc by the Asia-Pacific economies. The reason essentially was its Maoist isolationism and, therefore, autarkic orientation of its economy. China left this behind when it embarked on its 'open-door' modernisation strategy. The turning point came in 1980 when China launched its plan to quadruple its GDP by 2000, a goal that needed an average annual growth rate in excess of 7 per cent. In the same year, China also established a research institute for Asia-Pacific economic affairs at the prestigious Chinese Academy of Social Sciences. By 1984, in economic matters pragmatism got the better of the ideology. Scarcity of foreign exchange made a virtue of necessity. Its open-door strategy played a crucial role in expansion of foreign industrial investment. Setting up of special economic zones in coastal areas to attract foreign capital and technology and encourage trade made acceptance of capitalistic principles ideologically easier. Coastal cities like Shenzhen, Hutzhou and Shantou in the province of Guangdong, which is north of Hong Kong, have developed on the lines of Hong Kong. Likewise, Xiamen and Quanzhou in the province of Fujian, which is west of Taiwan, were taking it as their prototype for economic growth. Coastal China could well develop on the lines of the ANIEs. If Gorbachev's 1986 Vladivostok speech is any indicator, Russia is eager to be a part of the Pacific community. However, one has to wait and see how successful *perestroika* is before one can decide with how much effectiveness Russia will be able to join this community.

Another potential and vigorous member is Australia which has tried hard over the 1980s to integrate with the Asia-Pacific world culturally, geopolitically and economically. It has long had a significant economic presence in the region. It is its major resource supplier, has a GDP larger than all six ASEAN countries put together and is an important – sixth largest – trade partner of Japan.

As stated, the Asia-Pacific fora have been a subject of active interest and discussion among scholars, industrialists and bureaucrats which gave birth to several bodies. For instance, there is the academic-oriented Pacific Trade and Development Conference (PAFTAD) and the business-oriented Pacific Basin Economic Council (PBEC). The Pacific Economic Co-operation Conference (PECC) was started jointly by the governments of Australia and Japan. It has fifteen regional members and has adopted a tripartite structure of scholars, business people and government bureaucracy to enable it to take a pragmatic and flexible approach. Other than these, there is a large group comprising Japan, South Korea, Indonesia, Thailand, the Philippines, Malaysia, Singapore, Brunei, the United States, Canada, Australia and New Zealand which has been named the Asia-Pacific Economic Co-operation (APEC) forum. The most recent addition to this group has been that of the 'three Chinas', namely, China, Hong Kong and Taiwan. The APEC has received Japan's enthusiastic support. None of these fora have any semblance to a Pacific OECD or a customs union or a monetary union or a free-trade pact. They are all informal bodies for consulting, high-level exchange of views, organising support for the Uruguay round, and developing strategic co-operation in data collection and evaluation. Although to none of them the concept of a yen bloc is an unknown, none of them seems to be drifting towards it.

THE REGION'S ECONOMIC DYNAMISM

The foregoing section has made it obvious why the Asia-Pacific region recorded conspicuously high economic growth rates during the post-war period. It is frequently cited as the most dynamic in the world. As a group these economies display an impressive set of statistics for GDP growth rate, net investment, trade shares, resource endowment, industrial capital and other economic indicators. The total GNP of the region, that is of Japan, the ANIEs, the ASEAN-4, China, Australia and New Zealand, grew from 16.8 per cent of the world GNP in 1975 to 23.5 per cent in 1988.[2] Other than by their own endeavours, these economies were assisted by the climate of mutual economic co-operation which helped them in implementing their national economic strategies. Japan has dominated the flock and recorded an average real economic growth rate of 10.5 per cent as early as the 1960s. Its extraordinary regional presence is obvious from the volume of its foreign direct investment. Casual empiricism shows that in 1990 Japan outinvested the US for the fourteenth consecutive year in the Asia-Pacific, in some countries by as much as 10 to 1. The ANIEs were not far behind, their average decadal growth rate in the 1970s was 9.1 per cent. Of late, they have also developed into regional foreign investors of significance. The third sub-set, namely, the ASEAN economies grew in real terms by 7.5 per cent in the same decade. Even during the sub-periods when the economic rhythm of the world economy slowed, the economies of the Asia-Pacific region continued to grow at a commendable rate. The rapid growth of manufactured output and exports achieved by the ANIEs and the ASEAN economies imparted a good deal of economic strength to these two sub-sets of economies. During the 1970s, Japan, the ANIEs and the ASEAN-4 had emerged as a new industrial belt within the global economy. They also survived the second oil shock somewhat better and since 1983 embarked on a new period of rapid growth. If anything, their growth rate accelerated after the appreciation of the yen. China can be dovetailed with these countries. It had shown a lacklustre economic performance until the early 1980s but its average growth rate for 1982–90 was 9.5 per cent.

Thus, in terms of level of economic development and performance, the countries of the region make a cascade. Kaname Akamatsu used another simile, that of 'the flying geese' because they are known to form a purposeful and orderly formation while migrating.[3] This formation represents a special kind of dynamics, and when Akamatsu used it for the Pacific region economies of the 1930s he was taking the US as the lead goose of the flying formation and Japan the follower because it was trying to catch up with the US in the non-durable consumer goods, durable consumer goods and capital goods industries, in that order. In the contemporary setting, the ANIEs and ASEAN-4 are trying to catch up with Japan in a similar economic development sequence, followed by China.

The flying geese pattern is also called the 'multiple catch-up' process of development where the follower LDCs enter into sectors in which their comparative advantage is on the rise. LDCs that take-off late benefit from the access to the other's capital and technology which enables them to leap-frog some historical steps and telescope the growth process. They import technology from the leading or relatively more matured LDCs whose comparative advantage in these industrial sectors is on the wane. The latter country group moves into higher technology product lines in which they develop an innovative edge. Availability of large pools of inexpensive and trainable manpower resources in the ANIEs and the ASEAN-4 made it possible to shift the industrial structure along with movements in comparative advantage. This production dynamics can be explained by both the Heckscher-Ohlinian factor endowment theory as well as the product life cycle theory. According to the former, shift in production takes place due to shifts in factor endowments which work their way through the relative prices. The product life cycle theory dictates that the production facilities for standardised products shifts to the follower LDCs at a later stage of the product cycle. This process of movement of comparative advantage is far from smooth and calls for a good many supply-side changes in the economy.

The expansionary trend in the world economy, alluded to earlier, assisted the flying-geese pattern of development in the Asia-Pacific region. It has had a salutary influence over the LDCs that were following the export-oriented industrial development strategies. Between 1980 and 1988 world trade volume expanded by 35 per cent, it was far ahead of the 23 per cent growth in world output for the same period. International trade liberalisation during the Kennedy Round (1964–67) and the Tokyo Round (1973–79) of multilateral trade negotiations had something to do with it. Other reasons included the appreciating dollar and the booming US economy of the first half of the 1980s and the appreciating yen and the expansion of domestic demand in Japan during the latter half of the decade.

A complementary trading pattern progressively developed within the region, with Japan out-sourcing from the ANIEs and the ASEAN-4 chemical and metal products, machinery and transport equipment and construction materials. The continuing intra-firm specialisation and off-shore relocation of Japanese and the ANIEs firms in intermediate and heavy industries in the ASEAN-4 countries, which possess comparative advantage in resource-based industries, led to enhanced trade in the Asia-Pacific industrial belt. Japan's role as an absorber of industrial products manufactured by the Asia-Pacific region can only grow in the future. More Japanese firms will relocate overseas and Japan will import more from the relocated plants. Such out-sourcing will eventually develop into full-scale production. China's open door strategy has created both complementary and competitive elements in the regional trade. On the one hand China's market potential is likely to intensify complementarity while on the other its burgeoning drive towards manufactures and export of light consumer goods and the production of industrial raw materials is expected to enhance competition within the region.[4] The shifting comparative advantages in the ANIEs and the ASEAN-4 countries resulting from their race to catch up with the more advanced countries will bring further sophistication to their industrial and trade structures, which, in turn will strengthen the complementarity of their economies. The complementarity need not be limited to trade, the ANIEs investment in the ASEAN-4 countries will strengthen complementary ties in foreign direct investment as well.[5]

It is evident from the above exposition that at the regional and sub-regional level economies in this industrial belt are undergoing continuous structural change in moving up from labour-intensive industries to capital- and skill-intensive industries in accordance with changes in their comparative advantage. The pattern of shift in revealed comparative advantage for the Pacific economies has been empirically analysed using disaggregated long-term time series statistics. The well-known Balassa approach for measuring comparative advantage is utilised in such studies. The index of revealed comparative advantage for the Pacific LDCs changed significantly in case of the ANIEs and the ASEAN-4 countries. The latter gained comparative advantage in exporting several labour-intensive and moderately capital- and skill-intensive sub-sectors. A precondition for such structural transformation along with the movement in comparative advantage are regional and sub-regional co-operation in technology, a positive role of the transnational corporations and liberalisation of trade. The shift of comparative advantage was not found to be significant in the case of South Asian LDCs. It is not counter-intuitive because their economies have had a legacy of inward-orientation and are yet to be liberalised. The changes in the index of revealed comparative advantage for the ANIEs were greater during the pre-1973 period than in the post-1973 years, whereas the opposite was observed for the ASEAN-4 and the South Asian LDCs. This portends to the fact the the latter country groups were relatively slower in keeping in step with their changing comparative advantage and implementing dynamic industrialisation policies. These studies find considerable evidence of the existence of a flying geese pattern, that is, comparative advantage shifting from Japan to the ANIEs and further on to the ASEAN-4. This conclusion suggests that economic prosperity has been trickling down among these country groups.[6] The South Asian LDCs have not been able to participate in this game and have largely looked in from outside.

The region's economic dynamism is, first, reflected in the rapid increase in the export of manufactures as a proportion of total merchandise exports. Examples of ANIEs like the Republic of Korea and Taiwan show that the percentage of manufactures in total exports soared from around 15 per cent in 1960 to over 90 per cent in the mid-1980s.[7] Such rapid and radical economic transformation is unheard of in the history of industrialisation. It is impossible to locate another example of a country turning from agrarian to industrial in barely two decades. The ASEAN-4 do not provide such examples of rapid industrialisation but the proportion of manufactured exports for the Philippines and Thailand went up from 5 per cent to 40 per cent and from 8 per cent to 50 per cent, respectively, over the same period. Not many LDCs have been able to emulate this performance. The second indicator reflecting the vitality of the region is its unparalleled increase in merchandise exports as a part of GDP. Between 1960 and 1985, their proportion went up from 0.9 to 35.1 per cent for Korea, from 9.6 to 51.9 per cent for Taiwan, from 16.0 to 18.6 per cent for Thailand and from 9.0 to 14.0 per cent for the Philippines. These statistics have a correlation with two tendencies. First, the length of time for which the export-led growth policies have been followed by these economies and, second, the intensity with which they have been applied. The third feature of these economies is their high investment. The proportion of gross fixed investment to GDP increased rather rapidly. For Korea it increased from 10.8 to 36.4 per cent over the 1960–85 period, for Taiwan from 16.7 to 19.3 per cent (in 1980 it was 31.1 per cent), for Thailand from 14.0 to 22.3 per cent and for the Philippines from 13.5 to 20.9 per cent. These rapid climbs in exports and investment created a virtuous-circle, propelling these economies to new heights of economic achievement.

The economic vitality and its rippling effects are visible in the striking shifts in the pattern of world trade. Since 1970 the value of trade across the Pacific grew faster than that across the Atlantic. In 1980, for the first time, the value of trans-Pacific trade surpassed that of trans-Atlantic trade. The former grew to $309.9 billion in 1988, about 1.5 times the trans-Atlantic trade. The value of the trade among the countries on the Asian side of the Pacific rim should surpass trans-Pacific trade before 1995.[8] The economic vitality of the region generated not only greater intra-regional trade but also extra-regional trade recorded marked expansion. The intra-regional trade between the fifteen members of the PEECC increased from 54.4 per cent of their total exports in 1970 to 65.8 per cent in 1988. As for extra-regional trade, ANIEs' exports to the EC grew an average of 37.8 per cent per year over the 1985–88 period, which means that they outperformed Japan (34.6 per cent) and the US (20.8 per cent) in this respect.[9] Some commentators of the international economic scene feel that the economic centre of gravity is shifting from the Atlantic to the Pacific.

INTEGRATION

The rapid growth rates have brought about structural changes in production, trade and capital flows in the Asia-Pacific region and have worked towards economically integrating it. The progress in integration is in turn reflected in the region's progressive cohesiveness. Japan has supplied high-quality, low-priced capital goods for a long time and their demand has remained strong. Even in the late 1980s around 60 per cent of Japanese exports to the region comprised machinery and equipment which have enabled the ANIEs and the ASEAN-4 countries to improve the international competitiveness of their products. In recent years Japan has begun to provide more industrial co-operation and capital exports.[10] In addition, the ANIEs have now reached the stage where they can export their own consumer durables and some capital goods.

Traditionally, the ANIEs and the ASEAN-4 used to export their products largely to the US but their export market is now being diversified. In 1986, the ANIEs exported to the US $50.5 billion worth of goods, about half of their total exports. This proportion sagged to 37.0 per cent in 1987 and 31.0 per cent the next year. This was despite expansion in the volume and value of their exports to $62.2 billion in 1987 and $67.3 billion in 1988. As opposed to this, the value and share of exports to Japan have increased over this period. It rose from $13.8 billion or 11 per cent of the total in 1986 to $21.2 billion or 12 per cent in 1987 and further to $26.8 billion or 13 per cent in 1988.[11] The exports of ASEAN countries display a similar trend. Although the value of their exports to the US market increased from $8 billion to $11.8 billion during the 1986–88 period, its share fell from 21 per cent to 18 per cent over the same period. Conversely, their exports to Japan increased in terms of both value and share during this period. They increased from $2.1 billion or 6 per cent of the total to $8.2 billion or 13 per cent of the total.[12] Increasing integration of the region is also reflected in the doubling of Japan's trade with the ANIEs and the ASEAN between 1985 and 1988, when it reached $118 billion.[13] The structure of the regional trade has undergone radical transformation. Traditionally these countries used to export industrial raw materials to Japan and import intermediate and capital goods. Presently, more than 60 per cent of their exports to Japan are manufactured goods. ANIEs' exports to their ASEAN neighbours have also expanded. Exports within the ANIEs jumped to $22.4 billion or 10 per cent of their total exports in 1988 from $5.9 billion or 5 per cent of their total exports in 1986. Their exports to the ASEAN countries rose from $6.4 billion in 1986 to $14.5 billion in 1988 or from 5 per cent of the total to 7 per cent. Likewise, ASEAn exports to the ANIEs have also risen from $8.2 billion or 21 per cent of the total to $15.5 billion or 24 per cent over the 1986–88 period. Intra-ASEAN exports rose only in terms of value, from $1.5 billion $2.3 billion. The share of the internal market of the ASEAN countries remained constant and low at 4 per cent.[14]

Intra-regional investment, including investment by the ANIEs in each other's economies and in the ASEAN-4, is another important indicator of growing integration. For the Japanese FDI the ANIEs were the relatively more important group during the latter half of the 1980s. This state of affairs continued until 1989 when the ASEAN countries supplanted the ANIEs as the larger recipients of Japanese FDI. Hong Kong and Singapore were the largest recipients among the ANIEs. Japanese firms transferred production bases in several industrial sub-sectors to the ANIEs. During the latter half of the 1980s investment in labour-intensive industries declined while that in technology-intensive industries and services rose. The shift in import-ance from the ANIEs to the ASEAN-4 was largely due to rising labour costs in the ANIEs, manpower shortage and lack of suitable locations for production bases.

The accelerated growth rate of the ASEAN-4 is considerably attri-buted to direct foreign investment from Japan as well as the ANIEs. The latter's direct investment in ASEAN has outpaced that of Japan. In Malaysia ANIEs' direct investment increased to $709.3 million or 35.3 per cent of the total investment in the country in 1988. In 1986, it was a mere $101.3 million. Taiwan was the largest foreign investor among the ANIEs, its direct investment in Malaysia surpassed even that of Japan in 1988. Their investment in Indonesia also increased sharply, from $84.3 million or 10.5 per cent of the total in 1986 to $1373.4 million or 34.1 per cent in 1988. This was far ahead of Japanese investment in Indonesia. The direct investment of ANIEs outstripped that of Japan in the Philippines as well. It rose from $8 million to $132.5 million, which was 33.1 per cent of the total foreign direct investment. Likewise, although it was up from $14.3 million to $146.2 million in Thailand over the same two-year period, it did not surpass Japan's investment in Thailand which was $535 million in 1988.[15] Due to rising wage levels and appreciating currencies the ANIEs were losing their attractiveness for Japan during the latter half of the 1980s. The same reasons lay behind their own increasing investment in the ASEAN-4 countries. The result was that towards the end of the 1980s, the combined share of investment by Japan and the ANIES in the ASEAN-4 economies was 60 per cent of their total FDI receipts.[16] This shows the enormous impact of these economies over the ASEAN. The earlier waves of direct investment from Japan were in assembly plants or low-tech manufacturing. The surge this time, however, went into electronics, electrical components and other intermediate or even high-tech products which involved a wide range of technology transfer through licensing, production tie-ups and contracts of the supply of original equipment. Several large Japanese corporations manufactured their products in the ASEAN-4 or the ANIEs to import them for the domestic markets. Another noteworthy recent trend is that in the past only large corporations invested in the Asia-Pacific countries but in the current wave of foreign direct investment even medium- and small-sized firms are participating and shifting production abroad. Wage differentials and currency value configuration will sustain this trend.[17]

The heavy and sustained swell of Japanese investment in Asian equity towards the end of the 1980s was completely market determined (see Chapter 3). Beginning from almost zero in 1988, it came close to $1 billion in FY 1989/90[18] and had an upward trend. The sweep into Asian equity was *a fortiori* significant because it came about at a low period of the Japanese financial markets. This shift was caused, first, by a strong shift in the portfolio composition of the Japanese life insurance companies and, second, by a discernible deepening of the Asian equity markets. The ASEAN countries were favoured by the Japanese investors because of their strong growth prospects.

Thus viewed, a great deal of synergism has developed between the economies of the region and economic integration is progressing naturally. It seems that intervention by Kasumigaseki, the district that houses various ministeries in Tokyo, is superfluous. The trade and investment decisions of a large number of businessmen, and business firms and the operation of market forces is accelerating economic cohesion in the region. The activities and operation of the private sector is intertwining the economies in an efficient and pragmatic manner.

A new breed of blue chip corporate giants, with a mid-Pacific management style and a functional *modus vivendi*, has been born. Samsung, Daewoo, Sime Darby, Li-ka-Shing Group and Charoen Pokphand in association with Mitsubishi, Mitsui, Sumitomo and the like will form the corporate challenge of the 1990s. The Asia-Pacific region has grown into the largest market for autos, telecommunications equipment, airline seats, paint and a host of other products. Steel consumption in the region is higher than that in the US and the EC. By 1992, the consumption of semiconductors in the region is projected to exceed that in the EC.[19] In the foreseeable future the Asia-Pacific region will be the third most vibrant market after the US and the EC and economic integration brought about by market forces is likely to continue progressively. Therefore, it would be politically expedient to leave them to run their course. In the long run, economic factors will prevail over political ones and draw the region into a closer trade, monetary and currency related co-operation with the Japanese economy.

Spurring on the market forces for regional economic integration is being methodically done by the Ministry of International Trade and Industry (MITI). An Economic Planning Agency (EPA) study catches the drift of the official thinking in this regard.[20] The MITI strategy is to combine the resources of Japan's public sector (economic assistance, technical co-operation and measures to open Japanese markets) with private capital flows and technology transfer to encourage the development of carefully selected industrial sectors in the Asia-Pacific region. The former are intended to fill the infrastructural lacuna and pave the ground for the latter and then Japan will open its markets for the output of these industries. The study emphasised economic integration of the region at the exclusion of any kind of political integration. It talked of an 'Asian Brain' co-ordinating and controlling industrial investment in Japan, ANIEs and the ASEAN economies. Apparently the 'Asian Brain' was intended to be MITI. Implicit in this view is a well defined division of labour. For instance, according to MITI, Indonesia can pay special attention to textiles, forest products and plastics. Thailand has a great potential in producing furniture, toys and die-cast moulds. Malaysia can concentrate on sports shoes, copiers and television picture tubes. MITI sees potential for converting Malaysia into the world's foremost producer of word-processers, answering machines and facsimile machines. For Japanese corporations and MITI, Malaysia is of special significance. It has become a microcosm of precisely the sort of relationship Japan would like to have with its Asian neighbours. Elaborate documents have been prepared by MITI in concert with the planners in these countries. A complementary pattern of development has also been thought of. For instance, a regional auto industry might combine transmission made in the Philippines with steering mechanisms built in Malaysia and engines from Thailand. Each country would then do the final assembly. Toyota Motors has made impressive strides in this direction.[21]

The concept of a market-determined regional economic network is MITI's idea – albeit embryonic – of a regional economic community. MITI has taken a low-profile approach in this regard and has consulted not only countries within the region but also those outside. It is pursuing this plan because it seems more achievable in the short-term than the more grandiose regional initiatives put forward by Japanese politicians like Yosuhiro Nakasone. MITI is also careful to publicise that this regional economic network is not an exclusionist arrangement and need not be exclusively Asian in membership and will certainly not be inward-looking in its approach.

THE YEN APPRECIATION AND THE YEN BLOC

Most ANIEs recorded trade deficits up until the early 1980s but started to record surpluses since the mid-1980s which kept widening until 1987. The surplus was the largest for Taiwan (20 per cent of GNP) followed by South Korea. The surpluses of Singapore and Hong Kong were relatively much lower and of more recent vintage. The main reason behind their burgeoning trade surpluses was considerable under-valuation of their currencies. During the post Plaza accord years, when the yen began to appreciate and the dollar began to depreciate, the four Asian currencies remained pegged or closely tied to the dollar. Their exchange rates appreciated somewhat against the dollar. As discussed in Chapter 2, the Hong Kong dollar remained pegged to the dollar while the Singapore dollar appreciated by 12 per cent between 1986 and 1989 *vis-à-vis* the dollar, the won appreciated by 24 per cent and the New Taiwan dollar appreciated by 31 per cent. Over the same period, the real effective exchange rate depreciated by 8 per cent for the Singapore dollar, 5 per cent for the Hong Kong dollar, whereas it appreciated by 20 per cent for the won and 21 per cent for the New Taiwan dollar.[22] The exchange rates of these four currencies depreciated substantially *vis-à-vis* the yen. This gave exporters in the ANIEs large gains in competitiveness in real trade-weighted terms. Consequently, the post-appreciation Japanese market became most attractive for the ANIEs in terms of both relative prices and market growth. It has been noted in another context that their exports destined to the US grew but the growth rate of those to Japan was greater. Since 1987 their share of the Japanese market began to increase.[23] The result was that, as noted in Chapter 2, the growth of ANIEs' exports accounted for one quarter of the growth of total world exports in 1986 and 1987. The rapid growth of exports from ANIEs reflected increased domestic demand in industrialised countries and improved price competitiveness for their products due to the new currency value configuration. Since both the exogenous factors on the demand side also existed for other developing countries, it *a priori* suggests that the supply-side factors were more responsible for the outstanding performance of the ANIEs. The increasing presence of ANIEs in the US and the Japanese markets implies a greater international and regional role for these economies, which in turn means strengthened interdependence.

The Louvre accord (February 1987) called for the co-operation of the ANIEs in adjusting the current account imbalances. But even before the Louvre accord, the US had begun to pressurise the ANIEs to appreciate their currencies *vis-à-vis* the dollar to redress their bilateral trade balances. Initially they resisted the US pressure and kept the rate of appreciation low but after the Louvre accord, as stated above, the rate of appreciation of the won and New Taiwan dollar picked up momentum. Like Japan, South Korea and Taiwan took measures to deregulate and open their domestic markets. Average tariffs were cut from 28 per cent to 10 per cent in Taiwan over the 1986–89 period and from 24 per cent to 13 per cent in South Korea.[24] In order to redress their trade surpluses with the US they shifted the focus of their export drives to the Japanese and the EC markets. Although two of the four dragons began to look less fierce, Singapore and Hong Kong continued to have large current account surpluses when measured as a percentage of GDP. The reason was that their real exchange rates had depreciated relative to the dollar.

Rapid rise in domestic production, income and demand had created strong induced demand for imports in the ANIEs and generated upward pressure on wages. In dollar terms, the wage difference between Japan and Thailand was 100 to 8 in 1985, but widened to 100 to 5 in 1987 due to the yen appreciation. When Korea and Thailand are compared, Korean workers earned three times as much as their counterparts in Thailand in 1985 and three and a half times more in 1987, when the won had appreciated moderately.[25] Wage hikes coupled with gradual appreciation of currencies caused their industrial structure to shift from being labour-intensive to technology- and capital-intensive. Thus, first, their currencies strengthened dramatically against those of the ASEAN-4 countries. Second, wage differentials between the ANIEs and the ASEAN economies widened considerably. Third, the industrial structure and comparative advantage in the ANIEs underwent a good deal of transformation. All these were significant developments of far-reaching ramifications and were responsible for the development of a horizontally integrated trade pattern in the region. Japan's burgeoning demand-led domestic economy catalysed the process of horizontal integration. Not only the exports of manufactures to Japan from the ANIEs and the ASEAN-4 economies increased but those from the ANIEs also moved up-market. In so doing, they provided a niche into which the ASEAN exports could fit. Thus, the ANIEs-ASEAN division of labour became better defined.

The other mode of horizontal integration, as noted, was the

offshore movement of Japanese firms in response to the currency appreciation. The same offshore movement took place after a time lag among Korean and Taiwanese firms when their currencies were stung by appreciation. The ASEAN economies were eager hosts and introduced measures to promote foreign direct investment and deregulated business activities. Inward investments enabled the ASEAN economies to exploit their comparative advantage fully and benefit from their price competitiveness. Taiwan also discreetly invested in China through Hong Kong based front companies. South Korea was exploring similar possibilities.

The foregoing analysis indicates structural realignment in the regional economies followed by the currency value realignment. The ANIEs have become more significant than they were and have started playing a regional role commensurate with their post-appreciation economic and technological status. They have become an active intermediate stratum of the regional economic pyramid. They had accumulated impressive foreign exchange reserves through repeated current account surpluses over the 1980s. They were also recipients of foreign technology for a long time. This placed them in a position to transfer capital and technology to economies that belong to lower strata than their own. Regional economic integration will be stimulated by ANIEs' recent relinquishment of export-only strategy. The currency realignment has made them an attractive market for the ASEAN and Chinese exports. Be it noted that the total imports of the ANIEs were as large as those of Japan during the late 1980s and that they can contribute to the growth of export-oriented ASEAN economies by serving as import absorbers. Such a relationship has developed over the recent past between Thailand and Taiwan.[26]

THE SHORT- AND LONG-TERM PROSPECTS

The three necessary conditions for the formation of the yen bloc are: (1) the countries involved need to be sufficiently economically cohesive, (2) Japan must be able and willing to form the bloc, and (3) the countries involved must be willing to join the bloc.[27] The economic circumstances of the group show that none of the stipulations are totally fulfilled. First, although led by market forces a great deal of economic integration has taken place in the region over the 1980s, it is still fairly diverse and the diversity is not limited to the stages of economic growth. It extends to natural resource endowments, ethnic background and many other aspects of socio-economic life. The region presently comprises economies ranging from developed, rich and mature ones like Japan to underdeveloped and poor economies like China. The diversity precludes any possibilities of an EC-type structure of economic integration because it is incompatible with commonality of interests. Second, Japan's ability to lead the yen bloc is beyond dispute but its willingness to do so does not exist. To be sure, Japan's world view has undergone considerable change over the 1980s and the word 'international' is no longer taken as a synonym for the US or, at most, the OECD countries. The significance of the Asia-Pacific region, as we saw, has soared a great deal. Yet, since the first such proposal, when the United Nations Economic Commission for Asia and Far East (UNECAFE) mooted the establishment of an Asian Payment Union in 1954, Japan has opposed any proposal of Japan-led regional integration or formation of a yen bloc. Its disinterest is also clear from its several recent firm denials. For instance, when Karl Otto Poehl, the president of the Bundesbank, in Hamburg, suggested a yen-based Pacific zone in 1988, Japan remained cold to the idea. When Australia proposed the formation of an Asian-OECD in 1989, Japan made it obvious that it is against the idea of setting up a formal institution specially if it implies confronting other regional blocs like the EC. Likewise, the Malaysian proposal for the creation of an East Asian economic group in mid-1991 was rejected out of hand by Japan. Third, there is a marked lack of political will among the prospective members of the yen bloc to formally integrate their economies. Many members equate it to surrendering their economic sovereignty to Japan. The ANIEs, despite their closer nexus with the Japanese economy, were never warm to any proposition of a bloc formation. With the exception of the Malaysian initiative, the ASEAN countries were equally cold. When Japan tentatively offered to play a greater security role in the region in July 1991, it was rejected forthwith.[28] While these countries welcome the current economic role played by Japan, they have serious reservations about anything beyond it.

The official line regarding the last rejection of the idea of regional integration was that Japan is more committed to building a free trade system, and that it considers global integration superior to regional integration because it is trade-creating and does not divert trade. The 1991 White Paper on International Trade goes even further and mildly disapproves of the European Community's planned single internal market at the end of 1992 as well as the free-trade zone grouping of the United States, Canada and Mexico. It calls for a better GATT monitoring of the two.[29] At this point in time and in the current geopolitical ambience, it is important for Japan to demonstrate its eagerness for an open international economy and shun any idea of its being broken into regional blocs. Therefore, short-term prospects of the creation of a formal yen bloc range from slender to non-existent.

If this appears to be a pessimistic perspective, let us look at the other side. As alluded to earlier, during the last quarter century the ANIEs and the ASEAN economies have relied heavily on capital goods imports and technology transfer from Japan. This dependence varied from country to country. For instance, it was measured at 50 per cent on an average for the ANIEs in 1980 and at 40 per cent for the ASEAN countries.[30] Second, as stated, regional integration through trade and investment has progressed inexorably since the yen was appreciated. The 1991 White Paper cited in the preceding paragraph, while rejecting the idea of formation of a bloc, calls for enhanced economic ties between members of the Asia-Pacific region. It enlarges the region to include the US, Canada, Australia and New Zealand. Third, Japan's status as the largest creditor country and the largest provider of economic assistance is well established, both globally and regionally. Fourth, regional integration through trade and investment will continue and with that the economic diversity diversity in the region will decline. Without institutionalised efforts, if with the passage of time the region becomes an internally open market for capital and goods and services, harmonisation of economic and monetary policy may be the logical next step.

Over the remaining years of the century the soft-edged co-operation network on the lines of the MITI plan detailed on pp. 183–4 above is likely to continue. It would be a loose association of prospering and competing economies, voluntarily together because they see mutual gains in economic co-operation. A firmly structured trade-pact or a yen bloc does not seem to be even an intermediate-term possibility. One can, however, reasonably look forward to a yen bloc in the beginning of the next country when the ANIEs will have become quasi-advanced industrial economies and the ASEAN-4 will have reached the industrial status of the present-day ANIEs. The Asia-Pacific region will no longer be a pre-modern region. Japan will have become more sanguine about its status as an economic super-power. The size of the Chinese and Japanese markets will have made them important for the rest of Asia. Continued industrialisation and upgrading of industrial levels will have made the economies of the region more dependent on each other. Creation of a yen bloc will then be a reality.

SUMMING UP

The concept of an East Asian economic community or a yen bloc is not a new one. It has existed in one form or the other for over three decades. Those who supported it saw dynamic gains in mutual economic co-operation. Japan and the other Asia-Pacific economies, particularly the ANIEs and the ASEAN-4, have recorded conspicuously high economic and industrial growth rates in the past. Trade and investment have also grown faster within the region than in other parts of the world. These developments made the existing economic linkages among the Asia-Pacific economies stronger. The appreciating yen catalysed this economic dynamics which, in turn, resulted in the creation of several informal regional fora for economic consultations and co-operation. None of them, however, seems to be drifting towards the formation of a yen bloc.

In terms of the level of economic development and performance, the economies of the region make a cascade or a 'flying geese' pattern. Such a formation has become responsible for a special economic behaviour paradigm and has enabled countries to cash in better on their respective comparative advantages. In addition, their resource endowments supported this process and accelerated their industrialisation endeavours. This production dynamics was in accordance with the Heckscher-Ohlinian theory as well as the product life cycle theory. Consequently, a complementary trading pattern has developed within the region. The Asia-Pacific countries have emerged as the most successful traders in the world and they have made their mark on the international trade structure.

The changes that have come about in the pattern of production, trade and capital flows in the region have worked towards economically integrating it; with that the region is growing progressively cohesive. Traditionally the US used to be the most important partner of the economies in this region; now the Japanese economy is progressively supplanting it. It is *a fortiori* so after the yen appreciation. Intra-regional investment, that is, Japan's massive investment in the region as well as that made by the ANIEs, has worked as an integrating instrument. The ANIEs have become significant foreign investors, with Taiwan emerging as the largest foreign investor among them. Large dosages of FDI from Japan and the ANIEs has helped to bring about the economic transformation of the ASEAN countries. That apart, Japanese financial institutions began to invest in a sustained manner in the Asian equity markets. All these financial flows were market-determined. Thus viewed, economic integration of the region was advancing without any formal bloc formation and without government intervention. Under a MITI plan the market forces attempting regional integration were being methodically encouraged and supported. The strategy was to combine the resources of Japan's public sector with private capital flows and technology transfers to encourage the development of carefully selected industrial sectors in the region. The sector plans were to be country-specific and were to take into account the indigenous resource endowments.

The appreciating yen and the depreciating dollar affected the currency values of the ANIEs because they were closely pegged to the dollar. The post-appreciation Japanese market became most attractive for the ANIEs, as did the US and the EC markets. They began to have recurring surpluses in their current accounts, with Taiwan recording the largest surpluses. A rapid rise in domestic production and income created strong import demand in the ANIEs and as a group their imports became larger than that of Japan. A horizontal integration of trade became the regional pattern. Horizontal integration was also spurred on by the offshore movement of the Japanese firms first and those from the ANIEs later.

Although led by market forces a great deal of economic integration has taken place in the region over the decade of the 1980s, the region is still fairly diverse in many ways. The diversity precludes any possibilities of an EC-type structure of economic integration. Also, Japan's ability to lead the yen bloc is beyond dispute but its willingness to do so does not exist. Therefore, short-term prospects of the creation of a formal yen bloc range from slender to non-existent. This having been said, regional economic integration through trade and investment has made impressive strides over the 1980s, particularly during the post-appreciation period. Without institutionalised efforts, if with the passage of time the region becomes an internally open market for capital and goods and services, harmonisation of economic and monetary policies may follow as the logical next step. As regards the intermediate-term prospects, building of a soft-edged co-operation network on the lines of the MITI plan is likely to continue. This will result in a loose association of prospering and competing economies, voluntarily together because they see mutual gains in economic co-operation. A firmly structured trade-pact or a yen bloc does not seem to be even an intermediate-term possibility.

Notes and References

1 THE YEN APPRECIATION AND THE JAPANESE ECONOMY

1. Noguchi, Y., 'The Japanese Economy in a Changing World Environment' in *The JCIE Papers: Europe and Japan and their Co-operation in an Interdependent World* (Tokyo: Japan Center for International Exchange, 1988) pp. 17–38.
2. Roosa, R.V., *United States and Japan in the International Monetary System* (New York: Group of Thirty, 1986) pp. 43–44.
3. For instance, see Balassa, B., 'Japan's Trade Policies' *Weltwirtschaftliches Archiv* (Band 122, Heft 4, 1986) pp. 745–90. Bergsten, C.F. and W.R. Cline, *The United States–Japan Economic Problems* (Washington DC: Institute for International Economics, June 1988). Lawrence, R.Z., 'Imports in Japan: Closed Markets or Minds?' *Brookings Papers on Economic Activity* (no. 2, vol. III, 1987) pp. 517–54. Noland, M., 'An Econometric Investigation of International Protection' (Washington DC: Institute for International Economics) mimeo 1990. Saxonhouse, G.R., 'The Micro- and Macro-economics of Foreign Sales to Japan', in W.R. Cline (ed.) *Trade Policies in the 1980s* (Washington DC: Institute for International Economics, 1983) pp. 259–304.
4. Organisation for Economic Co-operation and Development, *OECD Economic Surveys: Japan 1988–1989* (Paris) pp. 86–92.
5. Barbone, L., 'Import Barriers: An Analysis of Time-Series Cross-Section Data', *OECD Economic Studies*, no. 11 (Autumn, 1988).
6. The Bank of Japan, *Balance of Payments Monthly* (Tokyo, December 1990).
7. Takeuchi K., 'Does Japan Import Less than it Should?', *The Asian Economic Journal*, vol. III, no. 2 (September 1989).
8. Down to 1990, Martin Feldstein, former chairman of the Council of Economic Advisers, pressed on with this logic. See Feldstein, M., 'Japan's Latest Export-Promotion Plan', *The Asian Wall Street Journal* (8 January 1990).
9. Porter M.E., *The Competitive Advantage of Nations* (London: Macmillan, 1990).
10. Burstein, D., *Yen: Japan's New Financial Empire* (New York: Fawcett Columbine, 1988) p. 140.
11. Bergsten, C. Fred, 'The Case for Leaning with the Wind', *The Financial Times* (24 October 1984).
12. Pine, A., 'To Avert a Trade War, US Sets Major Push to Drive Down Dollar', *The Wall Street Journal* (23 September 1985).

13. For instance, the US growth rate in 1985 was 2.4 per cent against the industrial market economics average of 2.7 per cent.
14. Funabashi, Y., *Managing the Dollar: From the Plaza to the Louvre* (Washington DC: Institute for International Economics, 1988) pp. 17–21.
15. The Bank of Japan, *Balance of Payments Monthly* (Tokyo, December 1989).
16. 'Japan Under Pressure', *World Financial Markets* (New York: Morgan Guaranty Trust Company, April 1987) pp. 2–4.
17. The Bank of Japan, 'Adjustment of the Japanese Economy under Strong Yen' (Tokyo: March 1987) Special Paper no. 149.
18. Economic Planning Agency, *Annual Report on National Accounts* (Tokyo, Various issues).
19. Economic Planning Agency, *Japanese Economic Indicators Quarterly* (Tokyo, 1990) no. 2.
20. The Japan Development Bank, 'Capital Investment Spending' (Tokyo, March 1989). See also Wagstyl, S., 'Japan's Capital Spending Grows at Fastest Pace for 15 years', *The Financial Times* (25 September 1989).
21. Robins, B., 'MITI Tries to Restrain Investment Spending', *The Asian Wall Street Journal* (19 March 1990).
22. Organisation for Economic Co-operation and Development, *Main Economic Indicators* (Paris, 1990).
23. Sargen, N. and K.L. Schoenholtz, 'Japan's Adjustment Miracle and its Implications for the Yen', *Japan and the World Economy*, no. 2 (1990) pp. 283–93.
24. Kohama, H. and S. Urata, 'The Impact of the Recent Yen Appreciation on the Japanese Economy', *The Developing Economics* (December 1988) pp. 323–40.
25. Blades, D. and W. Simpson, 'The OECD Compatible Trade and Production Data Base', Working Paper no. 18 (Paris: Organisation for Economic Co-operation and Development, January 1985).
26. Lawrence, R.Z., 'Imports in Japan: Closed Markets or Minds?' *Brookings Papers on Economic Activity*, no. 2 (1987) pp. 517–48.
27. Rising Ratio of Manufactured Imports, *The Journal of Japanese Trade and Industry*, no. 2 (1989) p. 34.
28. Ministry of International Trade and Industry, *White Paper on International Trade 1990* (Tokyo: June 1990).
29. Tokunaga, Y., 'An Anatomy of Japan's High Prices', *Economic Eve* (Spring 1990) pp. 20–25.
30. Ibid., p. 24.
31. 'A New Era of Japanese Trade Structure', *Mitsui Bank Monthly Review* (March 1988) pp. 1–8.
32. The Ministry of Finance, *Monthly Finance Review* (Tokyo, May 1991).
33. The Bank of Japan, 'Balance of Payments Adjustment Processes in Japan and the United States', Special Paper no. 162 (Tokyo, March 1988) Table 4.
34. Ibid.
35. All the statistics used here come from or are based on *International Financial Statistics* 1990 Yearbook of the International Monetary Fund.
36. Hickok, S., 'Japanese Trade Balance Adjustment to Yen Appreciation',

Federal Reserve Bank of New York Quarterly Review (Autumn 1989) vol. 14, no. 3, pp. 33–47.

37. Corker, R., 'External Adjustment and the Strong Yen: Recent Japanese Experience', *IMF Staff Papers*, vol. 36, no. 2 (June 1989) pp. 464–93.

38. Ohno, K., 'Export Pricing Behavior of Manufacturing: A US–Japan Comparison', *IMF Staff Papers*, vol. 36, no. 3 (September 1989) pp. 550–78.

39. Krugman, P.R., 'Pricing to Market when the Exchange Rate Changes' in S.W. Arndt and J.D. Richerdson (eds). *Real Financial Linkages Among Open Economies* (Cambridge MA: The MIT Press, 1987).

40. Baldwin, R.E., 'Some Empirical Evidence on Hysteresis in Aggregate US Import Prices'. NBER Working Paper no. 2483 (Cambridge MA: National Bureau of Economic Research, January 1988).

41. Ohno, K., 'Exchange Rate Fluctuations, Pass-Through and Market Share', *IMF Staff Papers*, vol. 37, no. 2 (June 1990) pp. 294–310.

42. For example, see Baldwin, R.E., 'Hysteresis in Import Prices: The Beachead Effect', *American Economic Review*, vol. 78 (1988) pp. 773–85. Also Marston, R., 'Pricing to Market in Japanese Manufacturing' (Philadelphia: University of Pennsylvania, 1989) mimeo.

43. Ohno (1990), op. cit.

44. Khosla, A. and J. Teranishi, 'Exchange Rate Pass-Through in Export Prices: an International Comparison', *Hitotsubashi Journal of Economics*, vol. 30 (1989) pp. 31–48.

45. Ohno (1989), op. cit.

46. The Bank of Japan, *Tankan: Short-Term Economic Survey of Enterprises in Japan* (Tokyo, November 1989) p. 8.

47. Hickok, op. cit., Table 1.

48. See also Ohno (1990), op. cit. His econometric exercise came to the same conclusion.

49. Based on the International Labour Organisation statistics cited by Hickok (1989).

50. 'A Hypothesis on the L-Curve Effect', *Japanese Finance and Industry*, Industrial Bank of Japan, no. 77 (I) (1989) pp. 1–19.

51. Economic Planning Agency, 'External Balance, Exchange rate Changes and Macroeconomic Policy', *Papers and Proceedings of the Fourth EPA International Symnposium* (Tokyo, March 1988).

52. The Bank of Japan, *'Tankan: Short-Term Economic Survey of Principal Enterprises'* (Tokyo, May 1987).

53. The Bank of Japan 'Corporate Management Under Strong Yen', Special Paper no. 159 (Tokyo, January 1988).

54. Ibid.

55. The Bank of Japan, *Tankan: Short-Term Economic Survey of Enterprises* (Tokyo, September 1988).

56. *The Economist*, 'Who are the Copy Cats Now?' (London, 20 May 1989) p. 109.

57. Reported in the *JEI Report*, 2 February 1990, p. 11.

58. Cited in Tatsuno, S.M., *Created in Japan* (New York, Harper & Row, 1990) ch. 1.

59. The Ministry of Finance, *Monthly Financial Review* (Tokyo, May 1991).

60. Itoh, S., 'Favourable Trend', *Journal of Japanese Trade and Industry*, no. 1 (1990) pp. 12–13.
61. Chandler, C., 'Japanese GNP Grew in Quarter at Rate of 11.2 per cent', *The Asian Wall Street Journal* (19 June 1991).
62. Kazutomo, I., 'Changes in the Japanese Economy' (Tokyo: Research Institute of International Trade and Industry, February 1990) Discussion paper no. 90.
63. Economic Planning Agency, *Economic Survey of Japan 1988–1989* (Tokyo, August 1989) pp. 44–48.

2 INTERACTION WITH THE INTERNATIONAL ECONOMY

1. *The Financial Times*, 'International Economic Indicators: National Accounts' (13 May 1991).
2. Ibid.
3. The Bank of Japan, 'Governor's speech Commemorating the 19th Annual General Meeting of Yomiuri International Economic Society' (Tokyo, 1 March 1990).
4. Organisation for Economic Co-operation and Development, *Development Co-operation: 1990 Report* (Paris, December 1990) p. 148.
5. *Fortune*, 'The Fortune Global 500' (29 July 1991) pp. 65–108.
6. This ratio has an unfortunate similarity to that of the shipping tonnage agreed among the US, Britain and Japan under the Washington Naval Treaty of 1922. As one of the world's three major naval powers, Japan was then in a position to share responsibility for the maintenance of international peace together with the US and Britain. However, it became over confident of its military strength and instead of defending the international order, chose the path of seeking to change the order by force. History testifies that this choice had tremendous tragic consequences for the entire world. This simile was recently drawn by Takakazu Kuriyama, deputy minister of foreign affairs and cited by Ian Roger in 'Japan: Still in Search of a Global Role', *The Financial Times* (9 July 1990).
7. Like when Japan offered to play a more active regional security role in July 1991, it was spurned by the neighbouring Asia-Pacific countries.
8. Das, Dilip K., *Migration of Financial Resources to Developing Countries* (London: Macmillan, 1986). See ch. 1.
9. The Economic Planning Agency, *Economic Survey of Japan 1987–1988* (Tokyo, August 1988) p. 101.
10. Peterson, P.G., 'Japan's Invasion: A Matter of Fairness', *The Asian Wall Street Journal* (6 November 1989). See also, Bhagwati, J.N., 'The Japanese: Not So Inscrutable to Adam Smith', *The Asian Wall Street Journal* (May, 1990).
11. Nester, W.R., *Japan's Growing Power over East Asian and the World Economy: Ends and Means* (London: Macmillan 1990). See ch. V for an impassioned culturalist view.
12. The Ministry of International Trade and Industry, *International Trade and International Policy in the 1990s* (Tokyo, 5 July 1990). See also

Murakami, Y. and Y. Kosai (eds) *Japan in the Global Community: Its Role and Contribution on the Eve of the 21st Century* (Tokyo: University of Tokyo Press, 1986).

13. Evans, G., 'Japan Takes over the IMF', *Euromoney* (September 1988), pp. 98–112.

14. The World Bank, *Annual Report 1990* (Washington DC, 1990) p. 225.

15. Loosely translated as groups of affiliated enterprises, corporate groups or development conglomerates of mutually co-operating firms. The Japanese economy is dominated by *keiretsu* arrangements which exist in production, distribution and finance. There are six of these, namely, Mitsui, Mitsubishi, Sumitomo, Fuji, Sanwa and Dai-Ichi Kangyo.

16. *The Economist*, 'America's Japanophobia' (18 November 1989).

17. 'The Intricacies of "Japanomics"', lecture delivered by C. Tait Ratcliff before the Kansai chapter of the American Chamber of Commerce, published by Keizai Koho Center, Tokyo, June 1990.

18. Quoted in 'The Unhappy Alliance: America and Japan', *The Economist* (17 February 1990) pp. 19–23.

19. Eguchi, T., 'US–Japan Trade Imbalance: Causes and Remedies', JCIF Policy Study Series no. 12 (Tokyo, May 1988) pp. 20–27.

20. Helliwell, J.F., 'The Effects of Fiscal Policy on International Imbalances: Japan and the United States', Paper presented at the Fourth EPA International Symposium (Tokyo, March 1988).

21. Sachs, J.D. and N. Roubini, 'Sources of Macroeconomic Imbalances in the World Economy: A Simulation Approach', Paper presented at the Third International Conference at the Bank of Japan (Tokyo, June 1987).

22. Ueda, K., 'Perspectives on the Japanese Current Account Surplus', *NBER Macroeconomics Annual 1988* (London, The MIT Press, 1988) pp. 217–67.

23. Noland, M., 'Fiscal Policies and the Japan–US Bilateral Current Account', *Japan and the World Economy* (July 1989) pp. 243–54.

24. Krugman, P.R., 'Exchange Rate and International Adjustment' (New York University Center for Japan–US Business and Economic Studies, September 1987) Working Paper no. 39.
Branson, W.H. and G. Marchese, 'International Payments Imbalances in Japan, Germany and the United States' in N.S. Fieleke (ed.) *International Payments Imbalances in the 1980s* (Boston: Federal Reserve Bank of Boston, 1988) pp. 195–230.

25. Bergsten, C.F. and W.R. Chine, *The United States–Japan Economic Problems* (Washington DC: Institute for International Economics, 1985).

26. Hooper, P. and C.L. Mann, 'The US External Deficit: Its Causes and Persistence', International Finance Discussion Paper no. 316 (Washington DC: Board of Governors of the Federal Reserve System, November 1987).

27. Krugman, P.R. and R.E. Baldwin, 'The Persistence of the US Trade Deficit', *Brookings Papers on Economic Activity*, no. 1, (1987) pp. 1–56.

28. Schlosstein, S.B., 'The New McCarthyism'. *The International Economy* (April/May 1990) pp. 12–15.

29. Organisation for Economic Co-operation and Development, *OECD Economic Survey: Japan 1989/1990* (Paris, 1990) pp. 60–61.
30. Riddell, P., 'SII Has Lived up to Expectations', *The Financial Times* (13 June 1991).
31. Balassa, B. and M. Noland, 'The Changing Comparative Advantage of Japan and the United States', *The Journal of the Japanese and International Economies*, no. 3 (1989) pp. 174–88.
32. Krugman, P.R., 'Discussion' in N.S. Fieleke (ed.) *International Payments Imbalances in the 1980s* (Boston: Federal Reserve Bank of Boston, 1988) pp. 51–53.
33. These disputes and tensions are properly chronicled in: Wilkinson, E., *Misunderstandings: Europe vs. Japan* (Tokyo, Chnokoronske, 1981). Hakishima, S., 'Mutal Ignorance and Misunderstanding: Causes of Japan–EC Economic Disputes', *Japan Quarterly*, no. 26 (1981).
34. Hakishima, op. cit.
35. Cecchini, P., *The European Challenge 1992: The Benefits of a Single Market* (Aldershot: Gower, 1988).
36. This expression is an American coinage.
37. The Japanese External Trade Organisation, *Current Management Situation of Japanese Manufacturing Enterprises in Europe: the 5th Report*. Cited in 'Japan–EEC Relations: More Ups and Downs', *JEI Report* (29 October 1990).
38. 'Japan–EEC Relations: More Ups and Downs', *JEI Report* (29 October 1990).
39. *The Asian Wall Street Journal*, 'Tokyo–EEC to Limit Japanese Auto Sales' (1 August 1991).
40. Rowley, A., 'A Partnership of Equals', *Far Eastern Economic Review* (20 June 1991) pp. 58–59.
    Islam, S. and R. Rowley, 'EC–Japan sign Charter to Upgrade Relations', *Far Eastern Economic Review* (1 August 1991) pp. 13–14.
41. Singapore is common to both the groups but for our purpose it will be treated as part of the first group, that is, the ANIEs. The tiny, oil-rich sultanate of Brunei does not count for much in this game. Therefore, ASEAN hereafter will mean only Indonesia, Malaysia, the Philippines and Thailand.
42. Smith, C. and L. do Rosario, 'Empire of the Sun', *Far Eastern Economic Review* (3 May 1990) pp. 46–48.
43. International Monetary Fund. *International Financial Statistics* (Washington DC, 1991).
44. Petri, P.P., 'Japanese Trade in Transition' (Brandeis University, Department of Economics, October 1989) Discussion Paper no. 248, Waltham, MA, pp. 8–11.
45. Balassa, B. and J. Williamson, *Adjusting to Success: Balance of Payments Policies in the East Asian NICs* (Washington DC: Institute of International Economics, April 1990) pp. 17–18.
46. Kitamatsu, K., 'Asian NICs Fill Export Vacuum Left by Japan', *The Japan Economic Journal* (12 September 1988).
47. The Bank of Japan, 'Greater Role of Asian Economies in the World and

Growing Interdependence Among Asia, the United States and Japan', Special Paper no. 166 (Tokyo, August 1988).

48. The US Treasury Department, *Report to the Congress on International Economic and Exchange Rate Policy* (Washington DC: 24 October 1988).

49. Sachs, J.D. and M.W. Sundberg, 'International Payments Imbalances of the East Asian Developing Economies' in N.S. Fieleke (ed.) *International Payments Imbalances in the 1980s* (Boston: Federal Reserve Bank of Boston, 1988) pp. 103–56.

50. The Asian Development Bank, *Asian Development Outlook 1991* (Manila, 1991) See Table A-1.

51. Levingston, S.E., 'Japanese Investment is Integrating Asia', *The Asian Wall Street Journal* (7 November 1989).

52. Shale, T., 'A New Crop of Tigers', *Euromoney* (September 1989) pp. 91–93.

53. Ibid.

54. *Far Eastern Economic Review*, 'Japanese Aid is Big Business in South Asia' (24 January 1991) pp. 42–43.

55. Nonaka, I., 'Managing Globalisation as a Self-Renewing Process: Experiences of Japanese MNCs' (New York: The Center for Japan–US Business and Economic Studies, New York University, October 1988) Working Paper no. 56.

56. The Economic Planning Agency, *Economic Survey of Japan 1988–89* (Tokyo, August 1989) pp. 161–62.

57. Nonaka, op. cit.

58. Nakakita, T., 'The Globalisation of Japanese Firms and its Influence on Japan's Trade with Developing Countries', *The Developing Economies* (December 1988) pp. 306–22.

59. Ibid.

60. *The Economist*, 'The Multinationals, Eastern Style' (24 June 1989) pp. 67–68.

61. Ibid.

62. *The Financial Times*, 'Japan's New Multinationals' (1 December 1989).

63. Tatsuno, S.M., *Created in Japan* (New York: Harper and Row, 1990) See ch. 14.

64. The Economic Planning Agency, *Economic Survey of Japan 1989–1990* (Tokyo, August 1990) pp. 183–85.

3 TRANSFORMATIONS IN THE WORLD OF INTERNATIONAL BANKING AND FINANCE

1. Sakakibara, E., 'The Internationalisation of Tokyo's Financial Markets' in A.H.H. Tan and B. Kapur (eds) *Pacific Growth and Financial Interdependence* (Sydney: Allen and Unwin, 1986) pp. 237–46.

2. Choi, S.P., A.E. Tschoegl and C.M. Yu, 'Banks and the World's Major Financial Centers 1970–1980', *Weltwirtschaftlisches Archive* (Bank 122, 1986) pp. 48–64.

3. Yoichi, S., 'Japan's Role as the World's Banker', *Economic Eye* (Summer 1990) pp. 22–29.
4. Bank for International Settlements, *International Banking and Financial Market Developments* (Basle, November 1990) p. 16.
5. *The AMEX Bank Review*, 'Japan's Capital Outflows: A Boost To Securitisation' (28 April 1986).
6. Mendelsohn, M.S., 'Japanese Banking's Global Challenge', *The Banker* (April 1986) pp. 46–47.
7. *Euromoney*, 'Big Four Become the Big Two' (May 1991) pp. 48–52.
8. Mitsui Bank and Taiyo Kobe Bank merged on 1 April 1990.
9. Source: Federation of Bankers' Association of Japan, cited in *The Financial Times* (19 April 1991) p. 29.
10. Myers, H.F., 'Japanese Banks are Building a Global Role', *The Asian Wall Street Journal* (12 September 1989. See also Goldberg, L.G. and G.A. Hanweck, 'The Growth of the World's 3000 Largest Banking Organisations by Country', *Journal of Banking and Finance*, vol. 15 (1991) pp. 207–23.
11. Myers, op. cit.
12. Kane, E.J., 'Competitive Financial Regulation: An International Perspective' in R. Portes and A. Swaboda (eds) *Threats to International Financial Stability* (Cambridge: Cambridge University Press, 1987) pp. 111–45. See also Kane, E.J. et al. 'Capital Positions of Japanese Banks', PRE Working Paper no. WPS 572 (Washington DC: The World Bank, January 1991).
13. Glynn, L., 'Japanese Banks Abroad: The Next Push', *Institutional Investor* (May 1990) pp. 94–97.
14. *Euromoney*, 'Leaders of the Pack' (December 1990) pp. 26–30.
15. *Institutional Investor*, 'Ranking the World's Largest Banks' (July 1990) pp. 149–51.
16. Rapoport, C., 'Tough Times for Japan's Banks', *Fortune* (16 July 1990) pp. 20–24.
17. Blanden, M., 'The Rising Sun', *The Banker* (July 1987) pp. 74–78.
18. Batten, D. et al., 'The Instruments and Operating Procedures for Conducting Monetary Policy in G-5 Countries', Occasional Paper no. 70 (Washington DC: International Monetary Fund, 1990).
19. Yakagi, S., 'The Changing Japanese Financial System', *Finance and Development* (March 1988) pp. 10–15.
20. Suzuki, Y., *Money, Finance and Macroeconomic Performance in Japan* (New Haven: Yale University Press, 1986).
21. Okumara, H., 'Japan's Financial Deregulation: Recent Developments and Future Outlook' (Tokyo: Nomura Research Institute, February 1990) mimeo.
22. *The Amex Bank Review*, 'Regulation of Financial Services' (3 April 1991).
23. Eken, S., 'Integration of Domestic and International Financial Markets: The Japanese Experience', *IMF Staff Papers*, vol. 31 (September 1984) pp. 499–548.
24. The *gensaki* transactions consist of short-term capital transactions using bonds as collateral. They essentially consist of resale or repurchase of

bonds at a fixed price after a fixed period, generally within three months. It is equivalent to the US repurchase or 'repo' agreement, where the seller of a debt instrument, usually a Treasury bill, agrees to repurchase it at a fixed price on a fixed date. Thus, while in form they resemble bond transactions, functionally they are short-term money transactions using bonds as collateral. The *gensaki* market developed parallel to the growth of the government bond market in the latter half of the 1970s.

25. The Ministry of Finance, *Financial Statistics of Japan 1991* (Tokyo, 1991).
26. Royama, S., 'Aspects of Financial Restructuring in Contemporary Japan', *Japan Review of International Affairs* (Spring/Summer 1990) pp. 42–65.
27. Important in-depth works on financial deregulation and liberalisation include: Frankel, J.A., *The Yen/Dollar Agreement: Liberalising Japanese Capital Markets* (Washington DC: Institute for International Economics, 1984). Osugi, K., 'Japan's Experience of Financial Deregulation Since 1974 in an International Perspective', *BIS Economic Papers*, no. 26 (Basle: Bank for International Settlements, January 1990). Suzuki, Y., *The Japanese Financial System* (Oxford: Clarendon Press, 1987).
28. Yamasaki, T., 'Japan's Foreign Securities Investment', *Tokyo Financial Review*, vol. 15, no. 4 (April 1990) pp. 1–7.
29. Koo, R.C., 'Japan and International Capital Flows' (Nomura Research Institute, April 1990) mimeo.
30. Kawai, M. and H. Okumura, 'Japan's Portfolio Investment in Foreign Securities', JCIF Policy Study Series no. 9 (Tokyo, January 1988).
31. The other cause of tightening the monetary policy was the interest rate hike in the other major industrialised economies.
32. Yu, D., 'Life After the Crash', *Asiamoney* (May 1991) pp. 10–16.
33. Cited in *The Annex Bank Review*, 'Japan as Global Creditor' (24 March 1988).
34. Wilcock, C.B., 'Japanese Investors Consider US Bonds', *The Wall Street Journal Europe* (2 April 1991).
35. Yamasaki (1990), op. cit.
36. Fukao, M., 'Liberalisation of Japan's Foreign Exchange Controls and Structural Changes in the Balance of Payments', *Bank of Japan Monetary and Economic Studies* (September 1990) pp. 101–61.
37. Ueda, K., 'Japanese Capital Outflows', *Journal of Banking and Finance*, no. 14 (1990) pp. 1079–101.
38. French, M., 'Behind the Japanese Myth', *Asiamoney* (May 1990) pp. 25–32.
39. Ibid.
40. A bankers' acceptance market allows a bank which has provided trade financing to a customer to resell his claim to a third party under his guarantee.
41. Sawai, Y., 'Internationalisation of the Yen: A Progress Report', *Tokyo Financial Review* (November 1989) pp. 10–16.
42. Ibid.
43. Tavlas, G.S., *On the International Use of Currencies: The Case of the*

Deutsche Mark (Princeton: International Finance Section, Princeton University, March 1991).

44. The next survey was scheduled for the last quarter of 1991.
45. McCallum, J., 'London, Tokyo and New York Dominate in their Time Slots: Big Three Battle it out', *The Financial Times* (29 April 1991).
46. Bank of International Settlements, *International Banking and Financial Market Developments* (Basle, February 1991).
47. *Euromoney*, 'Samurais Battle it Out' (April 1987) pp. 47–53.
48. Thorn, R.S., *The Rising Sun* (Singapore: Institute of Southeast Asian Studies, 1987) pp. 67–70.
49. Japan Economic Institute, *JEI Report* (5 October 1990) p. 9.
50. Tavlas, G.S. and Y. Ozeki, 'The Japanese Yen as an International Currency', IMF Working Paper no. WP/91/2 (Washington DC: International Monetary Fund, January 1991).
51. The Bank of Japan, *Economic Statistics Monthly* (January 1991).
52. *Tokyo Financial Review*, 'Internationalisation of the Yen: Where We Are', vol. 16, no. 3 (March 1991) pp. 1–8.
53. *Business Week*, 'The Tokyo Stock Market: How its Swing Affects You' (12 February 1990) pp. 18–24.
54. Terazono, E., 'Japanese Investors' Dividend Dilemma', *The Financial Times* (11 April 1991).
55. *The Economist*, 'International Financial Survey' (27 April 1991).
56. *The Economist*, 'International Financial Survey' (27 April 1991).
57. Hardouvelis, G.A., 'Evidence on Stock Market Speculative Bubble: Japan, United States and Great Britain' (New York: Federal Reserve Bank of New York, April 1988) Research Paper no. 8810.
58. Udea, K., 'Are Japanese Stock Prices Too High?' *Journal of Japanese and International Economies*, no. 4 (1990) pp. 351–70.
59. *Tokyo Financial Review*, 'Internationalisation of the Yen: Where We Are', vol. 16, no. 3 (March 1991) pp. 1–8.
60. Wagstyl, S., 'Japanese Financial Markets', *The Financial Times* (15 March 1990).
61. Shale, T., 'The Plot that Triggered Tokyo's Plunge', *Euromoney* (May 1990) pp. 32–36.
62. *The Financial Times*, 'Nikkei Beats Late Retreat as Interest Rate Hopes Fade' (9 April 1991).
63. *Asian Finance*, 'Banks Reel From Profit Crash' (15 August 1991) pp. 35–37.
64. Corrigan, T., 'Japanese Trust Banks Downgraded by S&P', *The Financial Times* (20 February 1991).
65. Brauchi, M.W., 'Japanese Securities Firms' Profits Plummet', *The Wall Street Journal Europe* (17–18 May 1991). Thomson, R., 'Sharp Falls at Japan's Securities Firms', *The Financial Times* (17 May 1991).
66. Shale, T., 'The Big Four Take a Beating', *Euromoney* (February 1991) pp. 38–41.
67. *Euromoney*, 'Big Four Become the Big Two' (May 1991) pp. 48–52.
68. Committee on Banking Regulation and Supervisory Practices, *International Convergence of Capital Measurement and Capital Standards* (Basle, July 1988).

69. Jones, C., 'Coming of the Crunch', *The Banker* (January 1991) pp. 31–33.
70. *The Economist*, 'International Finance Survey' (27 April 1991).
71. Thomson, D. and M. French, 'The Japanese Banks Retreat', *Asiamoney* (November 1990) pp. 25–30.
72. Vogl, F., 'Japan's SDR Plan Falls Flat', *Asian Finance* (15 June 1991) pp. 62–63.
73. Brauchli, M.W., 'Top Bankers Expect to Curb Lending in 1990s', *The Wall Street Journal Europe* (5 June 1991).

4 ACCELERATION IN FOREIGN DIRECT INVESTMENT

1. Ministry of Finance, *Statistics of Approvals/Notifications of Overseas Direct Investment* (Tokyo, Various years).
2. The Bank of Japan, *Balance of Payments Monthly* (Various Issues).
3. United Nations Centre on Transnational Corporation, 'World Investment Report 1991: The Triad in Foreign Direct Investment' (New York, 1991).
4. Julius, D., 'Foreign Direct Investment: The Neglected Twin of Trade' (New York: The Group of Thirty, 1991).
5. Ministry of Finance, *Zaisei Kinyu Tookei Geppo* (Tokyo, Various Issues).
6. The Ministry of Finance, *Statistics of Approvals/Notifications of Overseas Direct Investment* (Tokyo, 1990 and 1991).
7. Japan External Trade Organisation, *JETRO White Paper on Foreign Direct Investment 1991* (Tokyo, March 1991).
8. The Ministry of International Trade and Industry, *The Fourth Basic Survey on Japanese Business Activities Abroad* (Tokyo, March 1991).
9. Dunning, J.H., 'Explaining the International Direct Investment Position of Countries: Towards a Dynamic or Developmental Approach', *Weltwirtschaftliches Archive* (Band 117, Heft 1, 1981) pp. 30–64.
10. Lee, C.H., 'Direct Foreign Investment, Structural Adjustment and International Division of Labour', *Hitotsubashi Journal of Economics*, no. 31 (1990) pp. 61–72.
11. Das, Dilip K., 'The Challenge of Appreciating Yen and the Japanese Corporate Response', *The Columbia Journal of World Business* (forthcoming).
12. Ban, T., 'Factors Behind Japanese Direct Investment Abroad', *Japanese Finance and Industry*, no. 80 (1989) pp. 12–25.
13. These are: (1) The Union Bank, owned by the Bank of Tokyo, (2) the Bank of California, owned by the Mitsubishi Bank, (3) The Sanwa Bank of California, and (4) The Sumitomo Bank of California.
14. *The Banker*, 'Happy Together' (July 1990) p. 85.
15. Komia, R. and R. Wakasugi, 'Japan's Foreign Direct Investment', discussion paper no. 90 (Tokyo: Research Institute of International Trade and Industry, May 1990).
16. Japan External Trade Organisation, JETRO White Paper on *Foreign Direct Investment, 1991* (Tokyo, March 1991).

17. Ibid.
18. Ministry of International Trade and Industry, *The Fourth Basic Survey of Japanese Business Activity Abroad* (Tokyo, March 1991).
19. Takoaka, H., 'Global Management and Overseas Direct Investment' (Tokyo: Research Institute of Overseas Investment, The Export–Import Bank of Japan, January 1991).
20. Ibid.
21. The MITI survey cited above.
22. Wagstyl, S., 'Japanese Start to Shop More Cautiously Abroad', *The Financial Times* (2 January 1991).
23. Ministry of Finance, *Statistics of Approvals/Notifications of Foreign Direct Investment* (Tokyo, 1991).
24. Schlender, B.R., 'Japan's Buying Spree in the US', *Fortune*, vol. 112, no. 8 (1990) pp. 83–86.
25. *The Economist*, 'Japan's Big Property Grab' (13 January 1990) pp. 75–76.
26. Conclusions of a survey conducted by the University of Michigan and Ernst and Young in August 1991 and cited in *The Economist*, 'Fear of Foreigners' (10 August 1991) p. 21.
27. Graham, E. and P. Krugman, *Foreign Direct Investment in the United States* (Washington DC: Institute of International Economics, 1991).
28. Held on 24 and 25 January 1990.
29. The Ministry of Finance, *Fiscal Statistics of Japan 1991* (Tokyo, 1991).
30. Hirata, M., 'Japanese Corporate Response to EC Market Unification', *Hitotsubashi Journal of Commerce and Management*, no. 25 (1990) pp. 13–33.
31. Satake, T., 'Trends in Japan's Direct Investment Abroad in FY 1988' (Tokyo: Research Institute of Overseas Investment, The Export–Import Bank of Japan, January 1991).
32. Rapport, C., 'The Big Split', *Fortune* (6 May 1991) pp. 30–39.
33. Kanabayashi, M. and U.C. Lehner, 'Japanese Firms Shift Strategy in Southeast Asia, *The Wall Street Journal Europe* (9 January 1991).
34. Levingston, S.E., 'Japan Slows Direct Investment in Asia', *The Asian Wall Street Journal* (28–29 June 1991).
35. From various tables compiled by Takeuchi (1990).
36. Japan External Trade Organization, *JETRO White Paper on Foreign Direct Investment, 1991* (Tokyo, March 1991).
37. Blomstorm, M., I.B. Kravis and R.E. Lipsey, 'Multinational Firms and Manufactured Export from Developing Countries', National Bureau of Economic Research, Paper no. 2493 (Cambridge MA, January 1988).
38. Sibunruand, A. 1989 *Foreign Investment and Manufactured Exports in Thailand* (Bangkok: Social Science Research Institute, Chulalongkorn).
39. Takeuchi, K., 'Does Japanese Direct Foreign Investment Promote Japanese Imports from Developing Countries'? (Washington DC: The World Bank, International Economics Department, June 1990) Working Paper no. WPS 458.
40. The Ministry of International Trade and Industry, *The Fourth Basic Survey on Japanese Business Activities Abroad* (Tokyo, March 1991).

41. Tsukuda, C., 'Closing the Investment Gap', *Journal of Japanese Trade and Industry*, no. 6 (1990) pp. 8–12.
42. *Far Eastern Economic Review*, 'Japan Studies Ways to Balance Investment' (8 August 1991) p. 65. See also *The Financial Times*, 'Japan Aims to Set up Ten Free Trade Zones', (3 September 1991).

5 ECONOMIC ASSISTANCE TO THE DEVELOPING COUNTRIES

1. Formerly Burma.
2. Unless stated otherwise, all the statistics come from: (1) Ministry of Foreign Affairs, *Japan's Official Development Assistance Annual Report* (Tokyo, various issues), (2) Organisation for Economic Co-operation and Development, *Development Co-operation Report* (Paris, various issues), (3) Organisation for Economic Co-operation and Development, *Twenty-Five Years of Development Co-operation: A Review* (Paris, 1985).
3. The Ministry of Foreign Affairs, *Wagakumi no Seifu Kaihatsu Enjo 1990*, Japan's Official Development Assistance, 1990 Report (Tokyo, June 1990).
4. The Ministry of Foreign Affairs, *Outlook of Japan's Economic Co-operation* (Tokyo, February 1989).
5. The Ministry of Foreign Affairs, *Outlook of Japan's Economic Co-operation* (Tokyo, February 1990).
6. The World Bank, *Record IDA Funding for 1990–93* (Washington DC, 14 December 1989).
7. Ministry of Foreign Affairs, *Japan's Official Development Assistance: 1989 Annual Report* (Tokyo, March 1990).
8. Ozawa, T., *Recycling Japan's Surpluses* (Paris: Organisation for Economic Co-operation and Development, 1989).
9. They are entitled: (1) *The Potential of the Japanese Surplus for the World Economic Development* (18 April 1986). (2) *Japan Urged to Lead in Tackling International Economic Problems* (25 November 1986). (3) *Mobilising International Surpluses for World Development: A WIDER Plan for a Japanese Initiative* (7 May 1987).
10. Kinoshaita, T., 'Developments in International Debt Strategy and Japan's Response', *Exim Review*, vol. 10, no. 2 (1991) pp. 62–78.
11. Yasutomo, D.T., *The Manner of Giving: Strategic Aid and Japanese Foreign Policy* (Lexington MA: Lexington Books, 1986).
12. Ministry of Foreign Affairs, *The Philosophy of Economic Co-operation* (Tokyo, 1980).
13. *Business Week*, 'Is Tokyo As Generous As it Seems?' (2 October 1989) pp. 30–32.
14. In a somewhat different manner Nowels makes the same statement. See Larry Q. Nowels, 'Japan's Foreign Aid Program: Adjusting to the Role of the World's Leading Donor', in *Japan's Economic Challenge: Study Papers Submitted to the Joint Economic Committee*, The Congress of the United States (Washington DC: Government Printing Office, 1990) pp. 404–5.

15. Orr, R.M., 'The Rising Sun: What Makes Japan Give?' *The International Economy* (September/October 1989) pp. 80–83.
16. Asian Development Bank, *Annual Report 1989* (Manila) p. 52.
17. Asian Development Bank, *ADB New Release*, no. 126/89 (22 August 1989).
18. *The Economist*, 'Japan and the Third World' (17 June 1989) pp. 15–18.
19. Japan International Development Organization, *JAIDO 1991* (Tokyo, 1991).
20. Keizai Koho Center, 'Towards a New Development of Japan's Official Development Assistance Regime and the Role of the Private Sector' (Tokyo, October 1989).

6 THE YEN BLOC

1. Zerby, J., 'Prospects of Trading Bloc in the Asia-Pacific Region' (Montreal: Ecole des Hautes Etudes Commercials, July 1990) Cahier de Recherche, no. 90–09.
2. Okita, S., 'The Dazzle of the Asian Economies', *The International Economy* (August/September 1990) pp. 68–71.
3. Akamatsu, K., 'A Historical Pattern of Economic Growth in Developing Countries', *The Developing Economies*, no. 1 (March–August 1962).
4. Asian and Pacific Development Centre, *Decade of Discovery* (Kuala Lumpur, 1990).
5. Watanabe, T., 'Helping the NICs Help the World Economy', *Journal of Japanese Trade and Industry*, no. 4 (1988) pp. 10–14.
6. Rana, P.B., 'Shifting Revealed Comparative Advantage: Experiences of Asia and Pacific Developing Countries', report no. 42 (Manila: Asian Development Bank, November 1988). Watanabe, T. and H. Kojiwara, 'Pacific Manufactured Trade and Japan's Options', *The Developing Economies* (December 1983) pp. 313–39.
7. Das, Dilip K., *Korean Economic Dynamism* (London: Macmillan, 1991).
8. Petri, P.A., 'Japanese Trade in Transition: Hypothesis and Recent Evidence' (Waltham MA: Brandeis University, Department of Economics, 1989) Research Paper no. 248.
9. Okita (1990), op. cit.
10. Okita, S., *Japan in the World Economy of the 1980s* (Tokyo: University of Tokyo Press, 1989) pp. 225–26.
11. Kikutani, C., 'Dynamic Development', *Journal of Japanese Trade and Industry*, no. 6 (1989) pp. 12–13.
12. Ibid.
13. Smith C. and L. deRosado, 'Empire of the Sun', *Far-Eastern Economic Review* (3 May 1990) pp. 46–48.
14. Kikutani (1989), op. cit.
15. Smith, C., 'Seeking a New Role', *Far Eastern Economic Review* (8 June 1989).
16. Japan External Trade Organisation, *1991 JETRO White Paper on Foreign Direct Investment* (Tokyo, March 1991).

17. Noguchi, Y., 'Japan's Economic Policies and Their Regional Impact' in Robert A. Scalapino, et al. (eds) *Pacific–Asian Economic Policies and Regional Interdependence* (Berkeley: Institute of East Asian Studies, University of California, 1988).
18. French, M., 'Behind the Japanese Myth', *Asiamoney* (May 1990) pp. 25–32.
19. Kraar, L., 'The Rising Power of the Pacific', *Fortune*, vol. 112, no. 8 (1990) pp. 8–11.
20. The Economic Planning Agency, 'Promoting Comprehensive Economic Co-operation: Towards the Construction of an Asian Network' (Tokyo, 1988).
21. Wysocki, B., 'Tokyo Pushes Asian Economic Blueprint', *The Asian Wall Street Journal* (21 August 1991).
22. Balassa, B. and J. Williamson, *Adjusting to Success: Balance of Payments Policies in East Asian NICs* (Washington DC: Institute of International Economics, April 1990).
23. The Bank of Japan, 'Greater Role of Asian Economies in the World and Growing Interdependence Among Asia, the US and Japan', special paper no. 166 (Tokyo, August 1988).
24. Balassa and Williamson (1990). Op. cit.
25. The Bank of Japan, 'Greater Role of Asian Economies in the World and Growing Interdependence Among Asia, the US and Japan', special paper no. 166 (Tokyo, August 1988) Table 14.
26. Sakamoto, Y., 'NIEs' Economic Adjustment and Asia's Division of Labour', *Mitsui Bank Monthly Review*, vol. 34, no. 6 (1989).
27. Maidment, P., 'Together under the Sun', *The Economist* (15 July 1989).
28. *The Economist*, 'A Hesitant Patroller of the Pacific' (27 July 1991).
29. The Ministry of International Trade and Industry, *White Paper on International Trade 1991* (Tokyo, 1991).
30. Shinohara, M., 'Global Adjustment and the Future of Asian–Pacific Economies' in M. Shinohara and F. Lo (eds) *Global Adjustment and the Future of Asian-Pacific Economies* (Tokyo: Institute of Developing Economies, 1989) pp. 1–14.

Bibliography

Akamatsu, K. (1962) 'A Historical Pattern of Economic Growth in Developing Countries'. *The Developing Economies*, no. 1, March–August.

Amex Bank Review (1986) 'Japans Capital Outflows: A Boost To Securitisation', 28 April.

Amex Bank Review (1991) 'Regulation of Financial Services', 3 April.

Amex Bank Review (1988) 'Japan as Global Creditor' 24 March.

Asian Development Bank (1989) *ADB New Release*, no. 126/89, 22 August.

Asian Development Bank (1990) *Annual Report 1989* (Manila) p. 62.

Asian Development Bank (1991) *Asian Development Outlook 1991* (Manila).

Asian Finance (1991) 'Banks Reel From Profit Cash', 15 August, pp. 35–37.

Asian and Pacific Development Centre (1990) *Decade of Discovery* (Kuala Lumpur).

Asian Wall Street Journal (1991) 'Tokyo–EEC to Limit Japanese Auto Sales', 1 August.

Balassa, B. (1986) 'Japan's Trade Policies', *Weltwirtschaftliches Archiv*, (Band 122, Heft 4) pp. 745–90.

Balassa, B. and J. Williamson (1990) *Adjusting to Success: Balance of Payments Policies in the East Asian NICS* (Washington DC. Institute of International Economics) April, pp. 17–18.

Balassa, B. and M. Noland (1989) 'The Changing Comparative Advantage of Japan and the United States', *The Journal of the Japanese and International Economies*, no. 3, pp. 174–88.

Baldwin, R.E. (1988) 'Hysteris in Import Prices: The Beachead Effect', *American Economic Review*, vol. 78, pp. 773–85.

Baldwin, R.E. (1988) 'Some Empirical Evidence on Hysteresis in Aggregate US Import Prices', NBER Working Paper no. 2483 (Cambridge MA: National Bureau of Economic Research, January).

The Banker (1990) 'Happy Together' (July) p. 85.

Bank for International Settlements (1990) *International Banking and Financial Market Developments* (Basle, November), p. 16.

Bank of International Settlements (1991) *International Banking and Financial Market Developments* (Basle, February).

Bank of Japan (1987) 'Adjustment of the Japanese Economy under Strong Yen' (Tokyo Special Paper no. 149, March).

Bank of Japan (1988) 'Balance of Payments Adjustment Processes in Japan and the United States', (Tokyo, Special Paper no. 162, March) Table 4.

Bank of Japan (1989) *Balance of Payments Monthly* (Tokyo, December).

Bank of Japan (1990) *Balance of Payments Monthly* (Tokyo, December).

Bank of Japan (1988) 'Corporate Management Under Strong Yen' (Tokyo Special Paper no. 159, January).

Bank of Japan (1991) *Economic Statistics Monthly* (January).

Bank of Japan (1979) 'Governor's Speech Commemorating the 19th Annual General Meeting of Yomiuri International Economic Society' (Tokyo, 1 March).

Bank of Japan (1988) 'Greater Role of Asian Economies in the World and Growing Interdependence Among Asia the US and Japan' (Tokyo, Special Paper no. 166, August) Table 14.

Bank of Japan (1987) *Tankan: Short-Term Economic Survey of Principal Enterprises* (Tokyo, May).

Bank of Japan (1988) *Tankan: Short-Term Economic Survey of Enterprises* (Tokyo, September.

Bank of Japan (1989) *Tankan: Short-Term Economic Survey of Enterprises in Japan* (Tokyo, November) p. 8.

Bank of Japan (1990) *Tankan: Short-Term Economic Survey of Principal Enterprises* (Tokyo, August).

Barbone, L. (1988) 'Import Barriers: An Analysis of Time Series Cross-Section Data', *OECD Economic Studies*, no. 11 (Autumn).

Batten, D. *et al.* (1990) 'The Instruments and Operating Procedures for Conducting Monetary Policy in G-5 Countries', Occasional Paper no. 70 (Washington DC, International Monetary Fund).

Bergsten, C. Fred (1984) 'The Case for Leaning with the Wind', *The Financial Times* (24 October).

Bergsten, C.F. and W.R. Cline (1985) *The United States–Japan Economic Problems* (Washington DC, Institute for International Economics).

Bergsten, C.F. and W.R. Cline (1988) *The United States–Japan Economic Problems*, revised (Washington DC, Institute for International Economics, June).

Bhagwati, J.N. (1990) 'The Japanese: Not So Inscrutable to Adam Smith', *The Asian Wall Street Journal* (May).

Blades, D. and W. Simpson (1985) 'The OECD Compatible Trade and Production Data Base', Working Paper no. 18 (Paris, Organisation for Economic Co-operation and Development, January).

Blanden, M. (1987) 'The Rising Sun', *The Banker* (July) pp. 74–78.

Blomstorm, M., I.B. Kravis and R.E. Lipsey (1988) 'Multinational Firms and Manufactured Export from Developing Countries' (Cambridge MA, National Bureau of Economic Research, no. 2493, January).

Branson, W.H. and G. Marchese (1988) 'International Payments Imbalances in Japan, Germany and the United States' in N.S. Fieleke (ed.) *International Payments Imbalances in the 1980s* (Boston, Federal Reserve Bank of Boston) pp. 195–230.

Brauchi, M.W. (1991) 'Japanese Securities Firms' Profits Plummet', *The Wall Street Journal Europe* (17–18 May).

Brauchi, M.W. (1991) 'Top Bankers Expect to Curb Lending in 1990s', *The Wall Street Journal Europe* (5 June).

Burstein, D. (1988) *Yen: Japan's New Financial Empire* (New York, Fawcett Columbine) p. 140.

Business Week (1989) 'Is Tokyo As Generous As it Seems?' (2 October) pp. 30–32.

Business Week (1990) 'The Tokyo Stock Market: How its Swing Affects You', (12 February) pp. 18–24.

Cecchini, P. (1988) *The European Challenge 1992: The Benefits of a Single Market* (Gower, Aldershot, Hants).

Chandler, C. (1991) 'Japanese GNP Grew in Quarter at Rate of 11.2 Percent' (*The Asian Wall Street Journal* 19 June).

Chai, S.P., A.E. Tschoegl and C.M. Yu (1986) 'Banks and the World's Major Financial Centers 1970–1980' (*Weltwirtschaftlisches Archive*, Bank 122) pp. 48–64.

Corker, R. (1989) 'External Adjustment and the Strong Yen: Recent Japanese Experience' *IMF Staff Papers*, vol. 36, no. 2 (June) pp. 464–93.

Corrigan, T. (1991) 'Japanese Trust Banks Downgraded by S&P', *The Financial Times* (20 February).

Das, Dilip K. (1991) *Korean Economic Dynamism* (London: Macmillan).

Das, Dilip K. (1986) *Migration of Financial Resources to Developing Countries* (London: Macmillan) ch. 1.

Das, Dilip K. (Forthcoming) 'The Challenge of Appreciating Yen and the Japanese Corporate Response' (*The Columbia Journal of World Business*).

Dunning, J.H. (1981) 'Explaining the International Direct Investment Position of Countries: Towards a Dynamic or Developmental Approach' *Weltwirtschaftliches Archive* (Band 117, Heft. 1) pp. 30–64.

Economic Planning Agency (Various issues) *Annual Report on National Accounts* (Tokyo).

Economic Planning Agency (1988) *Economic Survey of Japan 1987–88.* (Tokyo, August) p. 101.

Economic Planning Agency (1989) *Economic Survey of Japan 1988–89* (Tokyo, August) pp. 44–48.

Economic Planning Agency (1989) *Economic Survey of Japan 1988–89* (Tokyo, August) pp. 161–62.

Economic Planning Agency (1990) *Economic Survey of Japan 1989–1990* (Tokyo, August) pp. 183–85.

Economic Planning Agency (1988) 'External Balance, Exchange Rate Changes and Macroeconomic Policy', in the *Papers and Proceedings of the Fourth EPA International Symposium* (Tokyo, March).

Economic Planning Agency (1990) *Japanese Economic Indicators Quarterly* (Tokyo) no. 2.

Economic Planning Agency (1988) 'Promoting Comprehensive Economic Co-operation: Towards the Construction of an Asian Network' (Tokyo).

Economist (1991) 'A Hesitant Patroller of the Pacific' (27 July).

Economist (1989) 'America's Japanophobia' (18 November).

Economist (1991) 'Fear of Foreigners' (10 August) p. 21.

Economist (1989) 'Japan and The Third World' (17 June) pp. 15–18.

Economist (1990) 'Japan's Big Property Grab' (13 January) pp. 75–76.

Economist (1989) 'The Multinationals, Eastern Style' (24 June) pp. 67–68.

Economist (1990) 'The Unhappy Alliance: America and Japan' (17 February) pp. 19–23.

Economist (1989) 'Who are the Copy Cats Now?' (London, 20 May) p. 109.

Eguchi, T. (1988) 'US–Japan Trade Imbalance: Causes and Remedies' (Tokyo JCIF Policy Study Series no. 12, May) pp. 20–27.

Eken, S. (1984) 'Integration of Domestic and International Financial Markets: The Japanese Experience' (*IMF Staff Papers*, vol. 31. September) pp. 499–548.

Euromoney (1991) 'Big Four Become the Big Two' (May) pp. 48–52.

Euromoney (1990) 'Leaders of the Pack' (December) pp. 26–30.

Euromoney (1987) 'Samurais Battle it Out' (April) 47–53.

Evans, G. (1988) 'Japan Takes Over the IMF' *Euromoney* (September) pp. 98–112.

Far Eastern Economic Review (1991) 'Japanese Aid is Big Business in South Asia' (24 January) pp. 42–43.

Far Eastern Economic Review (1991) 'Japan Studies Ways to Balance Investment' (8 August) p. 65.

Feldstein, M. (1990) 'Japan's Latest Export – Promotion Plan', *The Asian Wall Street Journal* (8 January).

Financial Times (1991) 'International Economic Indicators: National Accounts' (13 May).

Financial Times (1989) 'Japan's New Multinationals' (1 December).

Financial Times (1991) 'Nikkei Beats Late Retreat as Interest Rate Hopes Fade' (9 April).

Financial Times (1991) 'Japan Aims to Set up Tax Free Trade Zones' (3 September).

Fortune (1991) 'The Fortune Global 500' (29 July) pp. 65–108.

Frankel, J.A. (1984) *The Yen/Dollar Agreement: Liberalising Japanese Capital Markets* (Washington DC, Institute for International Economics).

French, M. (1990) 'Behind the Japanese Myth', *Asiamoney* (May) pp. 25–32.

Fukao, M. (1990) 'Liberalisation of Japan's Foreign Exchange Controls and Structural Changes in the Balance of Payments', *Bank of Japan Monetary and Economic Studies* (September) pp. 101–61.

Funabashi, Y. (1988) *Managing the Dollar: From the Plaza to the Louvre* (Washington DC, Institute for International Economics) pp. 17–21.

Glynn, L. (1990) 'Japanese Banks Abroad: The Next Push', *Institutional Investor* (May) pp. 94–97.

Goldberg, L.G. and G.A. Hanweck (1991) 'The Growth of the World's 3000 Largest Banking Organisations by Country', *Journal of Banking and Finance*, vol. 15, pp. 207–23.

Graham, E. and P. Krugman (1991) *Foreign Direct Investment in the United States* (Washington DC. Institute of International Economics).

Hakishima, S. (1981) 'Mutual Ignorance and Misunderstanding: Causes of Japan–EC Economic Disputes', *Japan Quarterly*, no. 26.

Hardouvelis, G.A. (1988) 'Evidence on Stock Market Speculative Bubble: Japan, United States and Great Britain' (New York, Federal Reserve Bank of New York, Research Paper no. 8810 April).

Helliwell, J.F. (1988) 'The Effects of Fiscal Policy on International Imbalances: Japan and the United States', paper presented at the Fourth EPA International Symposium: Japan (Tokyo: March).

Hickok, S. (1989) 'Japanese Trade Balance Adjustment to Yen Appreciation',

Federal Reserve Bank of New York Quarterly Review (Autumn) vol. 14, no. 3, pp. 33–47.

Hirata, M. (1990) 'Japanese Corporate Response to EC Market Unification', *Hitatsubashi Journal of Commerce and Management*, no. 25, pp. 13–33.

Hooper, P. and C.L. Mann (1987) 'The US External Deficit: Its Causes and Persistence', International Finance Discussion Paper, no. 316 (Washington DC: Board of Governors of the Federal Reserve System, November).

Institutional Investor (1990) 'Ranking the World's Largest Banks' (July) pp. 149–51.

International Monetary Fund (1990) *Direction of Trade Statistics Yearbook 1990* (Washington DC).

International Monetary Fund (1990) *International Financial Statistics, 1990 Yearbook.*

International Monetary Fund (1990, 1991) *Direction of Trade Statistics Yearbook 1990* and *Direction of Trade Statistics Monthly, August 1991* (Washington DC).

International Monetary Fund (1991) *International Financial Statistics* (Washington DC: April).

Islam S. and R. Rowley (1991) 'EC–Japan Sign Charter to Upgrade Relations', *Far Eastern Economic Review* (1 August) pp. 13–14.

Itoh, S. (1990) 'Favourable Trend', *Journal of Japanese Trade and Industry*, no. 1, pp. 12–13.

Japan Development Bank (1989) 'Capital Investment Spending' (Tokyo: March).

Japan External Trade Organisation (1991) JETRO White Paper on Foreign Direct Investment (Tokyo: March).

Japan External Trade Organisation (1990) *White Paper on Foreign Direct Investment 1990* (Tokyo).

Japanese External Trade Organisation (1990) *Current Management Situation of Japanese Manufacturing Enterprises in Europe: The 5th Report.* Cited in 'Japan–EEC Relations: More Ups and Downs', *JEI Report* (29 October).

Japanese Finance and Industry (1989) 'A Hypothesis on the L-Curve Effect' (Industrial Bank of Japan, no. 77) pp. 1–19.

Japan International Development Organisation (1991) *JAIDO 1991* (Tokyo).

'Japan Under Pressure' (1987) *World Financial Markets* (New York: Morgan Guaranty Trust Company, April) pp. 2–4.

JEI Report (1990) 2 February, p. 11.

Japan Economic Institute (1990) *JEI Report* (5 October) p. 9.

'Japan–EEC Relations: More Ups and Downs' (1990) *JEI Report* (29 October).

Julius, D. (1991) 'Foreign Direct Investment: The Neglected Twin of Trade' (New York: The Group of Thirty).

Kanabayashi, M. and U.C. Lehner (1991) 'Japanese Firms Shift Strategy in Southeast Asia', *The Wall Street Journal Europe* (9 January).

Kane, E.J. (1987) 'Competitive Financial Regulation: An International Perspective' in R. Portes and A. Swaboda (eds) *Threats to International Financial Stability* (Cambridge University Press) pp. 111–45.

Kane, E.J. et al. (1991) 'Capital Positions of Japanese Banks' PRE Working Paper No. WPS 572 (Washington DC: The World Bank, January).

Kawai, M. and H. Okumura (1988) 'Japan's Portfolio Investment in Foreign Securities' JCIF Policy Study Series no. 9 (Tokyo: January).

Kazutomo, I. (1990) 'Changes in the Japanese Economy', discussion paper no. 90 (Tokyo: Research Institute of International Trade and Industry, February).

Keizai Koho Center (1989) 'Towards a New Development of Japan's Official Development Assistance Regime and the Role of the Private Sector' (Tokyo: October).

Khosla, A. and J. Teranishi (1989) 'Exchange Rate Pass-Through in Export Prices: An International Comparison', *Hitotsubashi Journal of Economics*, vol. 30, pp. 31–48.

Kikutani, C. (1989) 'Dynamic Development', *Journal of Japanese Trade and Industry*, no. 6, pp. 12–13.

Kinoshaita, T. (1991) 'Developments in International Debt Strategy and Japan's Response', *Exim Review*, vol. 10, no. 2, pp. 62–78.

Kitamatsu, K. (1988) 'Asian NICs Fill Export Vacuum Left by Japan', *The Japan Economic Journal* (12 September).

Kohama, H. and S. Urata (1988) 'The Impact of the Recent Yen Appreciation on the Japanese Economy', *The Developing Economics* (December) pp. 323–40.

Komia, R. and R. Wakasugi (1990) 'Japan's Foreign Direct Investment', discussion paper no. 90 (Tokyo: Research Institute of International Trade and Industry, May).

Koo, R.C. (1990) 'Japan and International Capital Flows' (Nomura Research Institute, April) mimeo.

Kraar, L. (1990) 'The Rising Power of the Pacific', *Fortune*, vol. 112, no. 8, pp. 8–11.

Krugman, P.R. (1988) 'Discussion' in N.S. Fieleke (ed.) *International Payments Imbalances in the 1980s* (Boston: Federal Reserve Bank of Boston) pp. 51–53.

Krugman, P.R. (1987) 'Exchange Rate and International Adjustment' (New York: University Center for Japan–US Business and Economic Studies Working Paper no. 39, September).

Krugman, P.R. (1987) 'Pricing to Market When the Exchange Rate Changes' in S.W. Arndt and J.D. Richardson (eds) *Real Financial Linkages Among Open Economies* (Cambridge MA: The MIT Press).

Krugman, P.R. and R.E. Baldwin (1987) 'The Persistence of the US Trade Deficit', *Brookings Papers on Economic Activity*, no. 1, pp. 1–56.

Lawrence, R.Z. (1987) 'Imports in Japan' Closed Markets or Minds?" *Brookings Papers on Economic Activity*, no. 2, vol. III, pp. 517–54.

Lee, C.H. (1990) 'Direct Foreign Investment, Structural Adjustment and International Division of Labour', *Hitotsubashi Journal of Economics*, no. 31, pp. 61–72.

Levingston, S.E. (1989) 'Japanese Investment is Integrating Asia', *The Asian Wall Street Journal* (7 November).

Levingston, S.E. (1991) 'Japan Slows Direct Investment in Asia', *The Asian Wall Street Journal* (28–29 June).

Lincoln, E.J. (1990) *Japan's Unequal Trade* (Washington DC: The Brookings Institutions).

Maidment, P. (1989) 'Together under the Sun', *The Economist* (15 July).

Marston, R. (1989) 'Pricing to Market in Japanese Manufacturing' (Philadelphia: University of Pennsylvania) processed.

McCallum, J. (1991) 'London, Tokyo and New York Dominate in Their Time Slots: Big Three Battle it Out', *The Financial Times* (29 April).

Mendelson, M.S. (1986) 'Japanese Banking's Global Challenge', *The Banker* (April) pp. 46–47.

Ministry of Finance (1991) *Financial Statistics of Japan 1991* (Tokyo).

Ministry of Finance (1991) *Fiscal Statistics of Japan 1991* (Tokyo)

Ministry of Finance (1991) *Monthly Finance Review* (Tokyo, May).

Ministry of Finance (various years) *Statistics of Approvals/Notifications of Overseas Direct Investment* (Tokyo).

Ministry of Finance (1990 and earlier issues) *Statistics of Approvals'/Notifications of Overseas Direct Investment* (Tokyo).

Ministry of Finance (1990, 1991) *Statistics of Approvals/Notifications of Overseas Direct Investment* (Tokyo).

Ministry of Finance (1991) *Statistics of Approvals/Notifications of Foreign Direct Investment* (Tokyo).

Ministry of Finance (various issues) *Zaisei Kinyu Tookei Geppo* (Tokyo).

Ministry of Foreign Affairs (various issues) *Japan's Official Development Assistance* (Tokyo).

Ministry of Foreign Affairs (various issues) *Japan's Official Development Assistance: Annual Report* (Tokyo).

Ministry of Foreign Affairs (1990) *Japan's Official Development Assistance: 1989 Annual Report* (Tokyo, March).

Ministry of Foreign Affairs (1989) *Outlook of Japan's Economic Co-operation* (Tokyo, February).

Ministry of Foreign Affairs (1990) *Outlook of Japan's Economic Co-operation* (Tokyo, February).

Ministry of Foreign Affairs (1991) *Outlook of Japan's Economic Co-operation* (Tokyo, February).

Ministry of Foreign Affairs (1980) *The Philosophy of Economic Co-operation* (Tokyo).

Ministry of Foreign Affairs (1990) *Wagakumi no seifu Kaihatsu Enjo 1990*, Japan's Official Development Assistance, 1990 Report (Tokyo, June).

Ministry of International Trade and Industry (1990) *International Trade and International Policy in the 1990s* (Tokyo: 5 July).

Ministry of International Trade and Industry (1991) *The Fourth Basis Survey on Japanese Business Activities Abroad* (Tokyo, March).

Ministry of International Trade and Industry (1990) *White Paper on International Trade 1990* (Tokyo, June).

Ministry of International Trade and Industry (1991) *White Paper on International Trade 1991* (Tokyo, June).

Mitsui Bank Monthly Review (1988) 'A New Era of Japanese Trade Structure' (March) pp. 1–8.

Morgan Guaranty Trust Company (various issues) *World Financial Markets* (New York).

Murakami, Y. and Y. Kosai (eds) (1986) *Japan in the Global Community: Its*

Role and Contribution on the Eve of the 21st Century (Tokyo: University of Tokyo Press).

Myers, H.F. (1989) 'Japanese Banks are Building a Global Role', *The Asian Wall Street Journal* (12 September).

Nakakita, T. (1988) 'The Globalisation of Japanese Firms and its Influence on Japan's Trade with Developing Countries', *The Developing Economies* (December) pp. 306–22.

Nester, W.R. (1990) *Japan's Growing Power Over East Asian and the World Economy: Ends and Means* (London: Macmillan).

Noguchi, Y. (1988) 'Japan's Economic Policies and Their Regional Impact' in Robert A. Scalapino, et al. (eds) *Pacific–Asian Economic Policies and Regional Interdependence* (Berkeley: Institute of East Asian Studies, University of California).

Noguchi, Y. (1988) 'The Japanese Economy in a Changing World Environment' in *The JCIE Papers: Europe and Japan and their Co-operation in an Interdependent World* (Tokyo: Japan Center for International Exchange) pp. 17–38.

Noland, M. (1990) 'An Econometric Investigation of International Protection' (Washington DC: Institute for International Economics) mimeo.

Noland, M. (1989) 'Fiscal Policies and the Japan–US Bilateral Current Account', *Japan and the World Economy* (July) pp. 243–54.

Nonaka, I. (1988) 'Managing Globalisation as a Self Renewing Process: Experiences of Japanese MNCs' (Working Paper no. 56, (New York: The Center for Japan–US Business and Economic Studies, New York University, October).

Nowels, Larry Q. (1990) 'Japan's Foreign Aid Programme: Adjusting to the Role of the World's Leading Donor', in *Japan's Economic Challenge: Study Papers Submitted to the Joint Economic Committee*, The Congress of the United States (Washington DC: Government Printing Office) pp. 404–05.

Ohno, K. (1990) 'Exchange Rate Fluctuations, Pass-Through and Market Share', *IMF Staff Papers*, vol. 37, no. 2 (June) pp. 294–310.

Ohno, K. (1989) 'Export Pricing Behaviour of Manufacturing: A US–Japan Comparison', *IMF Staff Papers*, vol. 36, no. 3 (September) pp. 550–78.

Okita, S. (1989) *Japan in the World Economy of the 1980s* (Tokyo: University of Tokyo Press) pp. 225–26.

Okita, S. (1990) 'The Dazzle of the Asian Economies', *The International Economy* (August/September) pp. 68–71.

Okumara, H. (1990) 'Japan's Financial Deregulation: Recent Developments and Future Outlook' (Tokyo: Nomura Research Institute, February) mimeo.

Organisation for Economic Co-operation and Development (1990) *Development Co-operation: 1990 Report* (Paris, December) p. 148.

Organisation for Economic Co-operation and Development (various issues) *Development Co-operation Report* (Paris).

Organization for Economic Co-operation and Development (1990) *Main Economic Indicators* (Paris).

Organisation for Economic Co-operation and Development (1989) *OECD*

Economic Surveys: Japan 1988/1989 (Paris) pp. 86–92.

Organisation for Economic Co-operation and Development (1990) *OECD Economic Survey: Japan 1989/1990* (Paris) pp. 60–61.

Organisation for Economic Co-operation and Development (1985) *Twenty-Five Years of Development Co-operation: a Review* (Paris).

Orr, R.M. (1989) 'The Rising Sun: What Makes Japan Give? *The International Economy* (September/October) pp. 80–83.

Osugi, K. (1990) 'Japan's Experience of Financial Deregulation Since 1974 in an International Perspective', *BIS Economic Papers No. 26* (Basle: Bank for International Settlements, January).

Ozawa, T. (1989) *Recycling Japan's Surpluses* (Paris: Organisation for Economic Co-operation and Development).

Peterson, P.G. (1989) 'Japan's Invasion: A Matter of Fairness', *The Asian Wall Street Journal* (6 November).

Petri, P.A. (1989) 'Japanese Trade in Transition: Hypothesis and Recent Evidence'. Research Paper no. 248 (Waltham MA: Brandeis University, Department of Economics).

Petri, P.P. (1989) 'Japanese Trade Transition', Discussion Paper no. 248 (Waltham MA: Brandeis University Department of Economics, October) pp. 8–11.

Pine, A. 1985 'To Avert a Trade War, US Sets Major Push to Drive Down Dollar', *The Wall Street Journal* (23 September).

Porter, M.E. (1990) *The Competitive Advantage of Nations* (London: Macmillan).

Rateliff, C. Tait (1990) 'The Intricacies of "Japanomics" lecture delivered before the Kansai of the American Chamber of Commerce (Keizai Koho center, Tokyo: June).

Rana, P.B. (1988) 'Shifting Revealed Comparative Advantage: Experiences of Asian and Pacific Developing Countries', Report no. 42 (Manila: Asian Development Bank, November).

Rapport, C. (1991) 'The Big Split', *Fortune* (6 May) pp. 30–39.

Rapport, C. (1990) 'Tough Times for Japan's Banks', *Fortune* (16 July) pp. 20–24.

Riddel, P. (1991) 'SII Has Lived up to Expectations', *The Financial Times* (13 June).

Journal of Japanese Trade and Industry (1989) 'Rising Ratio of Manufactured Imports', no. 2, p. 34.

Robins, B. (1990) 'MITI Tries to Restrain Investment Spending', *The Asian Wall Street Journal*, (19 March).

Roger, Ian (1990) 'Japan: Still in Search of a Global Role', *The Financial Times* (9 July).

Roosa, R.V. (1986) *United States and Japan in the International Monetary System* (New York: Group of Thirty) pp. 43–44.

Rowley, A. (1991) 'A Partnership of Equals', *Far-Eastern Economic Review* (20 June) pp. 58–59.

Royama, S. (1990) 'Aspects of Financial Restructuring in Contemporary Japan, *Japan Review of International Affairs* (Spring/Summer) pp. 42–65.

Sachs, J.D. and M.W. Sundberg (1988) 'International Payments Imbalances of the East Asian Developing Economies' in N.S. Fieleke (ed.) *International Payments Imbalances in the 1980s* (Boston: Federal Reserve Bank of Boston) pp. 103–56.

Sachs, J.D. and N. Roubini (1987) 'Sources of Macroeconomic Imbalances in the World Economy: A Simulation Approach', paper presented at the Third International Conference at the Bank of Japan, Tokyo, June).

Sakakibara, E. (1986) 'The Internationalisation of Tokyo's Financial Markets' in A.H.H. Tan and B. Kapur (eds) *Pacific Growth and Financial Interdependence* (Sydney: Allen and Unwin) pp. 237–46.

Sakamoto, Y (1989) 'NIEs Economic Adjustment and Asia's Division of Labour', *Mitsui Bank Monthly Review*, vol. 34, no. 6.

Sargen, N. and K.L. Schoenhaltz (1990) 'Japan's Adjustment Miracle and its Implications for the Yen', *Japan and the World Economy*, no. 2, pp. 283–93.

Satake, T. (1991) 'Trends in Japan's Direct Investment Abroad in FY 1988' (Tokyo: Research Institute of Overseas Investment, The Export–Import Bank of Japan, January).

Sawai, Y. (1989) 'Internationalisation of the Yen: A Progress Report', *Tokyo Financial Review* (November) pp. 10–16.

Sanonhouse, G.R. (1983) 'The Micro- and Macro-economics of Foreign Sales to Japan, in W.R. Cline (ed.) *Trade Policies in the 1980s* (Washington DC: Institute for International Economics) pp. 259–304.

Schlender B.R. (1990) 'Japan's Buying Spree in the US', *Fortune*, vol. 112, no. 8, pp. 83–86.

Schlosstein, S.B. (1990) 'The New McCarthyism', *The International Economy* (April/May) pp. 12–15.

Shale, T. (1989) 'A New Crop of Tigers', *Euromoney* (September) pp. 91–93.

Shale, T. (1991) 'The Big Four Take a Beating', *Euromoney* (February) pp. 38–41.

Shale, T. (1990) 'The Plot that Triggered Tokyo's Plunge', *Euromoney* (May) pp. 32–36.

Shinohara, M. (1989) 'Global Adjustment and the Future of Asian–Pacific Economies', in M. Shinohara and F. Lo (eds) *Global Adjustment and the Future of Asian–Pacific Economies* (Tokyo: Institute of Developing Economies) pp. 1–14.

Shiraishi, T. (1989) *Japan's Trade Policies* (London: The Athlone Press).

Sibunruand, A. 1989 *Foreign Investment and Manufactured Exports in Thailand* (Bangkok: Social Science Research Institute, Chulalongkorn.)

Smith, C. (1989) 'Seeking a New Role', *Far Eastern Economic Review* (8 June).

Smith, C. and L. deRasado (1990) 'Empire of the Sun', *Far-Eastern Economic Review* (3 May) pp. 46–48.

Suzuki, Y. (1989) *Japan's Economic Performance and International Role* (Tokyo: University of Tokyo Press).

Suzuki, Y. (1986) *Money, Finance and Macroeconomic Performance in Japan* (New Haven: Yale University Press).

Suzuki, Y. (1987) *The Japanese Financial System* (Oxford: Clarendon Press).

Takeuchi, K. (1990) 'Does Japanese Direct Foreign Investment Promote

Japanese Imports from Developing Countries?' Working Paper no. WPS 458 (Washington DC: The World Bank, International Economics Department, June).

Takeuchi, K. (1989) 'Does Japan Import Less Than it should'? *The Asian Economic Journal*, vol. III, no. 2 (September).

Takoaka, H. (1991) 'Global Management and Overseas Direct Investment' (Tokyo: Research Institute of Overseas Investment, The Export–Import Bank of Japan, January).

Tatsuno, S.M. (1990) *Created in Japan* (New York: Harper and Row) ch. 14.

Tavlas, G.S. (1991) *On the International Use of Currencies: the Case of the Deutsche Mark* (Princeton: International Finance Section, Princeton University, March).

Tavlas, G.S. and Y. Ozeki (1991) 'The Japanese Yen as an International Currency', IMF Working Paper no. WP/91/2 (Washington DC: International Monetary Fund, January).

Terazono, E. (1991) 'Japanese Investors' Dividend Dilemma', *The Financial Times* (11 April).

Thomson, D. and M. French (1990) 'The Japanese Banks Retreat', *Asiamoney* (November) pp. 25–30.

Thomson, R. (1991) 'Sharp Falls at Japan's Securities Firms', *The Financial Times* (17 May).

Thorn, R.S. (1987) *The Rising Sun* (Singapore: Institute of Southeast Asian Studies) pp. 67–70.

Tokunager, Y. (1990) 'An Anatomy of Japan's High Prices', *Economic Eye* (Spring) pp. 20–25.

Tokyo Financial Review (1991) 'Internationalisation of the Yen: Where We Are', vol. 16, no. 3 (March) pp. 1–8.

Tsukuda, C. (1990) 'Closing the Investment Gap', *Journal of Japanese Trade and Industry*, no. 6, pp. 8–12.

Ueda, K. (1990) 'Are Japanese Stock Prices Too High'? *Journal of Japanese and International Economies*, no. 4, pp. 351–70.

Ueda, K. (1990) 'Japanese Capital Outflows', *Journal of Banking and Finance*, no. 14, pp. 1079–101.

Ueda, K. (1988) 'Perspective on the Japanese Current Account Surplus', *NBER Macro-Economics Annual 1988* (London: The MIT Press) pp. 217–67.

United Nations Centre on Transnational Corporation (1991) 'World Investment Report 1991: The Triad in Foreign Direct Investment' (New York).

US Treasury Department (1988) *Report to the Congress on International Economic and Exchange Rate Policy* (Washington DC, 24 October).

Voge, F. (1991) 'Japan's SDR Plan Falls Flat', *Asian Finance* (15 June), pp. 62–63.

Wagstyl, S. (1989) 'Japan's Capital Spending Grows at Fastest Pace for 15 Years', *The Financial Times* (25 September).

Wagstyl, S. (1990) 'Japanese Financial Markets', *The Financial Times* (15 March).

Wagstyl, S. (1991) 'Japanese Start to Shop More Cautiously Abroad', *The Financial Times* (2 January).

Watanabe, T. and H. Kojiwara (1983) 'Pacific Manufactured Trade and

Japan's Options', *The Developing Economies* (December) pp. 313–39.

Watanabe, T. (1988) 'Helping the NICs Help the World Economy', *Journal of Japanese Trade and Industry*, no. 4, pp. 10–14.

World Bank (1990) *Annual Report 1990* (Washington DC) p. 225.

World Bank (1989) *Record IDA Funding for 1990–93* (Washington DC, 14 December).

World Bank (1988) *World Tables 1987*, Fourth Edition (Washington DC).

Wilcock, C.B. (1991) 'Japanese Investors Consider US Bonds', *The Wall Street Journal Europe* (2 April).

Wilkinson, E. (1981) *Misunderstanding: Europe vs. Japan* (Tokyo: Chnokoronske).

Wysocki, B. (1991) 'Tokyo Pushes Asian Economic Blueprint', *The Asian Wall Street Journal* (21 August).

Yakagi, S. (1988) 'The Changing Japanese Financial System', *Finance and Deveopment* (March) pp. 10–15.

Yamasai, T. (1990) 'Japan's Foreign Securities Investment', *Tokyo Financial Review*, vol. 15, no. 4 (April) pp. 1–7.

Yasutomo, D.T. (1986) *The Manner of Giving: Strategic Aid and Japanese Foreign Policy* (Lexington MA: Lexington Books).

Yoichi, S. (1990) 'Japan's Role as the World's Banker', *Economic Eye* (Summer) pp. 22–29.

Yu, D. (1991) 'Life After the Crash', *Asiamoney* (May) pp. 10–16.

Zerby, J. (1990) 'Prospects of Trading Bloc in the Asia–Pacific Region' Cahier de Recherche, no. 90–09 (Montreal: Ecole des Hautes Etudes Commercials, July).

Index